Potluck on the Pedernales

Down Home Cooking From Deep in the Heart of LBJ Country

Compiled by

Community Garden Club of Johnson City
Johnson City, Texas

Motto: To Beautify and Serve

EAKIN PRESS   ★   **Austin, Texas**

Proceeds

The proceeds from the sale of *Potluck On The Pedernales* will be used for civic and community projects sponsored by the Community Garden Club of Johnson City.

A portion of the royalties from the sale of this cookbook is pledged to the National Wildflower Research Center in Austin, Texas. Lady Bird Johnson is a charter member of the Johnson City Community Garden Club and still participates in club activities when her schedule permits. It is in her honor that we make this pledge to the Wildflower Center because it is so special to her, and she is so special to us.

Disclaimer

The home remedies and household hints contained in this book are provided for historical and humorous purposes only. No express or implied warranties with regard to their efficacy or safety are made by the Community Garden Club of Johnson City. Do not use them without first consulting a physician or other appropriate medical professional. Community Garden Club of Johnson City or its members are not engaged in rendering medical advice.

"Where's It At?"

"KISSIN' DON'T LAST, COOKIN' DO!"

iii

"Much Obliged"

COOKBOOK COMMITTEE

Holly Lawson, Chairman	Thelma Elm
Peggy Arbon	Kittie Clyde Leonard
Joycelyn Carter	Ola Matus
Patty Casparis	Jane Mills
Mary Dyer	Cynthia Smith
Joyce Ellis	Janey Wiemers

PHOTOGRAPHY / Jeff Gatlin

COVER ART / Charles Shaw

COVER LOCATION / Pat Smith Ranch

COMPUTER / Joycelyn Carter

COMPUTER CONSULTANT / Dennis Bushnell

LEGAL ADVISOR / Dean Myane

DIVIDER PAGE ART

Elaine Lockhart	D. J. Whittington
Jane Mills	Margaret Withers
Gladys Stubbs	

NUTRITIONAL AID / Gail Rucker

FINANCE / Johnson City Bank

Members of the Community Garden Club of Johnson City and all the people of the Texas Hill Country for submitting recipes.

"What's Cookin'?"

Do we have a cookbook for you! You have just selected a cookbook for those inclined to the sheer joy-of-cookbook-reading or from which you can cook to your heart's content. The recipes and the colorful stories accompanying some of them are typical of the great cooks of this area . . . the Texas Hill Country.

There are recipes and remedies passed from generation to generation, family to family . . . food "so good, it'll make you want to slap yore Pappy," declares Mrs. Ava Johnson Cox, first cousin of Lyndon B. Johnson. The Cookbook Committee spent the better part of a day with "Miss Ava" as she is lovingly and respectfully called, as she talked and offered goodies from her pantry and we listened and ate . . .

Our cookbook features well-used favorites from old-timers and newcomers alike. You will find these culinary treats, cooked down-home style at the church supper, Women's Club meetings, Garden Club Membership Tea . . . wherever people meet and eat together.

Some recipes from long ago reflect history and customs pertaining to food from the past, while others are more current. And since the trend today is toward old-fashioned down-home cooking, these are recipes you will certainly want to try.

Included also, however, is a section on "Heart Happy" recipes . . . lower in calories, fat and cholesterol. These recipes carry the nutritional information you will be interested in, provided by the Blanco County Agricultural Extension Office.

"Ranch Road 1" features family favorites of Lady Bird Johnson and her daughters, Lynda Robb and Luci Turpin. Many of these recipes were used when visiting dignitaries came to the "Summer White House," the LBJ Ranch at Stonewall, Texas. Many of the favorites of the Johnson family were also used at the

White House in Washington, D.C., for family meals. Tillie Hahne of Stonewall has cooked for the Johnson family for many years and has given the committee recipes from the "Red Book" the official cookbook at the Ranch. Says Tillie, "although Mrs. Johnson rarely cooks these days, she always oversees the preparation and especially the final presentation of the food, often lending her special touch with garnishes, etc."

The pen and ink drawings done by local artists are renderings of historic structures in Johnson City and the area nearby. Included are drawings of the Blanco County Courthouse, the Johnson City Bank, the LBJ Ranch House in Stonewall, the Johnson Settlement, and the LBJ Boyhood Home. There is also a drawing of the building that formerly served as the LBJ Memorial Hospital. The Johnson City Community Garden Club originally was formed to take care of the planting and upkeep of the hospital grounds.

There is a section entitled, "This n' That" including everything from remedies to give a sick calf to something to make your arthritis "ease-up" a bit. A motto used often in the good old days was: "Eat it up, wear it out, make it do, or do without!" They did that very thing.

The Potluck Supper or sometimes it is called the Covered Dish Supper is one of the most practical traditions for sharing home cooked foods with your neighbor, friends or family. It is done a lot in the Hill Country. Originally it was an inexpensive way to entertain, so many families could "put in" together and what they ended up with would feed an army!

The dictionary says:

> **Pot-luck** (pot′luk′) "whatever food might have been prepared for the family . . . ordinary, nothing special"

. . . but taste these recipes and you will know better!

> **Pedernales River** (Perd′nālis local pronunciation), Spanish definition means: "River of Flint."

One of the last free flowing rivers in Texas with no major dams. The river bisects the LBJ Heartland, rising in S.E. Kimble county flowing eastward for 106 miles through southern Gillespie County, central Blanco County and onward to northern Hays

County, finally joining the Colorado River in western Travis county. The river cuts a rugged path that was home to pre-historic hunters, and determined pioneers who finally tamed the Hill Country. President Lyndon B. Johnson often referred to the Texas Hill Country and the "Perd'nalis" River as a builder of character and determination.

The Cookbook Committee is very proud to publish a book such as this containing local recipes and folklore. This is a true LBJ Country cookbook of *Pedernales Pot Luck* from the people who helped make the history of this area unique and the food so great. Enjoy!

When work seems rather dull to me
And life is not so sweet.
One thing at least can bring me joy
I simply love to eat.
— Submitted by Helen Mayfield

The recipe that is not shared with others
will soon be forgotten,
but when it is shared,
it will be enjoyed by future generations.

Appetizers

BLANCO COUNTY COURTHOUSE

The Blanco County Courthouse was built in Johnson City in 1915–1916 at a total cost of $28,900.00. It was constructed of rough-hewn rock transported by wagon from the Deer Creek area, about two miles south of town. Stones were hoisted into place by block-and-tackle pulled by mules. Though there have been improvements during the years to modernize the old structure, basically it has not changed and remains the hub of Blanco County.

1

ARMADILLO EGGS

Betty Wood

¹/₂ pound Monterey Jack
  cheese, grated
¹/₂ pound hot bulk Texas
  sausage
1¹/₂ cups buttermilk biscuit
  mix
15 medium jalapeño
  peppers, canned

¹/₂ pound Monterey Jack
  cheese, cubed (or with
  jalapeños)
1 box Shake 'n Bake for
  Pork
2 eggs, beaten

Mix cheese and sausage, add biscuit mix 1/2 cup at a time until thoroughly mixed. The mixture will become a very stiff dough and should be kneaded several minutes. Set aside. Slit and seed jalapeños. Stuff each pepper with a cube of cheese and pinch the pepper closed around the cheese. Pinch off a bit of the cheese-sausage mixture and pat into a flat pancake about 1/4 inch thick. Place the cheese stuffed pepper in the middle of the pancake and wrap pepper completely with dough, being sure that all edges and ends are sealed completely. Roll the dough covered pepper back and forth in your hands to mold egg shape. Roll each "egg" in Shake 'n Bake until coated. Dip armadillo eggs in beaten eggs and Shake 'n Bake again. At this point, the armadillo eggs may be baked or frozen. To serve, bake in slow oven about 300 degrees for 20 to 25 minutes. If the cheese begins to bubble out, remove from the oven. The "eggs" will seem soft to the touch but upon cooling will crust nicely. Best served slightly warm. Yield: 15 eggs.

BACON SWIRLS

Mariallen Moursund

6 slices bacon, cooked and
  crumbled
1 4-ounce can mushroom
  stems and pieces, drained
  and chopped
¹/₄ cup mayonnaise or salad
  dressing

¹/₂ teaspoon garlic powder
1 8-ounce can refrigerated
  crescent dinner rolls
2 3-ounce packages cream
  cheese, softened
1 egg white, lightly beaten
Poppy seeds

Combine bacon, mushrooms, mayonnaise and garlic powder; stir well and set aside. Separate crescent dough into 4 rectangles; press perforations to seal. Spread 1/4 of cream cheese over each dough rectangle, leaving 1/4-

inch margin on one long side and no margin on the other side. Spread 1/4 of bacon mixture evenly over cream cheese. Roll dough, jelly roll fashion, starting at long sides with filling spread to edge; pinch seams to seal. Cut rolls into 1/2-inch slices; place cut side down on a lightly greased baking sheet. Brush each slice with egg white and sprinkle with poppy seeds. Bake slices at 375 degrees for 9 minutes or until lightly browned. Serve warm. Yield: 3 dozen.

BACON WRAPS

Mariallen Moursund

¹/₄ **cup margarine**	**1 egg, slightly beaten**
¹/₂ **cup water**	¹/₄ **pound bulk pork sausage**
1 8-ounce package herb	¹/₂ **pound sliced bacon**
seasoned stuffing mix	**Cherry tomatoes, garnish**
(Pepperidge Farm)	**Parsley, garnish**

Mix margarine and water over heat and pour over stuffing mix, egg and sausage and mix well. Chill 1 hour and shape into oblong pieces about size of pecan. Cut bacon into thirds and wrap each piece of stuffing mixture with bacon and fasten with wooden toothpick. Bake at 350 degrees for 35 minutes; turn about halfway when cooking. When finished cooking drain on paper towels. Garnish with cherry tomatoes and parsley. May refrigerate or freeze before baking. Yield: 3 dozen.

LUCE'S CHEESE BALL

Vanessa Luce

2 8-ounce packages cream	**1 tablespoon onion, grated**
cheese	**1 tablespoon parsley, chopped**
1 cup cheddar cheese, grated	**1 tablespoon pimiento,**
2¹/₂-ounce can deviled ham	**chopped**
¹/₂ **teaspoon dry mustard**	**Seasoned salt**
Juice of 1 lemon	**Pecans, garnish**
2 tablespoons Worcestershire	**Maraschino cherries, garnish**
sauce	

Soften cream cheese. Mix all together and form into ball or Christmas wreath. Roll or put pecans on wreath with maraschino cherries and ribbon. Yield: 1 6″ cheese ball.

CHEESE WAFERS
Mary Dyer

2 cups Cheddar cheese,
   finely shredded
¹/₂ cup butter or margarine
1 cup flour

1 teaspoon salt
¹/₄ teaspoon red pepper
³/₄ cup nuts, finely chopped

Combine cheese and butter in mixing bowl; beat well. Add flour, salt, pepper and nuts; mix well. Divide dough in half; shape each half into 1 x 8-inch roll. Wrap in waxed paper, chill. Slice, bake at 400 degrees for 5–7 minutes. Makes about 6 dozen.

CHICKEN AND BEAN TOSTADITAS
Daisy Cox

3 7-inch corn tortillas, cut
   into 4 wedges each
Vegetable oil for frying the
   tortillas
1 16-ounce can red kidney
   beans, rinsed and drained
¹/₂ cup water
¹/₃ cup onion, finely
   chopped
1 teaspoon garlic, minced
1 teaspoon ground cumin
2 tablespoons olive oil

Salt and pepper to taste
1 tablespoon white wine
   vinegar
³/₄ cup chicken, cooked and
   shredded
¹/₂ cup romaine lettuce,
   finely shredded
Sour cream to taste, if
   desired
Tomato strips and black
   olive slices for garnish

Arrange tortilla wedges in one layer on baking sheet, cover them with kitchen towel and let stand for 1 hour. In a large heavy skillet heat 3/4-inch of vegetable oil to 375 degrees and fry the wedges in batches for 30 seconds to 1 minute, or until crisp. Transfer the chips with a slotted spoon to paper towels to drain and sprinkle them with salt. In a saucepan of boiling salted water blanch the beans for 2 minutes, drain well, and in a blender pureé them with 1/2 cup water. In skillet cook the onion, garlic, and cumin in one tablespoon of olive oil over moderately low heat, stirring, until the onion is soft. Add the bean pureé and salt and pepper to taste and cook the mixture over moderate heat, stirring for 5 minutes, or until mixture is very thick. Transfer the mixture to a bowl and let cool.

   In small bowl wisk together the vinegar, remaining one tablespoon olive oil and salt and pepper to taste until well blended. In two separate bowls, place chicken in one and romaine in the other. Divide dressing placing half in each bowl. Toss lightly. On each tortilla chip spread 1 heaping tablespoon of bean pureé and top with some sour cream, some of the romaine and a few strips of the chicken. Top the tostaditas with the tomato strips and black olive slices. Makes 12 appetizers.

EGG ROLLS
Janey Wiemers

This recipe was given to me by a neighbor in San Antonio who was from Viet Nam. She would share these with our family when she made some for her family and we all loved them. Then she began making them for their church when they had a fund raising Fall Festival. They were so popular she started making dozens beginning in September and freezing them.

- 2 pounds cooked chicken meat, ground
- 1 pound carrots, shredded
- 1 bunch green onions, chopped (optional)
- 1 package bean threads (soak in water about 20 minutes until soft-cut into 1 inch pieces)
- 4 teaspoons salt
- 1 teaspoon pepper
- 1/2 teaspoon Accent
- 2 eggs, beaten
- 1 package egg roll wrappers

Mix all the ingredients except wrappers thoroughly. Position an egg roll wrapper with one point toward you. Spoon about 2 to 3 tablespoons of filling diagonally across and just below center of wrapper. Fold bottom point of wrapper over filling; tuck point under filling. Fold side corners over center, forming an envelope shape. Roll up egg roll toward remaining corner; moisten point with a little water and press firmly to seal. Repeat with remaining wrappers and filling. Fry 1 to 2 egg rolls at a time in 365 degree oil until golden brown, about 2 to 3 minutes. Makes 30 large egg rolls.

STUFFED JALAPEÑO PEPPERS
Bradley Smith

Medium-large jalapeño peppers
1 6-ounce can tuna fish, drained

1 tablespoon cream cheese
1 tablespoon mayonnaise

5

Split and seed peppers. Mix mayonnaise and cream cheese together with drained tuna fish. Stuff into peppers and broil slightly or eat as is. Yield: enough to stuff 15 peppers.

KEEBLER'S NEEBLERS
Vanessa Luce

1 package Hidden Valley Ranch Salad Mix
1 teaspoon garlic powder
1 teaspoon dill weed
1 cup oil, warmed
2 12-ounce packages Keebler's Soup Crackers

Combine seasonings with oil. Put crackers in large bowl; pour oil and seasonings over crackers and stir well. Place seasoned crackers on cookie sheet, bake 15–20 minutes at 250 degrees, stirring occasionally. Store in metal containers. Yield: 4 cups.

APPETIZER MEATBALLS
Thelma Elm

1 egg
2 tablespoons water
1 package French's Hamburger Seasoning mix
1 pound ground beef
Fine dry bread crumbs

Combine all ingredients except bread crumbs and shape into small meatballs; roll in fine dry bread crumbs. Arrange on ungreased cookie sheet. Bake 10–15 minutes at 400 degrees. Makes 40–50 meatballs.

MUSHROOMS SANTA FE
Cynthia Smith

1 cup sharp Cheddar cheese, shredded
$1/4$ cup sour cream
3 teaspoons green onion, sliced
$2^1/2$ tablespoons cilantro or parsley, chopped
3 tablespoons green chilies, canned, diced
1 clove garlic, pressed
$1/4$ cup butter
16 2-inch fresh mushroom caps (about 1 pound)
Parmesan cheese, fresh, grated or canned

Mix Cheddar cheese, sour cream, onions, cilantro, and chilies. Set aside. Combine butter and garlic, warm to melt butter. Brush caps with garlic butter. Fill each mushroom cap with 1 tablespoon of Cheddar cheese mixture. Place in baking dish, sprinkle with Parmesan cheese. Broil until bubbly, about 3 minutes. Serves 16.

PIZZA NIBBLES
Dena K. Heider

1 pound Owens sausage, hot
1 teaspoon oregano
1 tablespoon ketchup
Salt to taste
Dash of garlic salt
Worcestershire sauce to taste

¹/₂ pound Velveeta cheese
1 14-ounce jar Ragu
  Spaghetti Sauce
1 loaf party rye bread,
  sliced
Parmesan cheese

Brown and drain sausage. Add seasonings, Velveeta, and Ragu sauce and stir to blend. Lay slices of bread on cookie sheet and spread sausage mixture over each slice. Top with Parmesan cheese. Bake at 350 degrees for 10–15 minutes. This can be frozen before baking and putting on Parmesan cheese. Freeze separately until frozen, then put in a bag or container. Yield: 24 slices.

QUESADILLAS
Cynthia Smith

2 cups mushrooms
4 slices low-cal Muenster
  cheese
¹/₄ cup green onions, chopped

¹/₄ cup cilantro, chopped
1 tablespoon green chilies,
  chopped
4 small flour tortillas

Spray skillet with Pam. Sauté mushrooms, set aside. Wipe skillet with paper towel, spray with Pam again. Combine mushrooms and cheese, green onions, cilantro, and green chilies. Divide mixture among tortillas. Spread mixture to edge of tortillas, fold in half and cut in 4 wedges. Fry in skillet slowly and keep mashing down until cheese is melted. Yield: 16 pieces.

HOLIDAY SANDWICH WREATH
Vanessa Luce

For all its beauty, this sandwich wreath is easy to prepare. It doubles as an attractive centerpiece as well as a delicious appetizer. By simply alternating rye bread and pumpernickel sandwiches filled with delicious spreads of deviled ham, liver pâté and chicken salad you get the contrast necessary to create a decorative wreath. Just place the mini sandwiches upright in a circle and then add a bright satin bow for the finishing touch.

Deviled Ham Spread: combine:
        1 4¹/₂-ounce can deviled ham
        ¹/₂ cup celery, chopped
        ¹/₂ teaspoon Worcestershire Sauce
Chicken Apple Spread: combine:
        1 4¹/₂-ounce can chicken spread
        ¹/₄ cup apple, chopped
        1 tablespoon sour cream
Nippy Pâté Spread: combine:
        1 4¹/₂-ounce can liverwurst spread
        ¹/₄ cup green pepper, chopped
        1 tablespoon mayonnaise

        Party Pumpernickel bread, sliced
        Party Rye bread, sliced
        Butter, softened

Prepare spreads as directed. Spread bread slices with softened butter. Spread half of bread slices with meat spread mixtures; close sandwiches with remaining slices. Each recipe makes 10 sandwiches. To form wreath, on a large round plate arrange sandwiches around the edge of plate. Decorate wreath with a satin or paper bow. Wreath contains 30 small sandwiches. Makes 30 appetizer or snack-size servings.

GLAZED SAUSAGE BITES
Janey Wiemers

1 egg, slightly beaten
1 pound bulk pork sausage
¹/₂ cup finely crushed
   saltines (14 crackers)
¹/₃ cup milk
¹/₂ teaspoon rubbed sage

¹/₂ cup water
2 tablespoons brown sugar
1 tablespoon soy sauce
¹/₄ cup ketchup
1 tablespoon vinegar

In mixer bowl, combine egg, sausage, crackers, milk, and sage and beat at high speed on electric mixer for 5 minutes. Shape into 1¹/₄-inch balls. (Mixture will be soft; wet hands to shape easily). In skillet brown meat on all sides, shaking pan occasionally to keep balls round, about 10 minutes. Pour off excess fat. Combine water, brown sugar, soy sauce, ketchup, and vinegar. Pour over meatballs. Cover and simmer 15 minutes stirring occasionally. To serve, keep hot in chafing dish. Yield: 16–24 balls.

SAUSAGE BALLS

Mary Pat Carter

3 cups Bisquick
1 pound hot sausage (raw)

10-ounces sharp cheddar
   cheese, grated

Blend together. Roll into small balls and place on cookie sheet and freeze. Bake at 375 to 400 degrees for 20 minutes or until brown. Makes 80 balls. They are very easy and good. They go fast especially when warm.

SAUSAGE ROLLS

Jewell Sultemeier

Good as hors d' oeuvres or as a breakfast dish with scrambled eggs and jelly or jam.

1 pound hot pork sausage
1 pound regular pork
   sausage

4 cups Bisquick
1/2 cup margarine, melted
1 cup milk

Mix two sausage meats together and set aside in refrigerator for about 30 minutes. Divide into three batches. Mix Bisquick, cooled margarine and milk. Divide into three parts. Roll each batch of dough into rectangular shape. Spread with sausage and roll as jelly roll. Wrap in plastic wrap and freeze. To prepare, thaw the roll a few minutes and slice thin. Bake at 350 degrees for about 15 minutes. Yield: 3 rolls at 24 slices per roll.

PEEL'EM–EAT'EM SHRIMP

Martha S. Combs

This was always one of our favorite things to serve when we lived on the ranch.

Water
Stale beer
Crab boil
Celery tops

1 onion, chopped
Seasoning of your choice
5 pounds fresh or frozen
   shrimp in shells

In large pot, put mixture of 2/3 water and 1/3 stale beer. Add crab boil, celery tops, onion (all in cheesecloth) and seasonings. Bring to boil and cook a couple of minutes. Add shrimp and bring to boil again until shrimp foams (but cook no longer than 3 minutes after water comes to boil). Can serve hot or cold with sauce and lots of napkins and let guest peel their own. Great served with green salad and hard bread. Yield: 10 servings.

SAUCE FOR SHRIMP
Martha S. Combs

1 bottle Heinz chili sauce
1 bottle Heinz ketchup
2 tablespoons Worcestershire
  sauce
$^1/_2$ cup good horseradish or
  to taste

Juice of 1 lemon
Dash Tabasco sauce
1 tablespoon sweet basil
Salt to taste
White pepper to taste

Combine all ingredients. Best made a day ahead. Store in a tightly covered container. Keeps well. Yield: 3$^1/_4$ cups.

SHRIMP MOLD
Lila Gene Hobbs

1 cup celery, chopped
$^1/_4$ cup onion, chopped
$^1/_4$ cup bell pepper, chopped
1 cup (2 cans) shrimp,
  chopped
1 8-ounce package cream
  cheese

1 can tomato soup
2 packages unflavored
  gelatin
$^1/_4$ cup cold water
1 cup mayonnaise

Chop the vegetables and shrimp first, leaving the shrimp in large chunks. Combine over low heat the cream cheese and soup, but do not boil. Soften the gelatin in 1/4 cup cold water and add to the soup mix. Add the chopped vegetables, shrimp and mayonnaise to the soup mixture. Pour into a 4-cup mold and chill until firm. Unmold and serve as a spread with crackers. Makes a 4 cup mold.

TORTILLA ROLLS
Anita Burg

2 8-ounce cartons sour cream
2 8-ounce packages cream cheese
2 4-ounce cans chopped green chilies
1 8-ounce jar hot taco sauce
1 2-ounce can chopped pimientos, drained
Dash of lemon
Flour tortillas

Mix and spread on tortilla and roll. Chill. Cut across rolls. Yield: 80 slices.

TORTILLA ROLL-UPS
Tracy Ulrich

2 8-ounce packages cream cheese
1 package large flour tortillas (8 burrito size)
1 8-ounce jar Pace Thick and Chunky Salsa
1 chopped green onion

Mix cream cheese, salsa to taste. Mix in green onion. Spread over tortilla. Roll. Set in refrigerator for at least 1 hour. Slice and serve with extra salsa for dipping. Yields: about 80 slices.

CRISP VEGETABLE MARINADE
Holly Lawson

This is very good, especially the olives. It does keep indefinitely. I made this 3 Christmases ago and put some in the back of the fridge and got it out this Christmas. It has the same good flavor and most of the vegetables are still crisp. Believe it or not!

1 small cauliflower, cut into flowerets
4 carrots, pared and sliced into bite-size pieces
4 celery ribs, cut into 1-inch slices
2 green peppers, cut into 2 inch strips
1 4-ounce jar pimientos, drained and cut into strips
1 6-ounce jar pitted green olives, drained
1 1/2 cups salad vinegar
1 cup salad or olive oil
1/4 cup sugar
1 teaspoon oregano
1 teaspoon parsley flakes
1/4 teaspoon pepper
2 teaspoons salt
1/2 cup water

Combine all ingredients in large pan. Bring to boil, stirring occasionally. Reduce heat; simmer, covered, for 5 minutes. Cool; refrigerate for at least 24 hours. Drain before serving. Keeps indefinitely in refrigerator. Serves 18 to 20 as a relish and at least 50 as an appetizer.

Dips

AUNT AMELIA'S DIP
Martha Combs

Know that you remember my darlin' Uncle Carl. He and his wife, Amelia, had no children . . . and sorta claimed me. Aunt Amelia was always so darn precise and proper . . . in fact, she was just a snob . . . with each new member of our family, that person was always given the job of seeing to Aunt Amelia. Our son-in-law, Lynn, was the last to be assigned Aunt Amelia . . . said he would just keep her, cause, in spite of all her snobbish ways, she did make a darn good dip . . . and so simple . . . And, although both Uncle Carl and Aunt Amelia are no longer with us, know that she is having a ball serving her dip to all those angels!!

- 1 **2-pound box Velveeta cheese**
- 1 **can Ro-Tel tomatoes with green chilies, chopped**
- 1 **pound ground round**

Melt Velveeta and add the Ro-tel tomatoes and green chilies. Cook ground round in skillet on top of stove (I put a little bit of Pam in the skillet, then add meat and do not overcook). (Always use ground round to avoid too much fat.) Add the cooked ground round to the cheese-Ro-tel mixture. Serve warm with Doritos, chips, etc. Very, very good!! Yield: 4 cups.

ARTICHOKE CHILI DIP
Daisy Cox

- 1 **14-ounce can artichoke hearts, drained and chopped**
- 1 **cup grated Parmesan cheese**
- 4 **ounce can green chile peppers, rinsed, seeded and chopped**
- 1 **cup mayonnaise or salad dressing**
- **Dippers such as pita wedges or tortilla chips**

In a small mixing bowl combine artichokes, cheese, peppers, and mayonnaise or salad dressing. Transfer mixture to an 8-inch round baking dish. Bake, uncovered, in a 350 degree oven about 20 minutes or until heated through. Serve warm with dippers. Makes about 2²/₃ cups.

Microwave directions: Prepare dip as directed, except transfer mixture to an 8-inch microwave-safe baking dish. Micro-cook, uncovered, on 70 percent power (medium-high) 4 to 6 minutes or until heated through, stirring once. Stir just before serving.

"OLE' LUTHER'S" AVOCADO DIP   *Helen Mayfield*

This recipe was sent to us from Shreveport, Louisiana, by Luther Cowan, Alvie's cousin.

2 ripe avocados
Juice of 1/2 lemon
1 3-ounce package cream
  cheese
1 large onion, grated
1 large garlic clove, grated

1 ripe tomato
2 tablespoons Worcestershire
  Sauce
¹/₂ teaspoon Tabasco Sauce
Salt and pepper to taste

Pulverize avocados with lemon juice, mash cheese, grate onion and garlic. Skin tomato and pulverize. Add other ingredients to avocados. Salt and pepper to taste, mix thoroughly. Serve on Ritz crackers or over shredded lettuce. Yield: 2 cups.

MEXICAN BEAN DIP   *Daisy Cox*

1 15-ounce can refried
  beans
4-ounces cream cheese,
  softened
1 12-ounce carton sour
  cream
1 bunch green onions,
  finely chopped
³/₄ cup picante sauce

4-ounce can diced green
  chiles
Salt, pepper and garlic
  powder to taste
1 cup Monterey Jack or
  Cheddar cheese, grated
Tortilla chips to serve

Combine beans, cream cheese, sour cream, onions, picante sauce, green

13

chiles, salt, pepper and garlic powder. Place in a 1¹/₂-quart baking dish. Sprinkle top with grated cheese. Bake 1 hour at 300 degrees. Serve with chips. Yield: 5 cups.

PRAIRIE FIRE

Agnes Stevenson

4 cups refried beans
1 cup butter or margarine
¹/₂ pound Provolone cheese, grated

4 to 6 canned jalapeño peppers, chopped
3 teaspoons jalapeño juice
2 onions, minced
1 tablespoon garlic, chopped

Place all ingredients in top of a double boiler, cook until cheese is melted and mixture is smooth. Serve with tortilla chips. Freezes well. Yield: 5¹/₂ cups.

FELIX'S CHILI CON QUESO

Cynthia Smith

¹/₂ cup vegetable oil
1 onion, finely minced
¹/₂ cup canned whole tomatoes
¹/₄ teaspoon cayenne (or to taste)
1 small garlic clove (optional)

3 tablespoons paprika
Salt and pepper to taste
¹/₂ cup flour
¹/₂ cup water
2 cups American cheese, grated

Mix oil, onion, tomatoes, cayenne, garlic, paprika, salt and pepper in a heavy pot and simmer for 25 to 30 minutes, or until well done. Mix flour and water and blend well. Melt cheese in microwave until soft and add to first mixture, stirring to keep from sticking or burning on low heat. Add flour mixture and up to ¹/₂ cup more water to get the right consistency. This is a thick spread. It is really better to spread it on large tortilla chips and heat to bubbly under broiler, but you can dip it. Freezes well. Yield: 4 cups.

YUMMY CHRISTMAS CRAB
Martha Combs

This crab dish is one of the prettiest you can have at Christmastime. However, lump crab is so expensive now, serving this has to be a very special occasion. My daughters, Terri and Wendy, have made it with the imitation crab, and they say it is almost as good. I've never figured out any way of serving this except in a Pyrex pie plate. I put the Pyrex plate on a silver tray, and put the Melba rounds around it. With the red and green colors, it is very festive (and, oh, so good!!)

1 pound lump crab
1 bottle Heinz chili sauce
1 8-ounce package cream cheese

1/2 cup mayonnaise
1/2 cup fresh parsley, chopped

Soften cream cheese with mayonnaise. Spread in bottom of Pyrex pie plate. Cover with chili sauce, then crab, then parsley. Serve with Melba rounds. Yield: 3 cups.

HOT CRAB DIP Á LÁ LIBERTY TEXAS
Cynthia Smith

Of course, it is best with lump fresh crab meat.

2 8-ounce packages cream cheese, softened
1/2 cup butter
2 tablespoons lemon juice
Dash of red pepper

2 tablespoons Worcestershire sauce
4 green onions, chopped
1 pound crab meat

Mix cream cheese and butter in double boiler with lemon juice, red pepper, Worcestershire sauce, onion, and crab meat last. Serve hot. Triscuits are good to dip with. Yield: 4 cups.

DILL DIP
Agnes Stevenson

2/3 cup mayonnaise
2/3 cup sour cream
1 tablespoon green onion, shredded

1 tablespoon parsley, shredded
1 teaspoon dill weed
1 teaspoon seasoned salt

Mix together mayonnaise and sour cream. Add onions, parsley, dill weed and salt. Mix well and chill for 1 hour to let flavors blend. Yield: 2 cups.

Cynthia Smith uses 1 cup each of mayonnaise and sour cream and Beau Monde seasoning instead of seasoned salt.

FRUIT DIP
Wanda Clark

1 7-ounce jar marshmallow
   cream
1 or 2 3-ounce packages
   cream cheese

1 8-ounce carton Cool Whip
   Amaretto or almond extract
   to taste

Mix all ingredients and serve with different fruits. Yield: 2 cups.

JENNI'S PICO DE GALLO
Jennifer Smith Marino

1 **large onion, chopped**
1 **tomato, chopped**
1 **tablespoon cilantro, chopped**
1 **tablespoon coriander**
Sprinkling of Tony Chachere's
   Cajun seasoning

1 **lime, squeezed**
1 **teaspoon white vinegar**
1 **tablespoon vegetable oil**
Dash red wine vinegar

Mix all ingredients together and serve with chips or over your food. Yield: 1 cup.

SPINACH DIP
Kittie Clyde Leonard

1 **package Hidden Valley Ranch Salad Dressing,**
   Original Buttermilk Recipe
2 **cups sour cream**
1 **10-ounce package frozen spinach, chopped, cooked**
   and drained
$1/4$ **cup onion, minced**
$1/4$ **teaspoon basil**
$1/2$ **teaspoon oregano**

Mix all ingredients well. Chill over night. Serve with chips, crackers, or your favorite raw vegetables. Yield: 3 to $3^1/2$ cups.

Beverages

APRICOT FROZEN PUNCH

Elva Shoemake

2 3-ounce packages apricot gelatin	1 cup lemon juice
2 cups boiling water	1 46-ounce can pineapple juice
2 cups sugar	1 cup apple juice
2 cups water	1 quart ginger ale

Dissolve gelatin in boiling water. Combine sugar and 2 cups water; bring to boil. Boil until sugar dissolves. Add to gelatin mixture. Set aside to cool. When cool, add lemon, pineapple and apple juices. Mix well. Pour into plastic containers with tight fitting lids. Freeze. To serve, place containers under hot water for a few minutes. Place frozen punch in punch bowl and add ginger ale. Stir to mix (mixture should be slushy). Serves 30.

FROZEN BANANA PUNCH

Ola Matus

Mrs. Snowie Teeters, our former Pastor's wife, gave me this recipe and I love to make it because it is so good and you can make it ahead of time.

4 cups sugar	Juice of 5 oranges
6 cups water	Juice of 2 lemons
1 46-ounce can unsweetened pineapple juice	5 bananas, mashed
	3 quarts ginger ale

Cook together sugar and water for 3 minutes. Cool and add to other ingredients except ginger ale. Freeze in containers. When ready to use, thaw about 1 1/2 hours or until mushy. Add about 3 quarts ginger ale. Serves 50.

MOCK CHAMPAGNE PUNCH

Daisy Cox

1 46-ounce can pineapple
juice
1 46-ounce can apple juice
or cider
1 12-ounce can frozen
lemonade, undiluted

$^1/_2$ cup granulated sugar
4 quarts ginger ale, chilled
Mint and lemon slices to
garnish

Combine juices, frozen lemonade concentrate and sugar. Stir well until sugar dissolves. Divide punch evenly into two plastic, 2 quart containers and store in freezer overnight or longer. When ready to serve, remove from freezer about 3 hours before serving so mixture becomes mushy. Break up and place in a large punch bowl ($2^1/_2$ to 3 gallon size) and add ginger ale. Do not add ice; the mushy juices keep the punch cold. Garnish as desired. Makes 40 six-ounce servings.

NOTE: I store the punch in 2 quart containers so a smaller quantity can be used. Use 2 quarts ginger ale for each 2 quart container of punch.

HOLIDAY CRANBERRY PUNCH

Daisy Cox

2 cups orange juice
$^1/_2$ cup lemon juice
$^1/_2$ cup sugar
2 28-ounce bottles ginger
ale, chilled

1 48-ounce bottle cranberry
juice cocktail
2 pints raspberry sherbet

Combine first 3 ingredients; stir until sugar dissolves. Add cranberry juice; mix well. Chill. Spoon scoops of sherbet on top of punch. Add ginger ale; gently stir to blend. Yield: $3^1/_2$ quarts.

ROSE GRAY'S PUNCH

Flora Cox

The following punch recipe was passed on to me by Rose Gray, a beautiful Christian lady, who served as hostess for the First Baptist Church of Borger for more than forty-five years. She served and catered many wedding receptions, anniversary parties, banquets, and bridal showers.

³/₄ cup sugar
Hot water
1 12-ounce can frozen orange
   juice

1 6-ounce can frozen limeade
1 46-ounce can pineapple juice

Melt sugar in small amount of hot water. Put juices in after thawing and just rinse out cans and stir, stir, and stir. Pour over about a quart and a half of ice cubes. Kool-Aid may be used for color. Serves 20–24.

FRUIT SURPRISE PUNCH

Vanessa Luce

6 cups water
4 cups sugar
1 46-ounce can pineapple
   juice
1 12-ounce can frozen
   orange juice

1 10-ounce package frozen
   strawberries, sliced
5 bananas, sliced
6 quarts 7-up
Fresh lime or lemon slices

Boil water and sugar 3 minutes. Add juices and freeze until used. Take out half hour before needed from freezer. Add strawberries, bananas, 7-Up and put slices of limes or lemons on top. Serves 40.

HAZEL'S FAST AND EASY PUNCH

Ola Matus

4 packages Lemon Lime
   Kool-Aid
4 quarts water

4 cups sugar
2 quarts pineapple juice
2 quarts ginger ale

Mix first four ingredients. Chill and serve with ice cubes. Add 2 quarts ginger ale just before serving. Serves 100.

SPICED TEA

Joy Watson

1 cup instant tea with lemon
1 11-ounce jar Tang

¹/₂ teaspoon ground cloves
1 teaspoon cinnamon

Mix together and keep stored in an airtight container. Use 2 teaspoons to 1 cup boiling water and 1 packet of Equal. Makes 2¹/₂ cups of tea mix.

SPICED TEA MIX
Addie Paul

1/2 cup instant tea
1 cup sugar
1 cup Tang
1 package Minute-Maid
   Lemonade mix

1 teaspoon cinnamon
1 teaspoon cloves
Pinch of salt

Mix together and store in jar. To make a cup of tea, add 2 teaspoons of mix to 1 cup of boiling water. Makes 1 1/2 cups of tea mix.

RUSSIAN TEA MIX
Thelma Elm

1 cup sugar
2 cups Tang
3/4 cup instant tea
1 package orange Jello

3 tablespoons lemon gelatin
1/2 teaspoon cinnamon
1/2 teaspoon allspice
1/2 teaspoon cloves

Mix together the sugar, Tang, tea, gelatin and spices, blending well. To make 1 cup of tea: add 2 teaspoons of tea mixture to 1 cup boiling water. Stir until blended. Makes 5 cups of tea mix.

JOYCE'S HOT FRUIT DRINK
Joyce Ellis

4 cups apple cider
2 cups cranberry juice
1 cup orange juice
1 12-ounce can apricot juice

1/2 cup sugar
2 sticks cinnamon
A few whole cloves
Orange slices, garnish

Mix all ingredients together in a large pot and heat 20 minutes. Garnish with orange slices. Serves 16–20.

WASSAIL
Addie Paul

2 quarts apple cider
2 cups pineapple juice
1 cup lemon juice
2 sticks cinnamon

6 whole cloves
Brown sugar or honey to
   taste

20

Place all ingredients in pot; bring to simmer and strain. Serve warm or it can be stored in refrigerator or freezer for future use. Serves 15.

Spirited Beverages

HILL COUNTRY BUTTERMILK
Norma Honeycutt

1 6-ounce can frozen pink lemonade
1 6-ounce can pineapple juice

1 6-ounce juice can tequila
Crushed ice

Blend until mushy. Makes 2¹/₄ cups.

STRAWBERRY CHAMPAGNE PUNCH
Cynthia Smith

1 quart ripe strawberries
Juice of 1/2 lemon
1 750 ml bottle Rhine wine or Chablis, chilled

1 750 ml bottle champagne, chilled
1 pint sparkling water, chilled

Place strawberries in punch bowl with lemon juice. Pour 1/2 bottle of wine over this and let stand in refrigerator for 3 hours. Just before serving place good size chunk of ice in bowl, add remainder of wine, champagne and sparkling water, all well chilled. Stir lightly and serve in punch glasses. Add strawberries to garnish. Makes 10 glasses.

CLARET PUNCH
Cynthia Smith

2 pounds sugar
Juice of 12 lemons
1 20-ounce can sliced pineapple, use juice
6 750 ml bottles Claret

1¹/₂ 750 ml bottles brandy
12 oranges, sliced
2 750 ml bottles champagne
2 quarts sparkling water

21

Dissolve sugar in fruit juices and pour over large piece of ice in 3 gallon punch bowl. Add wine, brandy, and sliced fruit. Let stand in refrigerator until guests arrive. Add champagne and sparkling water last. Serve in punch cups. Serves 40–50.

MEXICAN COFFEE

Bradley Smith

1 ounce Kahlúa	Dash cinnamon
½ ounce brandy	Hot coffee
1 teaspoon chocolate syrup	Whipped cream

Place Kahlúa, brandy, syrup and cinnamon in coffee cup, fill with hot coffee. Stir to blend. Garnish with whipped cream. 1 serving.

THE GODFATHER

Vic Marino

Two of these and Grandpa goes out on the town.

1 ounce Galliano	Juice of 1/2 lime
³/₄ ounce Drambuie	

Shake well and serve "on the rocks." 1 serving.

KAHLÚA

Cindy Abbit

2 vanilla beans (Spice Island)	7 cups boiling water
	1 liter brandy
7 cups sugar	1 pint bourbon
6 ounces instant coffee	

Use gallon jug with screw tight cap. Dark colored jug is best. Split vanilla beans lengthwise. Put in jug, mix sugar and coffee and add boiling water. Stir until sugar and coffee dissolve. Add brandy and bourbon. Pour into jug. Add enough water to fill jug. Let set for 30 days in a dark closet. Yields: 3 to 4 quarts.

PEACH FUZZ   *Holly Lawson*

I received a chain letter asking for recipes to be sent to the people on the list. Since I enjoy recipes so much and liked the idea of getting 36 recipes, I started writing my 6 letters. Out of all those letters this is the only recipe I received.

1¹/₂ ounces Amaretto	1 scoop vanilla ice cream
1 fresh peach	(or peach) or 2 ounces heavy cream
	1¹/₂ ounces grenadine

Blend and serve in a champagne glass. For a non-alcoholic drink, omit Amaretto and add 1 teaspoon almond extract. 1 serving.

FRESH PEACH MARGARITAS   *Cynthia Smith*

A different way to use our abundant peaches.

9 peaches, cut up	¹/₄ cup lime juice
2 ounces tequila	2 tablespoons sugar
2 ounces Triple Sec	10 ice cubes, cracked

Combine and whirl all in blender. Yields: 4 drinks, 5 ounces each.

ROSE AND LES TRUE'S MILK PUNCH   *Martha Combs*

Two of our very dearest friends were Rose and Les True, of the True Ranch in Wimberley. They could have lived any place in the world, but chose this beautiful part of Texas on the Blanco River. Rosie and True are no longer with us . . . but, during their lifetime, they were beyond a doubt the most gracious host and hostess I have ever known. I'll never forget an early morning visit to their ranch, Rosie and True greeted us with a huge silver tray with milk punch served in sterling mugs from one of the most beautiful sterling pitchers I have ever seen. This is the True's Milk Punch.

8 eggs
2 cups sugar
1 bottle (fifth) rum

1 bottle (fifth) brandy
1¹/₂ quarts milk or skimmed milk

In large bowl, beat eggs, slowly adding sugar. Continue beating until mixed well. Add rum, brandy and milk, stirring thoroughly. When ready to serve, fill blender 2/3 full. Add 1/2 cup ice and blend. Serves 15 to 20.

★　★　★　★　★

HINT:
Decorative ice molds will be clear if you draw up the water, stir it 4 or 5 times at 15 minute intervals to break up and expel air bubbles.

★　★　★　★　★

HINT:
A China coffee cup holds 6 ounces, a punch cup holds 4 ounces and a mug holds 8 ounces.

★　★　★　★　★

HINT:
Use muffin tins to make extra large ice cubes for punch.

★　★　★　★　★

HINT:
Freeze a portion of punch in ice tray or muffin cups to prevent diluting punch.

★　★　★　★　★

HINT:
A silver teaspoon in a glass of hot water or liquid will keep the glass from breaking. Put the spoon in first, then pour hot liquid.

★　★　★　★　★

HINT:
When making coffee for a crowd, allow 1 pound of coffee plus 2 gallons water for 40 servings.

Soups

D. J. Whittington '90

SAM EALY JOHNSON HOME

The Sam Ealy Johnson home, built in 1856, is a "dog-trot" log cabin, typical of early Hill Country dwellings, and is the oldest structure in the Johnson Settlement. Sam and his bride, Eliza Bunton Johnson, moved into it in 1867. It also served as headquarters for the Johnson brothers cattle business. In 1872, a year after the business failed, it was sold to Sam's nephew, James Polk Johnson, who became a prominent farmer and rancher. In 1879, he founded Johnson City, which was named in his honor.

CHEESE VELVET SOUP

Mary Amis

6 ounces Brie
2 ribs celery, finely
  chopped
2 carrots, finely chopped
1/2 onion, finely chopped
8 tablespoons butter
8 tablespoons flour

2 cups chicken broth,
  heated
1 bay leaf
1 teaspoon thyme
Salt and pepper to taste
1/2 cup whipping cream

Cut away rind on cheese and discard. Cut cheese into cubes and set aside. Sauté vegetables in butter over medium heat. Add flour and blend, making a roux. When butter is absorbed and the mixture thick, add broth and stir until thick again. Add bay leaf and thyme. Slowly add the cheese, stirring until melted. Add cream and heat thoroughly. Makes 6, 1/2-cup servings.

JENNI'S $5,000 CHEESE BROCCOLI SOUP

Cynthia Smith

Our daughter learned to make this soup one summer when she worked at Palmers Restaurant in San Marcos. The reason we call it $5,000 Cheese Broccoli Soup is this: It is about what it cost to send her to Colorado State University for about six weeks. She got homesick for her boyfriend and left school against our wishes. We told her since she had cost us greatly, she would have to support herself best she could until the next semester; she did, and for Valentines Day 1979 she wrote out this recipe and had it framed for me. It is the most expensive gift she ever gave me or ever will. It is terribly overpriced, but very good.

1 onion, chopped
1 carrot, chopped
2 stalks celery, chopped
1/4 cup margarine
1 can chicken broth
1 can Cheddar or Nacho
  cheese soup
1 soup can water

1 10-ounce package frozen
  broccoli, chopped
1/2 pound Velveeta cheese
Salt and pepper to taste
1 clove garlic, crushed
2 cups milk
3 tablespoons flour
3/4 cup water

Sauté onion, carrot, and celery in margarine. Add broth and bring to boil. Add cheese soup and water (1 can) and bring to a boil. Add broccoli. Add cheese, salt, pepper, garlic, and milk. Stir while simmering, until vegetables are soft. To thicken soup add flour with water. Makes 6, 1-cup servings.

CHICKEN SOUP

Holly Lawson

This chicken soup will make you feel so good, you won't need to call the doctor!

1 fryer
2 16-ounce cans tomatoes, undrained

2 10-ounce package frozen creamed corn
Salt and pepper to taste
Milk

Cook chicken in water: skin, debone and chop. Add tomatoes, corn and chicken to stock. Simmer 2 hours and just before serving add a little milk (2 tablespoons per bowl). Yield: 10 servings.

CORN CHOWDER

Cynthia Smith

Easier, Quicker and Cheaper

2 slices bacon, cooked crisp, crumbled
1 tablespoon bacon drippings
1/4 cup onion, chopped
2 tablespoons parsley

Dash of thyme
1/2 cup whole kernel corn
1 can cream of potato soup
1/2 soup can milk
1/2 soup can water
Salt and pepper to taste

Sauté onion, parsley, thyme in bacon grease; cook until onion is tender. Stir in rest of ingredients. Heat and stir now and then. Garnish with bacon. Serves 3.

AUNT ALICE'S FISH CHOWDER

Joycelyn Carter

1 can Chunky vegetable soup (any kind)
1 6-ounce can tomato juice or Snap-E-Tom

1 bay leaf
Black pepper to taste
1 1/2 pounds of fresh fish (any kind), cut in cubes

Mix all together and bring to a boil and simmer about 15 minutes. Remove bay leaf. Good with French bread. Serves 2–3.

FRENCH MARKET SOUP

Peggy Arbon

This is another delicious soup. Served with hot homemade baguettes (see breads) or rolls . . . what a feast.

9 Bean Soup Mix (see note)	1 large green pepper,
1 tablespoon salt	chopped
Ham hock	6 stalks celery, chopped
3 quarts water	2 tablespoons fresh cilantro
Bouquet garni (or use bay	1/2 cup dry wine
leaves, thyme, oregano	Salt and pepper to taste
and cumin)	1 pound smoked sausage
1 quart tomatoes	1/2 frying chicken
2 medium onions, chopped	Parsley, chopped

Wash dry bean mixture, drain. Add water to cover and add salt. Soak overnight. Drain. Add 3 quarts water, ham hock, bouquet garni or other. Cover and simmer 3 hours. Add all other ingredients except sausage and chicken and simmer uncovered 1 1/2 hours. Add sausage and chicken. Simmer until chicken is done. Remove chicken; skin, debone and cut into smaller pieces and return. Add parsley last ten minutes. Makes 9, 1-cup servings.

NOTE: May use 1/4 cup each of black beans, navy beans, red beans, garbanzo, pinto, split peas, barley lentils, black eyed peas, and baby limas.

HARVEST SOUP

Janey Wiemers

This is a quick and good soup for winter lunch or supper. Our family has enjoyed it for many years (we use one can of each soup for ample bowl of soup for six).

3 cans cream of chicken	3 cans tomato soup
soup	3 cans chicken gumbo soup

Blend the cream of chicken and tomato soups. Add 8 soup cans of water. Blend in cans of chicken gumbo soup. Heat until hot enough for serving. Stir occasionally. Makes 20, 1-cup servings.

HEARTY ITALIAN SOUP

Aline Slack

This recipe came from my late sister-in-law who took it from a magazine and it gets raves each time it's made.

1 pound sausage, bulk or link (if using links cut in $^1/_2$-inch pieces)
1 medium green pepper, chopped
1 medium onion, chopped
1 28-ounce can tomatoes, chopped

2 8-ounce cans tomato sauce
2 8-ounce sauce cans water
1 tablespoon granular or 3 cubes chicken bouillon
$^3/_4$ teaspoon garlic salt
$^3/_4$ cup small shaped macaroni or shell pasta
Cheese, shredded

In Dutch oven or large sauce pan, brown meat, green pepper and onion. Drain grease, stir in remaining ingredients, except macaroni. Cover and simmer for 15 minutes. Stir in macaroni, cover and simmer for 10 to 12 minutes until pasta is tender. Top with shredded cheese in each individual bowl. Makes 8 cups.

LONGORIA'S MEXICAN SOUP

Joycelyn Carter

This recipe was given to me by one of my nursing students in Corpus Christi. It can also be used as a dip or a sauce over tamales.

1 pound ground meat
1 pound bulk sausage, mild
1 can cream of mushroom soup

1 small onion, chopped
1 can Ro-Tel tomatoes and green chilies
2 pounds Velveeta cheese

Brown ground meat, sausage and onions, pour off grease. Place in Crockpot, add other ingredients. Heat on low. Yields 6 cups.

PINTO BEAN SOUP

Norma Honeycutt

This recipe was put together after being served as an appetizer in several Mexican restaurants in San Antonio. You can add what you like to suit you. If you want it spicier, add hot peppers or Ro-Tel tomatoes and green chilies. The more you put in the pot the better the soup.

29

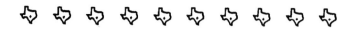

1 cup pinto beans	4 to 5 slices of bacon, diced
¹/₂ cup cilantro, chopped	Salt to taste

Cook beans in about 2 quarts of water. You want a lot of juice. About one hour before the beans are done add cilantro and bacon. Delicious with all Mexican dishes. Serves 6 to 8.

POTATO AND CARROT SOUP   *Vanessa Luce*

We were visiting with Robert's brothers and sisters and while sitting around the table we were discussing recipes. I told them how much I enjoyed cooking with Grandma Luce. Robert and I lived with her and Grandpa Luce for awhile and I spent a lot of time in the kitchen getting her recipes and cooking secrets. I am the only one of the family who had cooked with her and now cook like her. One of her favorite recipes was home made Potato and Carrot Soup which cured most any ailment. One of her secrets was a pinch of sugar. She always said it brought out the taste of any vegetable you cooked.

4 large potatoes, diced	2 cups hot water
2 large carrots, shredded	2 chicken bouillon cubes
2 onions, cut small pieces	4 cups milk
4 tablespoons butter	Salt and pepper to taste
1 tablespoon celery seed or	Pinch of sugar
1 cup chopped celery	

Sauté vegetables in butter until tender. Add two cups hot water with two chicken bouillon cubes dissolved in it. Cook until everything is tender, 45 to 60 minutes. When done add four cups of milk and heat. Yields: 6 cups.

TWIN SISTERS POTATO AND CHEESE SOUP   *Norma Honeycutt*

This is a favorite restaurant in San Antonio, famous for good food. This recipe is great. Can be made and eaten in a short time and I found if garnished with chopped bacon when served, it adds to the flavor. Bacon can be served on the side as a matter of choice. This is a hearty soup and tastes great on a cold day.

30

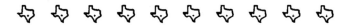

2¹/₂ **pounds Russet potatoes**
  (about 4 to 5 medium)
  thoroughly washed and
  left unpeeled and cut into
  bite-size pieces
6 **cups water**
1 **red bell pepper, chopped**

1 **green bell pepper,**
  chopped
1 **medium onion, chopped**
Salt and pepper to taste
2 **cups Cheddar cheese,**
  grated
1 **cup half and half**

Put cut potatoes in large stock pot. Add water, peppers, onion and salt and pepper. Bring to boil; reduce heat and simmer covered about 35 to 45 minutes or until potatoes are tender. Cool slightly. Put in food processor with steel blade. Pureé. Pour back in stock pot. Add cheese and half and half. Cook on low until cheese melts, stirring often to keep cheese from sticking and burning. Serves 6 to 8.

PORTUGUESE SOUP

Peggy Arbon

An Air Force friend, Jackie Pace, gave me this recipe several years ago, and I've enjoyed cooking and eating it. It is especially delicious on a cold winter day. It is excellent for feeding a large family.

2 **cups onion, chopped**
3 **cloves garlic, chopped**
2 **tablespoons oil**
1 **pound pork or beef Polish**
  sausage, garlic flavor
12 **small new potatoes,**
  quartered

10 **cups beef broth**
1 **small head cabbage,**
  coarsely chopped
2 **16-ounce cans pinto beans**
¹/₄ **cup cider vinegar**
1 **16-ounce bottle ketchup**

Sauté onions and garlic in oil. When transparent, add sausage that has been thickly sliced. Brown sausage slightly and add other ingredients. Simmer covered 30 to 45 minutes on low. Will keep one week in refrigerator. Freezes well except potatoes will disintegrate when soup is reheated. Yield: 4 to 5 quarts.

★　★　★　★　★

HINT:
A leaf of lettuce dropped into the pot absorbs the grease from the top of soup. Remove the lettuce as soon as it has served it's purpose.

★　★　★　★　★

CREAM OF SAUERKRAUT SOUP MIT LOVE   *Peggy Arbon*

While visiting our daughter, Leecia Rad, in Portland, Oregon, we frequently eat at a darling neighborhood restaurant where they have wonderful soups, salads and desserts. One of the soups they serve is cream of sauerkraut. I never asked for their recipe, but while here at home, I tried to duplicate it by memory of the taste.

2 tablespoons butter
1 small to medium onion, chopped
1 can cream of celery soup
1 16-ounce can sauerkraut, drained
1 to 2 cups milk

In pan you are going to cook your soup in, melt butter and sauté the onions until they are soft. Add the cream of celery soup and stir to blend. Add milk gradually, stirring to smooth the mixture. Add the sauerkraut. If you like mild kraut, rinse it before you add it to the pot. Cook it for several minutes, just until the onions are done. Simple!!! Yield: 5 cups.

SUMMER SQUASH SOUP   *Genevia Bushnell*

2 tablespoons butter or margarine
2 onions, chopped coarse (2 cups)
5 cups chicken broth
2 potatoes, peeled and cut in 3/4-inch chunks (1 cup)
2 pounds zucchini or yellow squash or combination, cut in 1-inch chunks (8 cups)
2 carrots, sliced thin (1 cup)
1$^1/_2$ teaspoons salt
$^1/_4$ teaspoon black pepper
2 tablespoons fresh basil, chopped or 1 teaspoon dried leaves
Garnish: squash blossoms

Melt butter in a 3 to 4 quart saucepan over medium-high heat. Add onions and cook 5 to 7 minutes stirring 2 or 3 times, until translucent. Add broth and potatoes. Bring to a boil, then cover, reduce heat and simmer 5 minutes. Stir in carrots and simmer 8 to 10 minutes until potatoes and carrots are almost tender. Stir in squash, salt and pepper. Simmer covered 10 to 15 minutes until vegetables are tender. Serve hot or cold. Makes 11 cups, 6 servings. 162 calories per serving.

TORTILLA SOUP   *Cynthia Smith*

Delicious Comida!

2 medium onions, chopped
2 cloves garlic, chopped
1 jalapeño pepper, chopped
1 stick butter
3 cans Ro-Tel tomatoes and green chilies, pureéd
2 cups chicken stock or broth
2 to 3 tablespoons cilantro, chopped
10 to 12 tortillas, cut into 1-inch squares or $1/4$-inch strips
Garnish with if desired:
Sour cream
1 **cup chicken, cooked and shredded**
Avocado, diced
Monterey Jack cheese, grated

Sauté onions, garlic, and pepper in butter. Add tomatoes, chicken stock, and cilantro, bring to boil, simmer. Fry cut tortillas in a little oil, drain. Top soup with tortilla strips and sour cream, shredded chicken, diced avocado or cheese, if desired. Makes 20, $1/2$-cup servings. **For milder soup:** Use $1/2$ jalapeño pepper, 2 cans Ro-Tel tomatoes and green chilies, pureéd.

LILLY AND COMPANY'S TORTILLA SOUP   *Dennis R. Bushnell*

1 yellow onion, finely chopped
2 tablespoons butter
4 cloves garlic, smashed with salt
4 cups kernel corn, fresh is best
3 tablespoons fresh cilantro, finely chopped
8 to 10 cups chicken stock or canned broth
1 cup chicken, cooked and shredded
1 8-ounce can tomato sauce
2 teaspoons cumin
Salt to taste
Black pepper to taste
Cayenne pepper to taste
10 to 12 corn tortillas
2 ounces Monterey Jack cheese, grated
Oil for frying tortillas

Sauté onion in butter until soft. Add garlic and corn and cook another 2 to 3 minutes. Add cilantro, chicken stock and pieces, tomato sauce, cumin, salt, pepper and cayenne and bring to boil. Reduce heat and simmer 15 minutes. Meanwhile cut tortillas into eights, then fry in hot oil until crisp. Remove from oil and drain on paper towels. Grate cheese, serve soup with several tortilla chips and about two tablespoons of grated cheese in each bowl. Makes 16, 1-cup servings.

Variations: Use parsley instead of cilantro, omit corn, cut into small pieces one avocado for each 4 servings and place into soup before serving, or use whole tomatoes instead of sauce.

Sandwiches

BEAN AND CHEESE OPEN FACED SANDWICH   *Cynthia Smith*

1 16-ounce can Ranch Style Beans	Bread
	Mayonnaise
1/4 cup ketchup	Mustard
Dash of Tabasco hot sauce	Velveeta or Cheddar cheese
Dash of garlic salt	

Mix beans, ketchup, Tabasco, and garlic salt and heat. Drain some of the juice off. Top bread that has been spread with mayonnaise and mustard with the beans. On top of this add cheese. Broil just until the cheese melts. We love Velveeta cheese but you can use either. Delicious! Serves 6.

MICROWAVE GRILLED CHEESE SANDWICH   *Daisy Cox*

2 to 3 slices processed cheese (see note)	2 slices bread (see note)
	1 teaspoon soft butter

Place cheese slices between slices of bread. Place sandwich on microwave-able plate in a microwave oven. Heat for about 30 seconds at high power, or until cheese begins to melt. Remove from microwave, and butter the exterior surfaces of both slices of bread. Place in a preheated, non-stick skillet, and grill for about 1 minute per side, until the surface browns slightly. Serve immediately. Makes one sandwich.

NOTE: Use your favorite variety of cheese and bread. Some good cheese options include low-cholesterol, Swiss-style, American or Muenster. Light or dark breads with firm texture work well.

Variations:

Southwest-Style sandwich — For cheese, use Monterey Jack flavored with jalapeño peppers. Add a tablespoon or two of hot salsa before heating in microwave. Butter the exterior of the bread slices and complete cooking as described in recipe above. Serve with guacamole and tortilla chips.

Taco Tuna Melt — Top cheese with 1/4 cup of well-drained, water-packed chunk tuna. Add 2 tablespoon of hot salsa. Heat in a microwave oven for one minute. Butter exterior of the bread slices and complete cooking as described in recipe above. Serve with tortilla chips.

Bacon Cheese Sandwich — Place two slices of crisp, cooked bacon with cheese between bread. Butter exterior of the bread slices and complete cooking as described in recipe above.

PIMIENTO CHEESE SANDWICH SPREAD   *Eloise Klein*

  2 **pounds Velveeta cheese, grated**
  1 **7-ounce can pimientos, chopped**
  1 **or 2 cups salad dressing**

Mix all ingredients thoroughly. May be used to stuff celery or as a dip. 2 tablespoons chopped onion and 2 medium jalapeño peppers chopped may be added. Makes 3–4 dozen sandwiches.

RAISIN SANDWICH SPREAD   *Lorraine Lanham-Mimi's Kitchen*

1 egg
1 cup sugar
Juice and rind of 1¹/₂ lemons

1 teaspoon butter
1 cup ground raisins
1 cup mayonnaise

Beat egg until light in color. Combine egg, sugar, lemon juice and rind in medium saucepan. Cook until thickened. Cool. Stir in raisins and mayonnaise. Spread on whole wheat bread. Yields: 2¹/₂ cups.

Sauces

FAJITA OR CHICKEN MARINADE

Peggy Arbon

Since I have been growing herbs, it has opened up a whole new experience for me in the kitchen. I thoroughly recommend both growing and cooking with herbs.

4 cloves garlic, chopped
3 tablespoons gold tequila
2 tablespoons fresh lime juice
2 tablespoons fresh orange juice
2 tablespoons red wine vinegar
1¹/₂ teaspoons orange zest
¹/₂ teaspoon black pepper, freshly ground

¹/₂ teaspoon dried red chilies, crushed
¹/₂ teaspoon dried Mexican oregano
¹/₂ teaspoon brown sugar
4 tablespoons olive oil
3 tablespoons cilantro, freshly ground

Mix ingredients together in a bowl. Marinate meat or chicken in mixture 2 to 4 hours or overnight. Makes 1 cup.

LEMON DILL SAUCE

Cynthia Smith

Sauce is super on any grilled or broiled meat; pork, chicken or beef.

3 tablespoons mayonnaise
2 tablespoons Dijon style mustard
2 tablespoons lemon juice

2 tablespoons fresh dill weed, snipped or ¹/₂ teaspoon dried dill

Mix mayonnaise, mustard, lemon juice and dill weed. Brush on meat one minute before removing from grill. Pass remaining sauce. Makes 1/2 cup, enough for 4 pieces of meat.

MUSTARD GRILLING SAUCE   *Daisy Cox*

$^1/_2$ cup margarine, melted
3 tablespoons prepared
   mustard

2 tablespoons parsley, chopped
1 tablespoon lemon juice
$^1/_8$ teaspoon pepper

In small bowl or saucepan stir together margarine, mustard, parsley, lemon juice and pepper until well blended. Brush on chicken or fish while grilling or broiling. Makes about 1/2 cup.

"CAJUN" REMOULADE SAUCE   *Cynthia Robichaux Smith*

A family recipe from my Acadian relatives in South Louisiana, near New Iberia where good food and good times prevail.

1 quart mayonnaise (not
   salad dressing)
4 hard boiled eggs
3 tablespoons Creole or
   dark mustard
4 tablespoons white vinegar
4 tablespoons fresh parsley,
   chopped

2 tablespoons paprika
2 tablespoons Worcestershire
   sauce
3 tablespoons horseradish
   sauce
4 garlic cloves, chopped
Salt and pepper to taste

Whirl all the ingredients in blender or processor, add salt and pepper to taste. Refrigerate 12 hours before using. Will keep several weeks in refrigerator. This sauce is basically for use over shrimp, as a cocktail but can be used for many other things such as: a great dip, a spread for chicken sandwiches and as a dressing for any green salad. Makes 6 cups.

Salads—Fruit

ANGEL SALAD

Jane Mills

1 8-ounce package cream
  cheese
1/2 cup sugar
1 teaspoon vanilla
1 16-ounce can fruit
  cocktail, well drained

1 20-ounce can crushed
  pineapple, well drained
1 envelope Dream Whip,
  prepared
1 cup pecans, chopped

Blend first 3 ingredients. Add fruits and mix gently. Fold in Dream Whip.
Put in serving bowl and top with chopped pecans. Chill at least 4 hours.
Serves 8–12.

CRANBERRY SALAD

Vanessa Luce

1 pound cranberries, ground
1 1/2 cups sugar, pour over
  cranberries while fixing the
  rest
1 pound marshmallows, cut
  in quarters

1 pound Tokay grapes,
  halved and seeded
1 cup chopped pecans
1 pint cream, whipped

Mix and refrigerate a few hours before serving. Serves 8–12.

CUP SALAD

Holly Lawson

1 cup pecans, chopped
1 cup pineapple chunks,
  drained
1 cup fresh apples, chopped
1 cup mandarin oranges,
  drained

1 cup miniature marshmallows
1 cup coconut
1 cup sour cream
Maraschino cherries, enough to
  add color (about 1/4 cup)

38

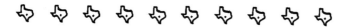

Mix all together in large bowl, refrigerate several hours or overnight. Serves 12.

ALDRICH FAMILY FRUIT SALAD　　　　*Joycelyn Carter*

Mrs. Aldrich was a friend of my mother. She said this was an old family recipe.

2$^1/_2$ cups fruit cocktail, drained (2 large cans)
$^1/_2$ cup marshmallows, cut or miniature
2 apples, peeled and diced
1 16-ounce can pineapple chunks, drained (save 2 tablespoons of juice)
1 cup angel flake coconut
$^1/_4$ pound Velveeta cheese, grated
6 maraschino cherries

Mix together first 4 ingredients. Make sauce.

Sauce:

1 egg
2 tablespoons pineapple juice
$^1/_4$ cup lemon juice
$^1/_4$ cup sugar
1 tablespoon flour
1$^1/_2$ teaspoon mustard (after sauce is cooked)

Cook eggs, sugar, flour, juices until thick. Cool, add mustard. Add cooled sauce to fruit mixture. On top of mixed salad add coconut. On top of coconut add cheese. (Velveeta cheese will grate better if frozen first). Cheddar cheese can be substituted. To garnish, cut cherries in half and put on top. Better if made a day ahead. Serves 8–12.

AUNT MARILEE'S FRUIT SALAD　　　　*Holly Lawson*

This recipe is made for just about every special occasion our family has. My Aunt Marilee started it.

12-ounces Cool Whip
1 can condensed milk
1 can Cherry pie filling
1 16-ounce can crushed pineapple, drained
1 cup miniature marshmallows
1 cup coconut (optional)
$^1/_2$ cup pecans, chopped

39

Mix Cool Whip and condensed milk and chill. Stir together other ingredients and chill. Add to cream mixture and chill. Serves 10–12.

BANANA SPLIT SALAD *Mary Pat Carter*

2 cups powdered sugar
1 teaspoon vanilla
1 cup margarine
3 eggs
2 to 3 bananas, sliced

1 16-ounce can crushed
   pineapple, drained
1 12-ounce carton Cool Whip
1/2 cup nuts, chopped

Crust:
4 1/2 cups crushed graham
   crackers or Rice Chex

1/2 cup margarine
1/8 cup sugar

Mix margarine and sugar, add crumbs. Press into a 9 x 13 inch pan. Bake at 325 degrees for 12–15 minutes. Cool. Mix powdered sugar, vanilla, eggs, and margarine. Beat 8 to 10 minutes on high speed of mixer. Put in cool crust. Cover with sliced bananas. Top bananas with pineapple. Cover with Cool Whip and chopped nuts. Refrigerate before serving. Serves 8–12.

FRUIT SALAD SUPREME *Ola Matus*

This is an old time recipe and was originally made with Queen Anne cherries instead of fruit cocktail. It was found handwritten in an old cookbook purchased in a thrift shop.

1 11-ounce can mandarin
   oranges
1 16-ounce can pineapple
   chunks
1 17-ounce can fruit cocktail

1 3 1/2-ounce package vanilla
   pudding mix (not instant)
12 large marshmallows
1 cup heavy cream
Lettuce cups

Drain fruit well, saving the juice. Measure 1 1/2 cups juice. Combine juice with the pudding mix, using the juice in place of the liquid called for in the pudding recipe, and cook until thickened, stirring constantly. While this mixture is hot, stir in marshmallows to dissolve. Cool to room temperature. Whip cream stiff and add the cream and drained fruit to pudding mixture. Keep covered in large bowl until serving time. To serve: put gen-

erous amounts of salad into lettuce cups. Serves 10–20 depending on portions.

GRANDMOTHER'S MARSHMALLOW DELIGHT *Cynthia Smith*

¹/₂ pound marshmallows
1¹/₂ cups crushed pineapple
2 cups whipping cream (1 pint)

2 tablespoons powdered sugar
1 teaspoon vanilla

Cut marshmallows in fourths, add pineapple and mix well. Let stand in refrigerator over night. Next day: Whip cream, add vanilla and powdered sugar. Mix well. Fold whipped cream into fruit and marshmallow mixture. Chill. The salad can also be served frozen but preferably chilled. Yield: 8–10 servings. Cool Whip may be substituted for whipping cream.

HOT FRUIT SALAD *Holly Lawson*

1 16-ounce can sliced peaches
1 16-ounce can sliced pears
1 16-ounce can apricot halves
1 16-ounce can pineapple chunks
1 17-ounce can fruit cocktail

¹/₂ cup margarine
1 cup fruit juice from cans
¹/₂ cup brown sugar
2 tablespoons apple pie spice

Drain fruit and put in baking dish. In saucepan mix butter, juice, sugar and spice. Bring to boil. Pour over fruit and bake 30 minutes at 300 degrees. Serves a crowd, 20–24.

JANEY'S FRUIT SALAD *Janey Wiemers*

I got this recipe from the wife of a couple who lived in the co-op with us in seminary. It has become a family tradition at holiday meals because it has always been a favorite. Notice the designation of "small size" and "commercial." I obtained this in 1958 before marshmallows were miniatures and all sour cream was commercial. I usually double and sometimes triple the quantities for family gatherings.

½ **pound marshmallows (small size)**

1 **20-ounce can fruit cocktail (No. 2)**

1 **20-ounce can crushed pineapple (No. 2)**

1 **cup sour cream (commercial)**

Drain fruit cocktail and pineapple thoroughly. Mix everything and chill 24 hours or overnight. Serves 8.

JOY'S 24-HOUR FRUIT SALAD

Joy Watson

3 **egg yolks, beaten**
½ **cups sugar**
Juice of 2 large lemons
½ **cup whipping cream, whipped**
1 **16-ounce can sliced pine- apple, drained and diced**

1 **16-ounce can pears, diced**
1 **16-ounce can Royal Anne cherries, pitted and drained**
2½ **cups miniature marshmallows**
3 **to 4 bananas, sliced**

Cook egg yolks, sugar, lemon juice in heavy saucepan or double boiler until thick, stirring constantly. Let cool completely, then fold into the whipped cream. Drain the fruit, then add to the whipped cream dressing. Add the miniature marshmallows. Let sit in the refrigerator overnight or for 24 hours. Just before serving, add the bananas. Serves 16–20.

TWENTY-FOUR HOUR SALAD

Mary Dyer

This is an old recipe of my mother-in-law's. This salad was always served at Christmastime.

2 **eggs, beaten**
4 **tablespoons vinegar**

4 **tablespoons sugar**
2 **tablespoons butter**

Mix eggs, vinegar and sugar; cook over low heat stirring constantly until thick and smooth. Add butter and cool. When cool, fold in the following and refrigerate 24 hours before serving. Serves 16.

1 **carton of cream, whipped**
1 **11-ounce can mandarin oranges, drained**
2 **bananas, sliced**
2 **cups small marshmallows**

1 **8-ounce can pineapple chunks, drained**
2 **apples, peeled and chopped**
1 **20-ounce can fruit cocktail, drained**

VALERIE'S SALAD

Holly Lawson

This recipe was given to me by a cousin, Valerie Schmid, at a family reunion but did not give the name, so I call it Valerie's salad. It is very good and soooo easy. My daughter, Lacey, won a blue ribbon with this salad at a 4-H Food Show.

1 16-ounce can apricot
   halves, drained and
   reserve juice
1 16-ounce can pineapple
   pieces, drained and
   reserve juice
3 bananas, sliced

1 teaspoon lemon juice
1 3½-ounce package vanilla
   instant pudding
1 cup milk
Pecan pieces
Poppy seeds

Mix juice of fruit, lemon juice, vanilla pudding and milk and pour over fruit. Add pecans, as much or as little as you like, and poppy seeds (a teaspoon goes a long way). Mix and serve. Serves 8–12.

GWEN'S FROZEN FRUIT SALAD

Gwen Pickett

1 quart Cool Whip
1 pint sour cream
1½ cups sugar
1 20-ounce can crushed
   pineapple, drained

1½ cups pecans, chopped
5 bananas, mashed
½ cup maraschino cherries,
   chopped

Mix well and freeze. Serves 12.

PEGGY'S FRUIT SALAD

Pam Lemons

Served at the Lemon's 50th Wedding Anniversary.

3-4 bananas, sliced
1 6-ounce can Awake or frozen
   orange juice, thawed
Fresh strawberries, sliced or
   1 package frozen, thawed
1 small can frozen lemonade

2 cups 7-Up or Sprite
1 16-ounce can sliced
   peaches, drained
1 20-ounce can fruit
   cocktail, drained

Mix all ingredients and freeze. Set out one hour before serving. Serves 15–20.

MY FAVORITE FROZEN FRUIT SALAD   *Joycelyn Carter*

This recipe came with our first refrigerator in 1952, an International Harvester. The refrigerator is still being used.

2 3-ounce packages cream cheese
1/8 teaspoon salt
2 tablespoons salad dressing
1 tablespoon lemon juice
1/2 cup crushed pineapple, drained (8-ounce can)
2 cups bananas, diced

1/2 cup maraschino cherries, chopped
1/2 cup pecans, chopped
1/2 cup marshmallows, diced
1 cup cream, whipped or 1 package Dream Whip prepared

Mash cheese with fork. Blend with salt, salad dressing, lemon juice and mix well. Fold in pineapple, cherries, nuts, bananas and marshmallows. Whip cream until thick, not stiff, and fold into cheese mixture. Turn into freezing trays. Freeze until firm. May place a half of a red and green maraschino cherries on top of salad to indicate serving. (This makes it a nice colorful Christmas salad). Serves 16.

WALDORF FROZEN SALAD   *Mary Pat Carter*

1 8-ounce can crushed pineapple drained, reserve juice
2 eggs, slightly beaten
1/2 cup sugar
2 1/2 cups chopped apples
2/3 cup miniature marshmallows

2/3 cup pecans, chopped
2/3 cup celery, chopped
1/4 cup mayonnaise
1/4 cup lemon juice
1 cup whipping cream, whipped

Combine pineapple juice, eggs, and sugar in a medium saucepan; cook over medium heat, stirring constantly, until thick and smooth. Cool slightly. Add pineapple and remaining ingredients except whipped cream; stir well. Fold in whipped cream. Place about 20 paper baking cups in muffin tins; spoon salad mixture into baking cups. Cover and freeze. Serves 20.

APRICOT DELIGHT

Holly Lawson

The topping is very rich.

2 3-ounce packages orange
  Jello or 1 6-ounce package
1³/₄ cups hot water
1 cup apricot and pineapple
  juice

1 20-ounce can apricots,
  chopped, drained, reserve
  juice
1 16-ounce can crushed
  pineapple, drained, reserve
  juice

Topping:
¹/₂ cup sugar
3 tablespoons flour
1 cup apricot and pineapple
  juice

1 egg, beaten
2 tablespoons butter
Cool Whip

Dissolve Jello in hot water, then add juices, and fruits. Chill until firm.
Mix topping ingredients and cook until thick. Cool, then fold in Cool
Whip. Spread on top of firm Jello mixture. Serves 12–16.

BARBARA'S ORANGE DELIGHT

Sallye Baker

1 6-ounce package orange
  Jello
1 cup boiling water
1 pint orange sherbet
1 8-ounce can crushed
  pineapple, drained

1 11-ounce can Mandarin
  oranges, drained
1¹/₂ cups Cool Whip
³/₄ cup pecans, chopped

Dissolve Jello in boiling water. Add sherbet to hot mixture and stir until
dissolved. Fold in remaining ingredients. Refrigerate. Serve on lettuce leaf
as a salad or use as a dessert. Serves 8–12.

CHERRY COKE SALAD

Holly Lawson

1 3-ounce package cherry
  Jello
1 cup hot water

1 16-ounce can pie cherries,
  drained, save juice
¹/₂ cup sugar
1 cup Coca Cola

Topping:

1 3-ounce package cream   ¹/₄ cup Miracle Whip
   cheese

Mix Jello with hot water, set aside. Mix cherry juice with sugar, boil. When cool, mix together with Jello and Coke. Topping: Mix softened cheese with Miracle Whip. Spread over top of salad when thoroughly jelled. Serves 8.

CONGEALED DESSERT SALAD   *Mary Pat Carter*

2 3-ounce packages   1 apple, chopped
   strawberry gelatin   1¹/₂ cups water
2 cups hot water   12 marshmallows, cut
1 cup coffee   ¹/₂ cup nuts, chopped
1 package condensed mince   ¹/₂ cup maraschino cherries,
   meat   chopped

Mix first three ingredients together. Mix mince meat, apple, water and cook until well blended. Add marshmallows, nuts, and cherries. Add mixture to gelatin mixture when it begins to set. Place in refrigerator. Serves 10–12.

CONVERSATION SALAD   *Ava Cox*

1 16-ounce can Bing   1 cup pecans, broken
   cherries, pitted, drained, 1 3-ounce bottle stuffed
   reserve juice   olives, sliced
¹/₃ cup cherry juice   1 pint cottage cheese
1 tablespoon lemon juice   (optional)
1 3-ounce package cherry
   Jello

Combine cherry juice and lemon juice. Add enough water to make 1³/₄ cups liquid. Heat liquid and pour over Jello and stir until dissolved. Chill until partially set. Add cherries, nuts, olives, and cottage cheese. Pour into mold and chill until firm. Yield: 8 servings.

EMERALD SALAD

Kittie Clyde Leonard

1 3-ounce package lime
  gelatin
1 cup hot water
2 3-ounce packages cream
  cheese
1/2 cup fruit juice
Few drops green food color
  (optional)

1 large can fruit cocktail,
  drained, reserve juice
1 cup nuts, chopped
1 can pineapple chunks,
  drained, reserve juice
1 cup marshmallows,
  chopped
1/2 pint whipped cream

Dissolve gelatin in 1 cup hot water. Blend cream cheese, and juice until smooth. Stir in gelatin. Beat until foamy. Add food coloring. Chill for 1 to 2 hours or until thickened. Fold in remaining ingredients. Chill until firm. Serves 10–15.

COUSIN FRANCES' GELATIN SALAD

Joyce Ellis

1 20-ounce can crushed
  pineapple, undrained
2 tablespoons sugar
1 6-ounce package orange
  Jello or sugar-free Jello

2 cups buttermilk
1 8-ounce carton Cool
  Whip, thawed
1 cup pecans, chopped
  (optional)

Combine pineapple and sugar in a saucepan; bring to a boil; stirring occasionally. Remove from heat; add Jello, stirring until dissolved. Cool. Add buttermilk, and stir until combined. Fold in Cool Whip and pecans if desired. Place in oblong glass dish and chill until firm. Serves 8.

SHIRLEY'S JELLO SALAD

Shirley Rosson

1 6-ounce package lemon
  Jello
2 cups hot water
2 apples, diced

Sauce:
1/2 cup sugar
2 egg yolks

1/2 cup celery, diced
1 cup pecans, chopped
1 8-ounce can crushed
  pineapple, drained

2 teaspoons lemon juice
1 8-ounce carton Cool Whip

Mix Jello with water. Cool. When thick, add apples, celery, pecans, and

47

pineapple. Sauce: mix sugar, egg yolks, and lemon juice in double boiler and cook until thick. Cool. Fold in Cool Whip and place on top of Jello mixture. Refrigerate. Serves 10–12.

STRAWBERRY CONGEALED SALAD

Norma Honeycutt

2 3-ounce packages strawberry Jello
1¹/₂ cups hot water
1 package frozen strawberries, sliced

1 16-ounce can crushed pineapple, undrained
1 large banana, mashed
1 pint sour cream (2 cups)

Dissolve Jello in hot water, add frozen strawberries (do not thaw), pineapple with juice and banana. Mix well. Pour half of mixture in mold or Pyrex dish, slightly oiled. Put in freezing compartment until firm, put other half in refrigerator. When half in freezer is firm spread with sour cream, pour other half on top and let set in refrigerator overnight or several hours. Serves 8 to 12.

Variation: Vanessa Luce uses half of recipe and omits bananas. Sour cream is placed on top. Serves 6.

STRAWBERRY-PRETZEL SALAD

Elaine Oliver

1 6-ounce package strawberry Jello
2 cups boiling water
1 large package frozen strawberries, slightly thawed
³/₄ cup margarine
3 tablespoons brown sugar

2¹/₂ cups crushed pretzels (not too fine)
1 8-ounce package cream cheese
1 cup sugar
1 8-ounce carton Cool Whip

Dissolve Jello in water and add strawberries. Cool until it begins to thicken. Combine margarine, brown sugar and crushed pretzels. Spread in a 13 x 9 Pyrex pan. Cream sugar with cream cheese; fold in Cool Whip and spread over crust. Pour Jello mixture over creamed mixture after it has begun to set. Refrigerate over night or until firm. Serves 12–14.

★ ★ ★ ★ ★

HINT:
Hull strawberries after washing to avoid them absorbing too much water.

Salads—Vegetable

HOT BEAN SALAD   *Daisy Cox and Flora Cox*

The following recipe was served to my husband and me by my niece about twenty-five years ago. I have never seen it in print in any cookbook, and since she is a homemaking major, I am sure that it is original with her. I have shared it with my teacher friends and my Sunday School class friends, and here is hoping that you, too, will enjoy it.

1 pound can kidney beans,
   drained
1 cup thinly sliced celery
¹/₃ cup chopped sweet pickles
³/₄ cup Cheddar cheese, diced
   (not grated) ¹/₄ pound

¹/₄ cup green onions, thinly
   sliced
¹/₂ teaspoon salt
¹/₂ cup salad dressing
¹/₃ cup rich round cracker
   crumbs

Combine all ingredients except the crumbs. Toss lightly. Spoon into four 8-ounce or six 5-ounce bakers or casserole dish. (I use one casserole dish). Sprinkle crumbs on top. Bake in very hot oven, 450 degrees, for 10 minutes or until bubbly. Garnish each with crisp bacon curls. Double for a luncheon. Yield: 4 to 6 servings.

BROCCOLI SALAD   *Pam Lemons*

Even men ask for this recipe. This was served at the 50th Wedding Anniversary for W. H. and Mavis Lemons on April 1, 1989, at the First United Methodist Church.

2 bunches fresh sliced
   broccoli (fairly small
   pieces)
1 3¹/₄-ounce can black
   olives, sliced
8 slices bacon, cooked and
   crumbled

1 bunch green onion, finely
   chopped
1 cup mayonnaise
¹/₄ cup salad dressing
³/₄ cup Parmesan cheese or
   less
   Italian dressing to thin

49

Combine vegetables and bacon. Combine ingredients for dressing. Pour dressing over vegetables and stir until all ingredients are moist. Chill 24 hours. May use less Parmesan cheese, 3/4 cup gives a strong flavor. Serves 12–16.

RAW BROCCOLI AND CAULIFLOWER SALAD   *Flora Cox*

The following recipe was served to Bill and me by one of our favorite students in her new home.

1 bunch fresh broccoli, washed and separated
1 head cauliflower, washed and separated
1 16-ounce can bamboo shoots, drained
1 8-ounce can water chestnuts, drained and sliced

1 pint box cherry tomatoes
1 stalk celery, sliced
1/2 pound fresh mushrooms
1/2 pound shelled green peas
2 green peppers, sliced
1 bunch green onions, sliced
Good Seasons Italian dry mix

Mix all ingredients. Dress with Good Seasons Italian mixed with lemon juice instead of vinegar. Sprinkle with garlic powder if desired. Best made 24 hours before serving to let flavors blend. Serves 12–16.

BROCCOLI RAISIN SALAD   *Thelma Elm*

This was served at a Home Extension luncheon in Ohio.

1 bunch broccoli, chopped
1 cup raisins
1 small onion, chopped
1 cup Miracle Whip

1/2 cup sugar
2 tablespoons cider vinegar
1 cup sunflower seeds, shelled and salted

Mix broccoli, raisins and onion in large bowl. Mix Miracle Whip, sugar and vinegar and fold into salad. Add sunflower seeds just before serving. Serves 6–8.

★   ★   ★   ★   ★

HINT:
Freshen wilted vegetables by letting them stand about 10 minutes in cold water, drain well and store in a plastic bag in the refrigerator.

12-HOUR CABBAGE SLAW

Vanessa Hale Luce

Many happy hours were spent on West Galveston Beach every 4th of July week. We had many family gatherings, both the Hale and Luce side of the family. One year we had over sixty people at the house for a day of fun and visiting and the fellowship and food was always wonderful. One of my favorite recipes and favorite of many is this slaw.

1 large cabbage, grated	1 large green pepper, cut in
2 large onions, sliced and	rings
separated into rings	1 cup sugar

Place a layer of cabbage, then onion rings and peppers. Sprinkle sugar over vegetables. Let stand while making dressing.

Dressing:

1 cup vinegar	1 tablespoon sugar
1 tablespoon celery seed	1½ teaspoons salt
1 tablespoon Dijon mustard	1½ cups salad oil

Bring vinegar, spices and sugar to a boil. Add oil and boil again. Remove from heat and pour over vegetables. Refrigerate 12 or more hours covered. The salad will keep for 2 weeks. Serves 8.

MARINATED CARROTS

Pam Lemons

OR COPPER PENNIES . . . Served at W. L. and Mavis Lemons' 50th wedding anniversary.

2 pounds carrots, scraped and sliced	³/₄ cup vinegar
1 green pepper, sliced	1 cup sugar
1 onion, sliced	1 teaspoon prepared mustard
1 can tomato soup	Pepper to taste
½ cup salad oil	
1 teaspoon Worcestershire sauce	

Cook carrots in salted water about 20 minutes. Cool. Alternate layers of carrots, green peppers, onions. Combine remaining ingredients. Stir until blended. Pour over vegetables and refrigerate for 24 hours. Serves 15.

Variation: Thelma Elm also gave this recipe. She omits the salad oil and Worcestershire sauce and uses only 1/2 cup vinegar and 1/2 teaspoon dry mustard for the prepared mustard. Serves 15.

Cynthia Smith submitted her mother, Louise Robichaux's recipe. Recipe is halved, the carrots are left crisp, and the tomato soup omitted. Serves 6–8.

CAULIFLOWER SALAD
Lucia Carbary

³/₄ cup sour cream
³/₄ cup mayonnaise
1 package Original Ranch dressing
1 head cauliflower, break in pieces

2 bunches radishes, chopped
2 bunches green onions chopped, use some tops
1 8-ounce can water chestnuts, chopped

Mix first three ingredients. Mix vegetables and chestnuts. Add dressing and mix. Serves 6–8.

CONGEALED CAULIFLOWER SALAD
Helen Mayfield

1 3-ounce package lemon Jello
2 cups hot water
Juice of 1 lemon
¹/₈ teaspoon salt

¹/₂ cup celery, diced
1 cup raw cauliflower flowerets
¹/₂ cup carrots, chopped
¹/₄ cup pecans, chopped

Make Jello as directed on package. Mix with vegetables and pecans, place in refrigerator. Serves 8.

★   ★   ★   ★   ★

HINT:
To prevent watery salads, place an inverted saucer in the bottom of the salad bowl. The excess dressing will drain under the saucer and keep the greens crisp.

★   ★   ★   ★   ★

CRUNCHY FOUR SEASON SALAD   *Jewell Sultemeier*

I've taken this to the Smorgasbord and it goes over really well.

1 cup green bell pepper, coarsely chopped
8 ounces ($^1/_2$ 16-ounce can) medium pitted ripe olives
9 ounces ($^1/_2$ 18-ounce jar) medium stuffed green olives
2 cups celery, sliced diagonally
2 $4^1/_2$-ounce cans mushrooms
3 stalks of broccoli, cut into small flowerets

1 medium head cauliflower, cut into small flowerets
12 green onions, coarsely chopped
1 medium zucchini, sliced $^1/_4$-inch thick, or use cucumber
$^1/_4$ teaspoon sugar
1 package dry Italian salad dressing.
1 6-ounce bottle Italian salad dressing

Mix vegetables and sugar together in a large bowl. Sprinkle with dry salad dressing then mix with liquid dressing. More olives can be used. Marinate for about four hours before serving. Will keep in refrigerator for several days. Serves 20.

CUCUMBER SALAD   *Jewell Sultemeier*

I have had this recipe since 1973 and we like it. Keeps well in refrigerator.

3 large cucumbers, sliced thin
$^1/_3$ cup vinegar
$^1/_3$ cup oil
$^1/_4$ cup sugar

1 teaspoon salt
$^1/_4$ teaspoon pepper
$^1/_8$ teaspoon garlic salt
1 tablespoon dill, minced (optional)

Slice cucumber wafer thin. Combine vinegar, oil, sugar and spices in a one-cup measure. Pour mixture over cucumbers. Refrigerate for at least one hour. At serving time drain off liquid. Sprinkle with dill. Serves 6.

MEXICAN DEVILED EGGS (SPICY)   *Robyn Henderson*

Most of all and maybe most important of what my Granny taught me is that after a meal is eaten, one should right away "do the dishes" as this helps in good digestion. I think Granny was pretty sharp and she never had a sink full of dirty dishes.

8 eggs, hard-boiled
1/2 cup sharp Cheddar
cheese, grated
1/4 cup mayonnaise

2 tablespoons green onion,
chopped
1 tablespoon sour cream
1/4 cup salsa, medium or hot
1/4 teaspoon pepper

Slice eggs in half lengthwise. Transfer yolks to medium bowl and add remaining ingredients. Mix thoroughly, then mound mixture into whites. Refrigerate. Serves 4–8.

DIG DEEP SALAD

Betty Wood

1/2 head lettuce, shredded or
fresh spinach or
combination
1 medium red onion, thinly
sliced
1/2 cup celery, chopped
1 8-ounce can water
chestnuts, sliced
1 10-ounce package frozen
green peas, thawed

Salt
1 pint mayonnaise
1 cup Romano or Cheddar
cheese, grated
4 hard cooked eggs,
chopped and salted
8 slices bacon, crumbled
8 cherry tomatoes
Buttered croutons

Layer first 7 ingredients in order listed, salting each layer. Cover and refrigerate 24 hours. Forty-five minutes before serving, take out of refrigerator and garnish with eggs, bacon and tomatoes. You may add buttered croutons as an additional garnish. Serves 8–10.

FRITO SALAD

Holly Lawson

This is a recipe from my sister Donna. It is very good.

1 large tomato, chopped
1 pound Cheddar cheese,
grated
1 15-ounce can ranch style
beans, drained

1 8-ounce bottle Catalina
dressing
1 head lettuce, chopped
1 onion, chopped
1 12-ounce package Fritos

Combine all ingredients except Fritos and let stand 1 hour. Just before serving add Fritos. Serves 6–8.

HOFFBRAU SALAD

Martha Combs

Everyone who has lived in Austin has eaten at the Hoffbrau. Yes, thank good-ness, it is still there!!! And, everyone loves the Hoffbrau Salad. Ellie Rucker was kind enough many years ago to publish this in the Austin paper . . . we have friends both here and in Colorado who have been most grateful!! I've changed it a bit . . . but, basically, this is it . . .

Iceberg lettuce, chopped
Tomatoes, chopped
1 3-ounce bottle of pimiento
  stuffed green olives, sliced
1 clove garlic, (I am often
  lazy and use a lot of garlic
  salt)

Corn oil (they use Mazola —
  I use olive oil)
Lemon juice
All of the juice from the
  olives
Salt and pepper to taste

Rub a wooden salad bowl with a cut clove of garlic. Add chopped lettuce, chopped tomatoes and sliced green olives, as much of each ingredient as pleases you. Make the dressing by combining equal amounts of corn oil and lemon juice (or maybe a little less lemon juice) to taste. Add the juice from the olives. Pour over salad and toss well. Add a little salt and pepper and you'll think you're dining outdoors at the Hoffbrau.

LAYERED GARDEN SALAD

Agnes Stevenson

1 head iceberg lettuce,
  washed and torn into bite-size pieces
1/2 pound fresh spinach,
  washed well and torn
2 cups fresh broccoli
  flowerets

1 10-ounce package frozen
  green peas
1 cup sour cream
1 cup mayonnaise
1 or 2 tablespoons sugar
1 pound bacon, cooked and
  crumbled
1 cup Swiss cheese, grated

Layer lettuce, spinach, broccoli and peas in a 3-quart glass bowl. Mix sour cream and mayonnaise well and spread evenly over top, sealing to edge of bowl. Sprinkle evenly with sugar; then bacon and cheese. Cover bowl tightly and refrigerate at least 2 hours for flavors to blend. Serves 12.

LAYERED SALAD Á LA RITA   *Peggy Arbon from Rita Ashford*

First Layer:

1 head lettuce, shredded
1 bunch spinach, torn
1 large Bermuda onion,
  sliced thin

Sprinkle ¹/₃ pound Swiss
  cheese, grated and
¹/₃ cup Italian or Parmesan
  cheese, grated

Second Layer:

1 large bell pepper,
  chopped
1 rib celery, chopped
1 bunch broccoli flowerets,
  small

Sprinkle ¹/₃ pound Swiss
  cheese, grated and
¹/₃ cup Italian or Parmesan
  cheese, grated

Third Layer:

1 can sliced water chestnuts
1 10-ounce box frozen
  English peas
¹/₂ pound mushrooms,
  sliced
6 eggs, boiled and sliced

8 slices bacon, fried and
  crumbled
Sprinkle ¹/₃ pound Swiss
  cheese, grated and
¹/₃ cup Italian or Parmesan
  cheese, grated

Mix 2¹/₂ cups mayonnaise and 5 tablespoons sugar together and spread over the top, making sure that the whole salad is covered and the dressing touches all sides of the bowl. This seals the salad. Cover bowl tightly. Refrigerate overnight. Serves 12–20.

GREEN PEA SALAD   *Thelma Elm*

1 16-ounce package frozen
  green peas, thawed
1 cup mayonnaise

¹/₂ cup sugar
¹/₃ cup wine vinegar
1 cup Spanish peanuts

Mix mayonnaise, sugar, vinegar and add to peas, mix well. Stir in peanuts. Refrigerate for several hours. Serves 6–8.

★   ★   ★   ★   ★

HINT:
Lemon juice poured into a spray bottle is easy to apply to the surfaces of cut fresh fruits or vegetables.

CALICO POTATO SALAD
Patty Casparis

3¹/₂ cups potatoes, cooked, peeled, and diced
2 tablespoons cooking oil
2 tablespoons wine vinegar
2 cups cabbage, shredded
1 4-ounce can ripe olives, chopped
¹/₄ cup dill pickles, chopped
¹/₄ cup carrots, shredded

2 tablespoons pimiento, chopped
3 tablespoons green pepper, chopped
²/₃ cup mayonnaise
1 tablespoon salad mustard
2 tablespoons onion, minced
Salt and pepper to taste

Mix potatoes, oil, and vinegar and refrigerate. Add the rest of ingredients and mix well. Refrigerate until ready to serve. Serves 8.

HOT POTATO SALAD
Ray Sultemeier

8 medium potatoes, boiled in jackets
8 slices bacon, diced
¹/₂ cup onion, diced
3 tablespoons flour

³/₄ cup water
³/₄ cup vinegar
5 to 6 tablespoons sugar
Salt and pepper to taste

Peel and slice boiled potatoes while warm. In skillet fry bacon to a light brown; remove from skillet, add onions and cook until clear. Stir in flour; add water, vinegar, sugar, salt and pepper. Cook until thickened; pour over potatoes, add bacon. May serve hot or cold. Serves 8.

GRANDMA HALE'S POTATO SALAD
Vanessa Luce

This is my Mom's recipe. She has continued the tradition of family gatherings which, in this time of history, might become a thing of the past. Mother always brought this to the beach, the Hill Country, made it at Christmas time and best of all made it anytime she could because it was my husband Robert's favorite.

57

5 large Irish potatoes, cooked, cut in 1/2-inch pieces
1 bunch crisp celery, cut in 1/2 inch pieces
2 whole bunches of green shallots, cut in 1/2-inch pieces
2 4-ounce jars of chopped pimientos
4 large green peppers, cut in 1/2-inch pieces
4 hard boiled eggs, chopped
1 8-ounce jar sweet pickles, chopped, with 1/2 cup or more of the juice
2 large white onions, cut in small bits
2 tablespoons of Dijon mustard with white wine
Juice of 1 lemon
2 tablespoons fresh parsley or 1 Tbs. McCormicks
2 tablespoons chopped chives, freeze dried, McCormicks
2 tablespoons or more seasoned salt
2 tablespoons or more of fancy paprika
2 tablespoons French's mustard
Hellmann's Light Mayonnaise to thoroughly moisten
Salt and pepper to taste
Black and green olives for garnish

Mix mustard with enough mayonnaise, add lemon juice and mix with all the rest of the ingredients. Add salt and pepper to taste. Mix, mix and mix some more. When everything looks good, pour into salad bowl and let stand about 1 hour. Serves 16.

AUNT JUNE'S RICE SALAD   *Joycelyn Carter*

All of my uncles are rice farmers. We eat a lot of rice. This is my favorite rice salad recipe.

2 cups Uncle Ben's rice
7 hard boiled eggs, chopped
3 dill pickles, chopped
3 green onions, chop all
3 ribs celery, chopped

1 2-ounce jar pimientos, drained
3/4 cup dill pickle juice
Salad dressing
Mustard

Cook rice according to instructions on box. Add next 6 ingredients. Mix

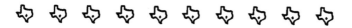

salad dressing and mustard; mix with salad. Let set in refrigerator over night. Serves 12.

CURRIED RICE SALAD
Vanessa Luce

Dressing:

1 cup peanut oil
$^1/_4$ cup fresh lemon juice
$^1/_2$ teaspoon ground coriander
2 teaspoons salt, or less

1 teaspoon ground cumin
$^1/_2$ teaspoon black pepper
1 tablespoon curry powder
Pinch of cayenne

Combine oil, lemon juice, salt, curry powder, cumin, coriander, pepper and cayenne; whisk together and set aside.

Salad:

2 cups raw regular long grain white rice
$^1/_2$ cup pistachios

2 6-ounce jars marinated artichoke hearts
$^3/_4$ cup raisins
4 to 6 scallions, chopped

Cook rice according to package directions, do not overcook. While rice is still warm, place in a large bowl and pour dressing over it — rice grains should be well-coated, but not floating. Toast pistachios in a preheated 350-degree oven 8–10 minutes. Let cool. (Can buy the roasted ones). Drain artichoke hearts, add raisins, pistachios, artichoke hearts and scallions. Add dressing. If necessary adjust seasoning to taste with salt and more lemon juice. Serve at room temperature or chill. Serves 8.

SAUERKRAUT SALAD
Dena Heider

1 16-ounce can sauerkraut, drained
1 cup onions, chopped
1 cup green peppers, chopped
1 small jar pimientos, chopped

1 cup celery, chopped
1 cup sugar
1 teaspoon pepper
1 cup water
$^1/_2$ cup vinegar
1 teaspoon salt

Mix sauerkraut and vegetables in large mixing bowl. Mix sugar, pepper, water, vinegar, and salt and heat. Pour hot liquid over sauerkraut and vegetables. Put in jars and refrigerate. It will keep indefinitely. Serves 6.

Variation: Norma Honeycutt omits the pimientos and for the dressing uses 1/4 cup oil, 1/3 cup vinegar and 1/4 cup sugar.

SENATOR'S SALAD   *Sallye Baker*

1 15-ounce can LeSeur peas	¹/₂ cup celery, chopped
1 16-ounce can French style green beans	¹/₄ cup green pepper, chopped
1 12-ounce can Shoe Peg corn	1 cup oil
	¹/₃ cup sugar
1 2-ounce jar pimientos	³/₄ cup vinegar
¹/₄ cup onions, chopped	Salt and pepper to taste

Mix vegetables in large bowl. Blend oil, sugar, salt and pepper and pour over vegetables and stir. Let it sit overnight. Drain before serving. Serves 8.

MOTHER'S COOKED SLAW   *Libby Casparis*

Mother said "This is guess work, but try it." I have found that her "guess work" is delicious.

¹/₂ head cabbage, shredded	1 teaspoon flour
Water	2 tablespoons sugar
Salt	2 tablespoons cream
1 tablespoon Crisco	1 tablespoon vinegar

Shred cabbage and put on to cook with a very little water, salt, and the Crisco. Cook until tender then mix flour and sugar together, then add cream and vinegar (enough vinegar to suit your taste) and pour over the cabbage. Let come to a boil. Serves 4.

SPAGHETTI SALAD   *Thelma Elm*

1 pound thin spaghetti	3 to 4 tomatoes, cut small
Green onion, chopped	1 jar McCormick Salad Supreme
1 16-ounce Wishbone Italian dressing	

Cook spaghetti according to instructions on the box. Let cool and add all ingredients and toss to mix. Serves 8.

SPINACH-EGG SALAD   *Libby Casparis*

Another recipe Katherine Wel Feltman copied from the Minneapolis paper.

1 **pound fresh spinach**	1 **teaspoon onion, finely grated**
1/2 **cup salad oil**	1/4 **teaspoon dry mustard**
1/4 **cup sugar**	6 **slices bacon, cooked crisp,**
2 **tablespoons vinegar**	**drained and crumbled**
1/2 **teaspoon salt**	1 **egg, hard cooked, sliced**
5 **hard cooked, chopped eggs**	**(garnish)**

Wash spinach thoroughly in lukewarm water, drain, chill to crisp. Combine oil, sugar, vinegar, onion, salt and mustard. Beat or blend in blender until dressing becomes thick and syrupy and sugar is thoroughly dissolved. Tear spinach into bite size portions. Place in large salad bowl. Add bacon and chopped eggs. Pour dressing over and let stand about 1/2 hour. Toss salad thoroughly to mix. Garnish with sliced egg. Prepare dressing ahead and refrigerate. Serves 6.

MARINATED BLACKEYED PEAS   *Sadie Sharp*

Texas Caviar . . .

1 **15-ounce can blackeyed**	1 **tablespoon salad dressing**
peas, drained	1 **tablespoon vinegar**
1 **rib celery, chopped**	1/4 **teaspoon salt**
1 **tablespoon onion, chopped**	**Dash of black pepper**
1 **tablespoon salad oil (Puritan)**	1 **large tomato, diced**

Drain blackeyed peas and rinse with cold water; drain well. Add celery and onion. Combine oil, vinegar, salad dressing, salt and pepper. Mix well. Pour over peas. Stir gently. Allow to chill in refrigerator several hours or overnight. At serving time add tomato. Mix carefully. Serve as a relish with meat or on a lettuce leaf as a salad. Serves 4–6.

TEXMATI SALAD

Vanessa Luce

1 cup Italian Salad dressing
³/₄ cup water
1 cup uncooked rice
1 10-ounce package frozen
  green peas, unthawed
1 4-ounce can sliced
  mushrooms, drained

¹/₂ cup green onions,
  chopped
1 8-ounce can water
  chestnuts, chopped
1 cup mayonnaise, optional
1 cup cooked cubed ham

Combine rice, dressing and water. Bring to a boil; turn to simmer; cover and cook 20 minutes or until rice is done. Remove from heat and let stand 10 minutes. Fluff rice with fork. Place in large bowl and combine with peas. Chill. When cool, add remaining ingredients and return to refrigerator. May need to add more Italian Salad dressing. Serves 8.

Meat–Salads

JOY'S CHICKEN SALAD

Ola Matus

Joy Watson always made Chicken Salad Sandwiches for our Garden Club Teas. They were always soooo good!

1 chicken, cooked, boned
  and chopped
1 cup celery, chopped
1 cup sweet pickles,
  chopped

1 apple, peeled or unpeeled,
  chopped
2 boiled eggs, chopped
Salt and pepper to taste
Mayonnaise

Combine first five ingredients and add salt and pepper to taste. Moisten with mayonnaise. Chill before serving. Can be used as a luncheon salad or on sandwiches. If you like it crunchy, add some chopped pecans. Serves 8.

CHICKEN MUSHROOM SALAD

Ava Cox

$^1/_2$ cup mayonnaise
2 tablespoons lemon juice
1 can condensed mushroom soup
1 envelope unflavored gelatin
$^1/_4$ cup cold water

$1^1/_2$ cups chicken, cooked and shredded
$^1/_2$ cup celery, cut fine
$^1/_2$ cup apple, cut fine (optional)
$^1/_2$ cup pecans, cut fine (optional)

Add mayonnaise and lemon juice to soup. Soften gelatin in cold water, dissolve over hot water. Add gelatin to soup mixture and mix well; add chicken and celery to soup mixture. Add apple and pecans, if desired, and mix well. Put in molds and refrigerate until set. Unmold on platter of lettuce leaves. Serves 6–8.

CHICKEN TARRAGON SALAD

Peggy Arbon

4 chicken breasts, cooked and diced
$^1/_2$ cup finely chopped green onion

$^1/_2$ cup sliced almonds
$^1/_2$ cup chopped fresh tarragon

Dressing:
2 tablespoons fresh lemon juice
2 tablespoons capers
1 tablespoon Dijon-style mustard

1 teaspoon yellow prepared mustard
$^1/_2$ cup Miracle Whip

Combine chicken, green onions, almonds, and tarragon in a large bowl. Combine remaining ingredients in a blender or food processor. Mix on high speed until ingredients are thoroughly combined. Pour dressing over chicken mixture and mix well. Refrigerate several hours or overnight. Tarragon may be processed with dressing ingredients, turning the dressing a lovely spring green. Serves 4–6.

RITA'S CHICKEN SALAD

Rita Reiner

1 pound boneless, skinless chicken breasts, cut into 1-inch cubes
2 tablespoons olive oil
Juice of one lime
1/8 teaspoon cayenne pepper or to taste
Ground black pepper and salt to taste
1 small onion, diced fine

1 rib celery, diced fine
1 jicama, about 1/4 pound, peeled and diced fine
4 large dates, pitted and chopped
1/4 cup pecans, roasted slightly and chopped
1/4 cup chopped fresh cilantro
1/2 cup mayonnaise

Place the cubed chicken in a glass bowl and toss with olive oil, lime juice, cayenne pepper, black pepper and salt. Spoon mixture into a baking pan and bake 15 minutes at 375 degrees, until chicken is cooked completely. Place chicken in refrigerator to cool, then add remaining ingredients, toss well to incorporate and serve. Serves 4.

SHRIMP-TUNA SALAD

Joycelyn Carter

1 pound shrimp, cooked, peeled, deveined, and cut in small pieces, or use canned shrimp
1 cup chopped celery
1/2 cup chopped shallots
1/2 cup chopped bell pepper

3 hard boiled eggs
1 2-ounce jar chopped pimientos
2 6-ounce cans tuna, drained
2 cups cooked rice
1/2 cup mayonnaise or more

Mix all together. Serve with crackers. Serves 10–12.

★   ★   ★   ★   ★

HINT:

When serving cantaloupe, cut and remove seeds and sprinkle evenly with a dusting of sugar and allow to stand until ready to serve. By the time the fruit is ready to be eaten the sugar has been absorbed into the fruit and the result is delicious.

★   ★   ★   ★   ★

Salad Dressings

BLUE CHEESE DRESSING

Mary Amis

2 teaspoons instant minced
  onion
2 tablespoons water
1 3-ounce package Blue
  Cheese, crumbled

³/₄ cup mayonnaise
2 tablespoons lemon juice
¹/₂ teaspoon paprika
¹/₄ teaspoon ground white
  pepper

Rehydrate onion with water 10 minutes. In small bowl crumble cheese, should be about 1/3 cup. Stir in mayonnaise, lemon juice, paprika, pepper and onion. Mix. Makes 1¹/₄ cups of dressing.

DILL DRESSING FOR SLAW

Daisy Cox

¹/₂ cup sour cream
¹/₂ cup mayonnaise
2¹/₂ tablespoons red wine
  vinegar

1 tablespoon sugar
¹/₂ teaspoon salt
2 tablespoons dill weed
¹/₃ teaspoon pepper

Thoroughly combine all ingredients. Can be stored in refrigerator in a glass jar. Makes 1 cup dressing.

FRENCH DRESSING

Daisy Cox

1 can tomato soup
²/₃ cup cider vinegar
²/₃ cup Wesson oil

¹/₂ cup sugar
1 onion, diced
1 green pepper, diced

Combine ingredients in glass jar and shake until thoroughly mixed. Use as dressing on all kinds of salad greens. Makes about 2¹/₂ cups.

REDUCED CALORIE FRENCH DRESSING   *Cynthia Smith*

³/₄ cup salad oil   ¹/₂ teaspoon paprika
¹/₄ cup vinegar   ¹/₄ teaspoon dry mustard
1 teaspoon salt   Pepper to taste
1 teaspoon sugar

Combine all ingredients in tight glass jar. Shake until blended. Chill. Makes 1 cup.

HONEY DRESSING FOR FRUIT SALAD   *Mary R. Davis*

Good when you are low on sugar.

¹/₂ cup honey   A pinch of ground ginger
¹/₂ cup lime juice

Mix and pour over fruit. Makes 1 cup.

LOUISE'S DRESSING   *Cynthia Smith*

(HORSERADISH HERB DRESSING) . . . Try this for your carrots, tossed greens, tomatoes, and cucumbers. For the carrots, I add a little carrot water to thin. It is delicious.

1¹/₂ tablespoon horseradish   1 teaspoon dried dill
1 cup sour cream   1 tablespoon sugar
1 tablespoon Tarragon   ³/₄ teaspoon salt
  vinegar   ¹/₄ teaspoon paprika
1 tablespoon snipped chives

Mix horseradish, sour cream and vinegar until smooth. Stir in chives, dill, sugar, salt and paprika. Refrigerate covered at least 15 minutes. Makes 1 cup.

★   ★   ★   ★   ★

HINT:
Submerge a lemon or orange in hot water for 15 minutes before squeezing to yield more juice.

MARITA'S SALAD FIXINGS

Peggy Arbon

from Marita Woodruff

> 1 4-ounce package Parmesan or Romano cheese, coarsley grated
> 1 3-ounce jar capers, drained
> 1 pint sweet cherry pickles, drained and save 1/2 cup juice
> 1 large can pitted black ripe olives
> 1 pint green salad olives, drained and save 1/2 cup juice
> 2 cans rolled anchovies, leave whole and use oil
> 3 cups tender celery, sliced
> 1 cup red or green bell pepper, sliced
> 2 packages Good Seasons Italian salad dressing
> 1 16-ounce Garbanzo beans, drained
> 1/4 cup good olive oil
> 1 medium purple onion, quartered and sliced
> Red wine vinegar (optional)

In a non-metal bowl, mix together the beans, olives, cherry pickles, cheese, anchovies, capers, celery, peppers and onions. Sprinkle with dressing mix and toss just enough to mix. Add the oil, and both vinegars (red wine and olive juice). Toss again to mix. Add enough wine vinegar to have the desired tartness. I use about 1/2 cup. Let stand overnight unrefrigerated so that the flavors blend. Serve as a dressing over any salad greens. Put in a small bowl and add about 2–3 heaping spoonsful of the dressing. Makes 2 to 3 quarts.

I like to use a mixture of Iceberg lettuce, Romaine lettuce, chopped red and green bell pepper, green onions, tomato and one carrot grated coarsely. Toss together.

★ ★ ★ ★ ★

HINT:
Place fresh unwashed cranberries in refrigerator for up to one month. Wash before serving.

★ ★ ★ ★ ★

67

HERBED MAYONNAISE

Jenni Marino

You can store this delicious homemade mayonnaise up to one month in a tightly covered jar in the refrigerator.

1/4 cup loosely packed
   watercress leaves
1/4 cup loosely packed
   parsley sprigs
1 green onion, sliced
1/2 teaspoon Dijon style
   mustard

1 cup salad oil
3 egg yolks
2 tablespoons lemon juice
Pepper to taste

In a blender or processor, place watercress, parsley and green onion, cover and blend. Add egg yolks, mustard and lemon juice and blend until smooth; with appliance running, add oil in a very slow steady stream. Scrape sides often. Add pepper to taste. Transfer to covered container and store in refrigerator. Makes 1 1/3 cups.

ROQUEFORT–BLUE CHEESE DRESSING

Cynthia Smith

1 quart Hellmann's
   mayonnaise
1/2 cup Sauterne wine
Juice from 1 lemon
8-ounces Roquefort cheese,
   crumbled

Salt to taste
1 teaspoon MSG
1/4 teaspoon white pepper
1 packet Sweet'n Low

Mix all ingredients together. Makes 4 cups.

★   ★   ★   ★   ★

HINT:
Sprinkle lemon juice on freshly cut bananas, apples, peaches and avocados to prevent darkening.

★   ★   ★   ★   ★

Main Dishes

EXPANSION OF
JOHNSON CITY BANK
JOHNSON CITY.   TEXAS

WAGNER & KLEIN, INC.
ARCHITECTS
FREDERICKSBURG.   TEXAS

THE JOHNSON CITY BANK

The Johnson City Bank building was constructed in 1885. James Polk John-
son, the founder of Johnson City, was the builder and architect. He died before
the building was completed. In 1890, when the Blanco County seat was moved
from the city of Blanco to Johnson City, the building was used as a temporary
Courthouse until 1916 when the new Courthouse was finished. On June 15,
1944, a charter was granted for a bank. It opened as the Citizens State Bank
on August 1, 1944. In June 1965, the name was changed to the Johnson City
Bank.

MEAT

The following is a story the committee received concerning recipes passed from generation to generation, maybe you've heard it: Daughter inquires of her mother, "How do you cook a roast?" Mother to her Daughter, "First you season the meat with salt and pepper, a little garlic, roll the meat in flour and cover it well with the flour, cut off about 1/3 of the roast, then brown the two pieces of meat in bacon grease. Next you add a little water and cook covered in a pan in a 350 degree oven 30 minutes per pound and test for doneness, uncover and continue to cook 15 minutes till the roast is browned on top." Daughter to her Mother, "Mom, why do you cut off 1/3 of the roast?" Mother to her daughter, "I don't know but that's how your grandmother told me to do and that's how I've always done it." Daughter being unsatisfied with the answer, asks of her grandmother, "Grandmother, Mother cuts off 1/3 of the roast before she cooks it and she doesn't know why, except you always did, what is the reason for that?" Grandmother to granddaughter, "I can't imagine why your mother cuts off part of her roast, but the reason I do is because I have a small pan and the whole roast won't fit in one big piece!" So you see some things are done without our ever understanding the reason, it is just passed on from generation to generation.

The following is a recipe belonging to a committee member written by her grandmother with all the particular details written out.

How to Prepare a Roast

Wipe the meat with damp cloth, sprinkle unseasoned or seasoned tenderizer (Adolph's), salt and pepper — not too much salt (the tenderizer has salt already in it). Let this set on the meat about 30 minutes, or you can start right away — I usually let mine set awhile. You do not have to use the tenderizer if you know the meat is tender. It is just a little insurance against a tough roast.

Put about 3 tablespoons of shortening in roasting pan (I use fried meat or bacon grease). Flour the meat on all sides, brown on all sides — push back enough to get about 3 tablespoon of flour into the grease and stir till this is browned. Have some hot water ready and put a little (not much, about 2 or 3 cups) hot water in pan and cover. Do not use cold water, it will steam up and burn you. The cover of the roasting pan should fit tightly and then put the pan in a 325 degree oven and cook about 2^1/$_2$ hours for a 3 to 5 pound roast. Test meat for doneness. I have never had a recipe, I just cook it like any thing you roast. Be sure it is browned all over before you put the water in it for the gravy, you might have to thin the gravy. You might like the seasoned tenderizer best, I do. I haven't always used the tenderizer, but I like it. (Do not burn yourself turning the meat, you can though if you aren't very careful). It might take three hours to cook — after 2 hours test it with a fork. If you do not have a lid for your roaster you can use foil. But be careful! It is hard to tell you just how to do it, as I just experiment, browning the meat all over is important though.

Good luck, you can do it — just take your time. Your oven may vary from mine, I use 300 to 325 degrees to preheat the oven.

Love, Grandmother

This was the recipe I received in 1955 as a young bride just learning to cook. My grandmother, Pearl Tarver, left me all her cookbooks with the most detailed instructions written in the margins, such as, "this is Granddaddy's favorite," "I never use Sage in dressing because it gives me indigestion" and ever so many wonderful hints. When I read Grandmother's recipes it is just like talking to her. She left little to chance and she sure didn't want me to hurt myself!

Cynthia Smith

Beef

AUSSIE MEAT PIE

Helen O'Bryant

I am from Australia and this is the way recipes are written down under. Have a good time figuring it out.

71

750 grams topside steak,
    diced
1 tablespoon cooking oil
2 beef stock cubes
2 tablespoons cornflour
500 grams puff pastry

2 lambs kidneys, diced
1 onion, diced
1 teaspoon Vegemite
Salt and pepper
1 egg, beaten

Cook steak and kidney in oil until brown. Add onion, stock cubes and Vegemite. Add enough hot water to cover the meat, cover and simmer for 1¹/₂ hours. Mix the cornflour with cold water, enough to make a thin cream, and add this to the meat slowly. Bring to the boil until the mixture has a jelly consistency. Add more cornflour if necessary. Season with salt and pepper. Roll out puff pastry and line six individual pie tins which have been buttered. Fill the tins with the meat mixture. Cover the top of pies with more pastry, make a small slit in the top and brush with beaten egg. Cook until golden brown. (The recipe does not give the oven temperature. Vegemite is a black paste that can be obtained in specialty stores.) Serves 6.

CARNE GUISADA (COWBOY STEW)   *Norma Honeycutt*

This is my husband's favorite breakfast, great for company, deer camps and brunches. Serve with warm flour tortillas.

1¹/₂ pounds lean chuck or
      venison, cut bite size
1 10-ounce can Ro-tel
    tomatoes and green
    chilies, diced
¹/₂ cup onions, diced
¹/₂ cup green pepper,
    chopped

1 rib of celery, chopped
1 teaspoon garlic powder or
    2 cloves, crushed
1 teaspoon cumin
1 teaspoon salt
1 teaspoon black pepper
    (may adjust)
3 tablespoons flour

Salt and pepper meat well and add flour coating each piece of meat. Cook meat in a small amount of oil, just to keep from sticking. After meat is browned add a small amount of water and simmer about 20 minutes. In bowl you floured meat in, add onion, pepper, celery, and garlic. Mix with any remaining flour. Add to meat mixture, along with salt, pepper, cumin, and can tomatoes. Simmer on low heat covered 30 or 45 minutes, stir occasionally. You will love the way this smells while cooking. If you prefer more juice, just add water to tomatoes when you add them. Serves 6–8.

CHINESE PEPPER STEAK

Jeanne Hardy

1 pound beef chuck	1 can beef consommé
4 tablespoons cooking oil	1/2 teaspoon salt
4 medium green peppers, diced	Dash of pepper
	Minced garlic
2 tablespoons pimientos, chopped	2 tablespoons cornstarch
	1/4 cup water
1/4 cup green onions, chopped	2 teaspoons soy sauce
1 cup celery, sliced	

Cut beef into thin slices; then cut slices into thin slivers. Heat oil in large skillet. Add beef, cook and stir over high heat until meat is browned, about 5 minutes. Add salt, pepper, garlic, green peppers, pimientos, onion, celery, and consommé. Cover and cook over low heat until meat and vegetables are tender, about 10 minutes. Blend cornstarch, water and soy sauce and stir into meat mixture. Cook and stir until mixture is slightly thickened. Serve over rice. Serves 4–6.

GREEN CHILI STEW

Mary A. Thurlkill

A good wintertime supper dish. Popular in New Mexico. Pork may be used instead of beef.

2 pounds lean chuck, cut into 1/2 inch cubes	12 large green chilies, roasted, peeled, and cut into pieces or a 7-ounce container frozen chilies or two 4-ounce cans chopped green chilies
Cooking oil	
1/2 medium onion, chopped	
4 medium potatoes, peeled and diced	
1 teaspoon salt	1 teaspoon garlic salt
	6–7 cups water

Brown meat in a little oil in a large, deep heavy pan. Add the onion and potatoes and brown with meat. When browned, drain off excess fat. Add the chilies, garlic salt, salt, and water. Bring to a boil and simmer for at least half an hour. Serve in soup bowls with homemade bread. Serves 6–8.

SWISS STEAK "ARMY-STYLE"   *Maurice (Hoot) Gipson*

Hoot Gipson was for a time during World War II, a cook. This is one of the recipes he remembers using quite often. It could certainly be cut down for use in a regular family.

100 pounds round steak, cut in individual servings	4 bunches celery, chopped
6 16-ounce cans tomatoes	Water, as much as needed
1 dozen onions, chopped	2-3 clumps garlic, chopped

Pound steak to tenderize; season with salt and pepper and flour it thoroughly. Cook the canned tomatoes, chopped onions, chopped celery, and garlic in a little water just enough to make it limp. Then strain through a "China Cap." This liquid then goes in the pan with the meat. Bake at 350 degrees for an hour or until the meat is tender. This makes its own gravy. Serves an Army.

BARB'S MEXICAN CASSEROLE   *Barbara Smith*

1 pound tenderized round steak, cut in small pieces	1 clove garlic, chopped
$1/4$ cup flour	2 tablespoons cumin or comino
Salt and pepper to taste	1 16-ounce can stewed tomatoes
$2/3$ cup oil	$1^1/2$ cups water
1 box Mexican noodles (Fideo Enrollado)	

Cut meat into small pieces; dredge in flour seasoned with salt and pepper. Brown meat in oil. Add raw noodles and stir until they are browned. Add seasonings, water and tomatoes; cover and cook about 30 to 45 minutes until noodles are tender and liquid is absorbed. Serves 6-8.

BEEF CHEESE CASSEROLE

Jeanne Hardy

1¹/₂ pounds ground beef
1 medium onion, chopped
   (3/4 cup)
1 teaspoon salt
¹/₈ teaspoon pepper
2 8-ounce cans tomato sauce

8-ounces noodles, cooked
   and drained
1 cup cottage cheese
¹/₄ cup dairy sour cream
¹/₃ cup green peppers,
   chopped
¹/₃ cup green onions, chopped

Combine ground beef and onion in skillet and cook until beef is browned. Add salt, pepper and tomato sauce and simmer slowly while preparing remaining ingredients. Mix together cottage cheese, sour cream, green peppers, and green onions. Place half the noodles in bottom of greased 3-quart casserole. Top with cheese mixture, then remaining noodles. Pour meat mixture over the top. Bake in moderate oven, 350 degrees, for 30 minutes. May use two 1¹/₂-quart casseroles. It can be assembled in advance and refrigerated until ready to use, then bake for half an hour. Serves 8–10.

BEEF-STUFFED POTATOES

Betty Wood

6 large potatoes
2 tablespoons vegetable oil
2 tablespoons butter
3 tablespoons onion,
   chopped
1 pound ground meat
¹/₂ teaspoon chili powder
¹/₂ teaspoon garlic powder

Paprika
1 teaspoon salt
¹/₂ teaspoon pepper
2 tablespoons A-1 Sauce
¹/₂ cup bell pepper, chopped
¹/₂ teaspoon sage
1 cup Cheddar cheese,
   grated

Scrub and dry potatoes, then rub with oil. Bake at 350 degrees for 50 minutes or until tender. While the potatoes are baking prepare the meat. When potatoes are done, cut a slice from the top of each potato and carefully scrape out most of the center, leaving a thin layer around outside of potato. Melt butter in a skillet; sauté the onions and pepper 5 minutes. Mix in the beef and cook until browned. Stir in salt, pepper, A-1 Sauce, bell pepper, chili powder, garlic and potatoes removed from the skin. Taste for seasonings. Stuff the shells and sprinkle with paprika. Add grated cheese to top and bake for 10 minutes at 350 degrees, or until very hot. If aluminum potato boats are used, cover with aluminum foil and freeze until ready to use. Add cheese just before baking. Serves 6.

SAVORY BEANS AND MEAT BALLS   *Joycelyn Carter*

1 pound lean ground meat
$^1/_4$ cup onion, finely cut
$^1/_2$ cup nonfat dry milk
$1^1/_4$ teaspoons salt
$^1/_2$ teaspoon chili powder
$^1/_8$ teaspoon pepper

1 tablespoon shortening
$^1/_2$ cup onions, finely cut
1 16-ounce can baked beans
2 tablespoons brown sugar
$^1/_4$ cup ketchup
$^1/_4$ teaspoon dry mustard

Mix ground meat, 1/4 cup onion, dry milk, salt, chili pepper and pepper well. Wet hands and shape meat mixture into 12 balls. Place shortening and 1/2 cup onions in skillet, add meat balls and brown slowly on all sides. Spoon off any fat and add a mixture of beans, brown sugar, ketchup and dry mustard. Cover and cook over low heat for 10 minutes. Serves 4.

QUICK CHINESE COMBO   *Aline Slack*

A good, quick and easy dish.

1 pound ground beef
2 cloves garlic, chopped
1 cup celery, diagonally cut
1 10-ounce can cream of
   mushroom soup
$^2/_3$ cup water
1 8-ounce can cut green
   beans, drained

1 5-ounce can water chestnuts, drained and sliced
1 tablespoon soy sauce
1 16-ounce can tomatoes,
   drained and cut up or 2 fresh
   tomatoes, cut in wedges
Chinese noodles

In wok or skillet cook beef with celery and garlic until celery is crisp tender. Drain off fat. Add soup and next 4 ingredients. Simmer 5 minutes, stirring occasionally. Add tomatoes; heat through. Serve over noodles with extra soy sauce. Serves 6.

HEARTY BEEF AND POTATO CASSEROLE   *Cathy Woods*

Great for a quick and filling evening meal.

    4 cups frozen potato rounds (¹/₂ 30-ounce bag)
    1 pound ground beef
    1 10-ounce package frozen chopped broccoli, thawed
    1 2.8-ounce can Durkee's French fried onions
    1 medium tomato, chopped (optional)
    1 10³/₄-ounce can condensed cream of celery soup
    ¹/₃ cup milk
    1 cup (4-ounces) shredded Cheddar cheese
    ¹/₄ teaspoon garlic powder
    ¹/₈ teaspoon black pepper

Place potatoes on bottom and up sides of 8 x 12 inch casserole. Bake, uncovered at 400 degrees for 10 minutes. Brown beef in large chunks, drain.
Place beef, broccoli, 1/2 can onions, and tomatoes in potato shell that lines
the dish. Combine soup, milk, 1/2 cup cheese and seasonings, pour over
beef mixture. Bake covered at 400 degrees for 20 minutes. Top with remaining cheese and onions. Bake uncovered 2 to 3 minutes longer. Serves 6.

BUTCH'S LASAGNE   *Norma Honeycutt*

*Having tried several lasagna recipes and never satisfied, I happened on this
one and it worked. Lasagna was firm, but moist, and freezes well. I make full
recipes. We eat half and I freeze the other half.*

1 cup onions, minced	2¹/₂ cups tomato juice
2 teaspoons salad oil	1 16-ounce can tomato paste
1 pound ground round	¹/₂ cup Parmesan cheese
2 cloves garlic	3 quarts boiling water
1¹/₂ teaspoons salt	¹/₂ pound lasagne noodles
¹/₄ teaspoon each, pepper,	³/₄ pound Mozzarella cheese
parsley flakes and oregano	1 pound cottage cheese

Sauté onions in salad oil; add beef and cook until slightly brown; mash
garlic with salt; add meat with pepper, oregano, parsley, tomato juice, tomato paste, and 2 tablespoons Parmesan cheese. Simmer, covered 30 min-

utes. Cook noodles until tender; cool with cold water bath. Layer noodles lengthwise; layer grated Mozzarella cheese, cottage cheese, Parmesan cheese and sauce; repeat ending with sauce. Bake at 350 degrees for 1 hour or until done. After you take it out of oven let it sit at least 20 minutes to set. Slice and serve. Serves 8.

OPEN-FACE ENCHILADAS   *Dena K. Heider*

This is great served with a green salad.

Sauce:

2 to 4 tablespoons New Mexico chili powder or to taste
3 tablespoons flour
1/4 teaspoon oregano
1/4 teaspoon garlic powder

2 tablespoons oil
1 teaspoon salt
1/4 teaspoon cumin
1/8 teaspoon pepper
2 cups water

Other ingredients:

1/2 pound Longhorn cheese,
  grated
1/2 pound Monterey Jack
  cheese, grated

1 small onion, grated
4 corn tortillas
Hot oil

Combine sauce ingredients and cook about 15 minutes. Soften tortillas in hot oil. Dip a tortilla in sauce and place in a pie dish. Divide cheeses and onions equally and spread on top of each tortilla. Pour remaining sauce on top and bake 10–15 minutes at 350 degrees. Serves 4.

MEXICAN CORNBREAD   *Gail Rucker*

1 cup yellow cornmeal
2 eggs, beaten
1 cup sweet milk
1/2 teaspoon soda
3/4 teaspoon salt
1 16-ounce can cream-style
  corn

1/4 cup bacon drippings or oil
1 1/2 pounds hamburger
1 large onion, chopped
1 jalapeño, chopped
1/2 pound Cheddar cheese,
  grated

Combine cornmeal, eggs, milk, soda, salt, corn and drippings and set aside. Sauté hamburger, onion and jalapeño. Drain well on paper towels. Grease large casserole, 9 x 13 x 2-inch. Pour 1/2 of cornbread batter in

casserole; spread meat mixture over batter, then layer of grated cheese. Pour remaining batter over this. Bake one hour at 325 degrees. Serves 6–8.

MEXICAN LAYERED DISH
Joycelyn Carter

Our eleven-year-old grandson said on eating this, "Mom, get this recipe, it is good."

1 10-ounce package big flour tortillas
2 pounds ground beef
Salt and pepper to taste
1 can Ranch Style beans
1 onion, chopped
1 8-ounce package Velveeta cheese or Cheddar cheese
2 cans cream of chicken soup
1 can Ro-Tel tomatoes with chilies, chopped, juice and all

Lightly grease bottom and sides of 9 x 13 x 4-inch pan. Brown beef in skillet; drain. Salt and pepper to taste. Layer in order: 5 tortillas, torn; beans; meat; onions; cheese; 5 torn tortillas; 2 cans of soup, undiluted; and tomatoes, sprinkled over top. Cover with foil and bake 60 minutes at 350 degrees. Freezes well. Can be made in two pans. Serves 8 to 12.

MEAL IN ONE
Lucille Newman

1½ pounds ground beef
½ cup onion, chopped
1 16-ounce can tomatoes, chopped
1 can cream of mushroom soup
½ can of water
Generous dash of black pepper
1 10-ounce package frozen cut green beans, cooked and drained
1 cup carrots, cooked and sliced
3 cups cooked potatoes, mashed
Shredded mild processed cheese to cover

Brown beef and cook onions until tender; pour off fat. Add soup, water, tomatoes, pepper and vegetables except potatoes. Pour into shallow baking dish 12 x 8 x 2-inch. Spoon mashed potatoes in diagonal lines across top of casserole; sprinkle with cheese. Bake at 350 degrees for 30 minutes. Serves 6.

MEAT LOAF

Liz Carpenter

2 pounds very lean ground beef
$^1/_2$ pound raw bacon, chopped, save 2 strips
2 eggs, slightly beaten
1 cup milk
1 cup soft bread crumbs
1 tablespoon prepared horseradish
2 cloves garlic, minced fine
3 tablespoons onion, minced
1 tablespoon salt
$^1/_2$ teaspoon pepper
$^1/_2$ cup ketchup
1 tablespoon Worcestershire sauce
1 teaspoon lemon juice
Fresh parsley, minced

Sauce:

1 cup ketchup
1 tablespoon Worcestershire sauce
1 teaspoon lemon juice

Mix beef and chopped bacon with eggs, milk, bread crumbs, and remaining ingredients. Shape in an 8 x 11 baking pan, and cover with sauce. Place strips of bacon on top, and bake at 350 degrees for about one hour. Serves 8.

PEGGY'S MEAT LOAF

Peggy Stieler

$1^1/_2$ pounds ground beef
1 onion, grated
$^1/_2$ cup bread crumbs

1 egg, beaten
Salt and pepper to taste
1 8-ounce can tomato sauce

Mix well and place in oiled pan.

Sauce:

$^1/_2$ cup water
2 tablespoons dry mustard
2 tablespoons Worcestershire sauce

3 tablespoons vinegar
3 tablespoons brown sugar
1 8-ounce can tomato sauce or more

Mix well and pour over meat. Bake 1 hour and 30 minutes at 350 degrees. Baste several times while baking. Serves 8.

MINI MEAT LOAVES
Betty Wood

1-ounce package spaghetti sauce mix
1 egg
3/4 cup plain yogurt or sour cream
1/2 bell pepper, chopped
1 pound ground beef
1 cup soft bread crumbs
1/2 cup onions, chopped
1/4 cup Cheddar cheese, shredded
1 3-ounce can sliced mushrooms, drained
1 16-ounce can stewed tomatoes

Stir egg, yogurt, and spaghetti sauce mix together. Mix yogurt mixture with meat, bread crumbs, onions and bell pepper. Shape into 4 or 5 patties. Cook in skillet until brown. Pour mushrooms and stewed tomatoes over patties and simmer until sauce thickens. Place cheese on top. Serves 4 or 5.

OATMEAL MEAT BALLS
Libby Casparis

My daughter copied this recipe from the Minneapolis paper, and we have enjoyed it.

Meatballs:
1 1/2 pounds ground beef
1 3-ounce can mushrooms, sliced
1 egg
1/4 cup onions, chopped
3/4 cup rolled oats
1/2 cup milk
1 1/2 teaspoons salt
1 cup dry bread crumbs
Seasonings to suit your taste

Sauce:
1 cup sour cream
1/4 cup mayonnaise
2 teaspoons chives
1/2 teaspoon sugar
4 drops Tabasco sauce
2 bouillon cubes
1/2 to 1 cup hot water

Mix all meatball ingredients thoroughly and shape into balls. Place on

81

baking sheet and bake at 375 degrees until done. Combine bouillon cubes and hot water; stir until cubes are dissolved. Add rest of sauce ingredients and mix well. Heat thoroughly. Pour over cooked meatballs. I find that this makes an attractive and tasty dish served with rice. Place the rice on a platter, place meatballs on top of rice and cover with the sauce. Serves 6.

ROLLED TACOS   *Wanda Clark*

1 pound ground beef	4 slices bread
1 small raw potato, grated	1 teaspoon salt
1 large tomato, grated	1/2 teaspoon black pepper
1 medium onion, grated	1 dozen tortillas
2 cloves garlic, grated	Oil for deep frying

Slightly brown beef. Grate potato, tomato, onion, and garlic. Break up bread and add to meat with vegetables. Fry until potatoes and onions are done. Heat tortillas, add meat mixture to tortillas and roll tight. Secure with a toothpick. Fry in deep hot shortening or oil until crisp. Serve with grated cheese and salad. Freezes well. Serves 4–6.

SUPPER ON A BREAD SLICE   *Joycelyn Carter*

2/3 cup evaporated milk	1 1/2 teaspoons salt
1 1/2 pounds ground beef	3/4 teaspoon Accent
1/2 cup cracker crumbs	1/8 teaspoon pepper
1 egg	2 cups cheese, grated
1/2 cup onion, chopped	1 loaf French bread
1 tablespoon prepared mustard	Heavy Duty Reynolds Wrap

Combine all ingredients except bread and Reynolds Wrap and mix well. Cut 1 loaf of French bread in half lengthwise or use French rolls. Spread meat mixture evenly over top surface of bread or rolls. Wrap Reynolds Wrap around crust of each half, leaving top uncovered. Place on cookie sheet. Bake at 350 degrees for 25 minutes. Garnish with strips of cheese and bake 5 minutes longer. To serve loaf, cut slices across or diagonally. Freezes well. Serves 8.

TEXAS HASH
Wanda Clark

2 pounds ground beef
Salt and pepper to taste
1 large onion, chopped
1¹/₂ cups celery, chopped
¹/₂ cup regular rice, uncooked

1¹/₂ teaspoons chili powder
1 16-ounce can tomato sauce
1 8-ounce can tomato pureé
Cheese, grated

Brown beef and season to taste. Place meat in casserole dish, and sprinkle onions and celery over meat. Place rice over vegetables. Mix chili powder in tomato sauce and pureé and pour over mixture. Bake at 350 degrees for 1 hour 30 minutes or until done. Add cheese on top and melt. Serves 6 to 8.

SALAMI
Mavis Lemons

5 pounds cheapest ground meat
5 heaping teaspoons Morton's Quick Salt
2¹/₂ teaspoons mustard seed
2¹/₂ teaspoons cracked pepper
2¹/₂ teaspoons garlic salt
1¹/₂ teaspoons hickory smoked salt
(DO NOT SUBSTITUTE SALTS)

Mix thoroughly. Refrigerate 3 days, kneading once a day (running through a coarse food grinder does a better job than kneading by hand). Form into rolls (about 3) and place on broiler rack and pan and bake at:
> 350 degrees for 15 minutes
> 150 degrees for 5 hours and 45 minutes
> 200 degrees for 2 hours

Turn meat every 2 hours as it cooks. Cool and wrap (wax paper or foil). Let meat cure for seven days in refrigerator. May be eaten as soon as it cooks and cools, however, the taste improves each day. If you have a smoker grill, the last 2 hours of cooking on such smoker gives a much better, smokier taste. Makes 3 rolls.

Pork

DEPRESSION SPAGHETTI
Vanessa Hale Luce

This is Grandma Maury Haltom Teamer Hale's recipe. In 1930 Grandpa made $9.00 per week. Five dollars went for rent and the rest for food. At that time you could buy only what you needed. So she bought:

3 slices of bacon, sliced thin (cheaper)
2 medium size onions
1 large can tomatoes or tomato sauce (whichever cheaper)
1 package of spaghetti
1 tablespoon sugar, if you had it!

Cook spaghetti according to directions on container. Cut bacon in 2-inch pieces and fry in skillet until crisp. Remove from grease. In skillet with grease, add onions cut in small bits and cook a few minutes. Add can of tomatoes or tomato sauce. If using tomato sauce add a small amount of water in can, can get all of tomato sauce out, and cook a little longer. Add cooked spaghetti, stir well and cook a little bit. Add crisp bacon, stir and serve. Don't cook too long. Serve with bread and butter. Serves 4–6.

BAVARIAN CHOPS
Thelma Elm

4 boneless pork loin chops, 1/2 to 3/4 inch thick
Flour as needed
1 tablespoon butter
1/2 cup green onion, chopped
2 cloves garlic, minced
8-ounces fresh mushrooms, sliced
1/2 teaspoon thyme
8-ounces beer, room temperature
Salt and pepper to taste
Buttered noodles
Parsley, minced

Lightly flour chops. Melt butter in heavy skillet over medium-high heat until foamy. Sauté chops and brown quickly on both sides. Remove, reserve. Sauté onions and garlic until soft; add mushrooms and thyme and sauté one minute. Return chops to pan; add beer; bring to boil. Reduce heat; cover and simmer 7 to 8 minutes. Season with salt and pepper. Serve with buttered noodles, garnished with parsley, if desired. Serves 4.

HONEY APPLE PORK CHOPS
Thelma Elm

4 4-ounce boneless loin
  chops 1-inch thick
1¹/₂ cups apple cider
¹/₄ cup lemon juice

¹/₄ cup soy sauce
2 tablespoons honey
1 clove garlic, minced
¹/₄ teaspoon pepper

Combine all ingredients except pork chops. Mix well. Place chops in a shallow dish. Pour marinade over chops. Cover and refrigerate 6 to 24 hours. Prepare covered grill with drip pan in center, banked by medium-hot coals. Grill chops for 20 to 25 minutes, turning once and basting occasionally with marinade. Serves 4.

HAM AND BROCCOLI CASSEROLE
Daisy Cox

1 10-ounce package frozen
  broccoli spears, cooked
  and drained
3 cups medium wide egg
  noodles, cooked and drained
1 11-ounce can Cheddar cheese
  soup

²/₃ cup milk
1 teaspoon prepared mustard
2 cups cubed ham, cooked
¹/₃ cup slivered almonds,
  toasted

Cut broccoli stems into chunks, leaving flowerets whole. In small saucepan, heat together soup, milk and mustard, stirring until well blended. Place noodles in bottom of 8 x 12-inch (2-quart) baking dish. Pour half of soup mixture over noodles, stirring gently. Layer ham and broccoli chunks over noodles. Pour remaining soup mixture over all. Top with broccoli flowerets. Cover; bake at 375 degrees for 30 to 35 minutes or until thoroughly heated. Sprinkle with almonds before serving. Serves 6.

FRIED COUNTRY HAM
Jerry Parsons

DO NOT trim fat off of slice before frying — it will fry itself. You can make a few slices on the outer edge to ensure that the slice lays flat during cooking. Add no shortening. Put slices in medium hot, heavy skillet, turning several times while frying. CAUTION: Do not over fry, as slices will become hard and dry.

RED-EYE GRAVY
Jerry Parsons

After country ham is fried and removed, pour 1/2 to 3/4 cup of water into the pan. If desired, 2 tablespoons brewed coffee can be added to water. Increase the heat to moderate and simmer 3 to 5 minutes, stirring until gravy is reddish. This is the red-eye gravy. Pour over biscuits and the ham. Makes about 1 cup.

RIBS WITH BBQ SAUCE
Agnes Stevenson

Pork finger ribs
1 bottle Cattleman's Smoke
  flavored BBQ sauce
1¹/₂ tablespoons Spice
  Island orange peel

1 cup honey
¹/₃ cup syrup
1 to 2 tablespoons butter
¹/₃ cup soy sauce
Liquid smoke

Mix all ingredients except ribs and liquid smoke and heat to boiling point. Trim all fat from ribs. Brush ribs with small amount liquid smoke. Brush on sauce and marinate several hours or overnight. Place ribs in foil lined shallow baking pan and bake at 275 degrees for 1 hour. Turn, drain off fat and baste again. Bake for another hour or longer until ribs begin to get dark and smoked looking. This freezes well. Serves 6–8.

BREAKFAST SAUSAGE AND EGG CASSEROLE
Ola Matus

This is Elaine Oliver's recipe which we use at our Sunday School Class Brunch every year at Christmas.

1 pound Owens sausage
1 package crescent rolls
2 cups Mozzarella cheese,
  grated

6 eggs, beaten
³/₄ cup milk
¹/₄ teaspoon salt
¹/₂ teaspoon black pepper

Brown and drain sausage. Set aside. Line a 13 x 9 x 2 inch glass Pyrex dish with crescent rolls, bring up 1/2-inch on sides of dish and sealing seams together. Spread browned sausage over raw crescent rolls. Then spread the cheese over the sausage. Mix eggs, milk, salt and pepper and pour over cheese. Bake at 425 degrees for 15 minutes or until set.
  Gertrude Whittington made one of the casseroles this past year and

used the hot Owens sausage, 4 eggs, 1/2 teaspoon oregano, 2 tablespoons chopped bell pepper and Monterey Jack cheese for the Mozzarella. She baked hers at 350 degrees for 18 to 20 minutes. I think among our class members we have three or four versions of this recipe but they are all basically the same. Serves 6–8.

BAPTIST CASSEROLE (Sausage and Rice)   *Daisy Cox*

2 pounds bulk sausage, 1 regular and 1 hot
1 green pepper, chopped
2 cups celery, chopped
2 large onions, chopped
2 cups raw rice, long cooking
1 cup slivered almonds, toasted
8 cups water
1 small can water chestnuts, chopped
3 packages Lipton's chicken noodle soup mix

Brown sausage slowly and drain off excess grease. Sauté in microwave the onions, pepper, and celery. Add to the sausage. Add the rice, almonds, water, chestnuts and soup mix. Place in roaster and stir well. Cover. Bake 1 hour in 375 degree oven. Serves 12–16.

DINNER IN THE CROCKPOT   *Agnes Stevenson*

1 15-ounce can whole white potatoes, drained
1 16-ounce can French style green beans, undrained
1 pound Kielbasa sausage, cut in several pieces

Drain the potatoes and rinse with cold water and drain again. Put in crockpot and pour in green beans with the liquid in the can. Cut the sausage in several pieces and push down into the vegetables. Cook all day on low heat. Your favorite sausage can be used. Serves 3.

★   ★   ★   ★   ★

HINT:
When cooking bacon crumble extra pieces of cooked bacon and freeze. Use as a topping for casseroles, baked potatoes or in omelets.

★   ★   ★   ★   ★

ITALIAN SAUSAGE BAKED RICE
Cynthia Smith

1 onion, chopped
8-ounces fresh mushrooms, sliced
1 pound bulk sausage, Italian or Owens
$1/4$ cup butter
1 9-ounce package frozen artichokes or 1 14-ounce can

1 10-ounce package frozen green peas
1 $10^1/2$-ounce can beef bouillon, divided
3 cups cooked rice
Parmesan cheese

Sauté onion, mushrooms, sausage in butter. Add artichokes, peas, and 1/2 of bouillon and simmer uncovered 10 minutes. Stir in rice. Add remaining bouillon and toss lightly. Pour into greased $1 1/2$ quart casserole. Sprinkle with Parmesan cheese. Bake 15–20 minutes until browned at 375 degrees. Serves 6–8.

SAUSAGE RICE
Bonnie Hayes

$1/2$ pound bulk sausage, mild or spicy
$1/3$ cup green pepper, diced
$1/3$ cup green onion, diced
$1/4$ cup celery, sliced thin

$1/4$ teaspoon salt
$1/4$ teaspoon pepper
$1^1/2$ cups instant rice, uncooked
$1^1/2$ cups water

Crumble sausage in skillet and sauté until browned. Add onions, celery, and green pepper and sauté lightly. Add salt, pepper, rice, and water. Bring mixture to a boil, reduce heat, cover and simmer on low heat for 5 minutes. Fluff with fork and serve. Serves 6.

SAUSAGE UPSIDE DOWN CORNBREAD
Agnes Stevenson

1 cup onion, chopped
$1/3$ cup green pepper, chopped
1 pound bulk sausage
2 tablespoons flour
1 8-ounce can tomato paste
1 8-ounce can tomato sauce
1 tablespoon chili powder (optional)

Salt and pepper to taste
1 carrot, chopped
$1/2$ pound cheddar cheese, grated
$1/2$ cup black olives, sliced or chopped
2 packages corn muffin mix

Brown onions, peppers and sausage. Stir in flour, tomatoes, seasonings, carrot, cheese and olives. Pour into 9 x 13 casserole. Prepare cornbread mixture as directed on package and spread over sausage mixture. Bake at 400 degrees for 35 minutes. Let stand 5 minutes, loosen edges and invert on serving platter. Serves 6 to 8.

Chicken and Turkey

CHICKEN AND BROCCOLI STROGANOFF *Daisy Cox*

1 10-ounce package frozen broccoli
1 tablespoon margarine
1/2 cup onion, chopped
3 tablespoons flour
1/4 teaspoon salt
1/4 teaspoon white pepper

1 can chicken broth
2 cups chicken, cooked and cubed
1 3-ounce jar sliced mushrooms, drained
1 8-ounce carton sour cream
Hot cooked noodles

Cook broccoli according to package directions; drain and set aside. Place margarine in a 2-quart, round microwave safe casserole. Microwave at HIGH 35 seconds or until melted. Stir in onion. Cover tightly with heavy-duty plastic wrap; fold back a small edge of wrap to allow steam to escape. Microwave at HIGH 2 minutes. Add flour, salt and pepper, stirring until smooth; gradually add chicken broth, stirring well. Microwave at HIGH, uncovered, 4 to 6 minutes or until thickened and bubbly, stirring at 2-minute intervals with a wire whisk. Stir in broccoli, chicken, and mushrooms; microwave at High 2 minutes. Stir in sour cream; microwave at High 1 minute. Serve stroganoff over noodles. Serves 6.

BAKED BUTTERMILK CHICKEN *Betty Wood*

1 chicken, cut up
3/4 cup flour
1 1/2 teaspoons salt
1/4 teaspoon pepper

1 1/2 cups buttermilk
1/4 cup butter
1 can cream of chicken soup

89

Mix flour, salt and pepper. Dip chicken in 1/2 cup buttermilk and roll in flour mixture. Melt butter in 13 x 9 x 2 pan. Put chicken in pan, skin side down and bake 30 minutes at 425 degrees. Turn and bake 15 minutes. Mix soup and remaining 1 cup of buttermilk and pour over chicken. Bake additional 15 minutes or until golden brown. Serves 6.

JUANITA'S CHICKEN CHOW MEIN *Janey Wiemers*

1 large onion, chopped
1 cup celery, sliced
1 tablespoon oil
2 cups chicken, cooked and cubed
1 can cream of mushroom soup

¹/₃ cup chicken broth
1 tablespoon soy sauce
1 16-ounce can bean sprouts
¹/₃ cup toasted almonds
1 5-ounce can chow mein noodles

Sauté onion and celery in a small amount of oil. Stir in remaining ingredients except noodles. Add 1/3 of the noodles. Sprinkle the remainder of the noodles over the top. Bake for 30 minutes at 350 degree. Serves 6.

L'DON'S CHICKEN AND DUMPLINGS *Cynthia Smith*

1 chicken, cooked, chopped
¹/₂ white onion, chopped
3 ribs celery, chopped
1 can cream of mushroom soup
1 can cream of chicken soup
1¹/₂ cups stock or broth

Salt and pepper to taste
1 can biscuits
1 bunch green onions, chopped
8-ounces fresh mushrooms, chopped

Place chicken in large pot and cover with water, add onions, and celery and cook until chicken is done. Remove chicken, bone and tear meat into small pieces. Reserve 1¹/₂ cups stock. Drain rest. Mix soups, stock, salt and pepper and bring to a good boil. Open biscuits and tear into small pieces. Toss into boiling ingredients. Add chicken, onions and mushrooms and simmer. Top with green onions.

90

OLD-FASHIONED CHICKEN AND DUMPLINGS   *Martha Combs*

LULA BELL'S . . . .

1 chicken, 3 to 4 pounds
1 medium onion, chopped
1 clove garlic, chopped

2 ribs celery with tops, chopped
Salt and pepper to taste

In Dutch oven, place chicken. Add plenty of water with onion, garlic, celery, salt and pepper. Bring to boil; reduce heat and simmer about 1 hour or until tender. Cool in broth overnight. Next day, remove chicken; strain broth. Bone chicken and cut in bite-size pieces. Set aside.

Dumplings:

2 cups all-purpose flour
1/2 teaspoon salt
1/2 teaspoon soda

3 tablespoons shortening
3/4 cup buttermilk

Combine flour, soda and salt. Cut in shortening until mixture resembles coarse meal. Add buttermilk. Stir with fork until dry ingredients are moist. Turn dough out onto a well floured surface and knead lightly 4 or 5 times. Pat dough to 1/2-inch thickness. Pinch off dough in 1 1/2-inch pieces. Bring broth to boil. Drop pieces of dough into boiling broth. Reduce heat and cook on medium-low about 10 minutes, stirring occasionally. Stir in chicken. Heat and serve.

CHICKEN ENCHILADAS   *Cathy Woods*

2 whole chickens, boiled, boned and shredded, save broth
1 16-ounce can hominy, crushed
Picante sauce to taste
Salt and pepper to taste
1 package 8-inch flour tortillas

2 blocks Monterey Jack cheese, grated
1 block Mozzarella cheese, grated
2 cans cream of chicken soup
1 pint carton sour cream

Mix chicken, hominy, picante sauce, salt and pepper together and set aside. Mix cheeses, soup and sour cream together and set aside. Dip each tortilla in warm chicken broth (this will make the tortillas very pliable and easy to work with) and fill. Fill each tortilla with the chicken mixture and then top with cheese mixture. Cook at 350 degrees for 30 minutes or until bubbly. Serves 10.

SPECIAL OCCASION CHICKEN ENCHILADAS   *Norma Honeycutt*

This recipe is time consuming, thus it is really good to make for very special dinner guests, or to show off your cooking skills. I suggest you read the recipe over very carefully before you begin. You will not be sorry you went to the trouble.

Chicken Filling:
1/4 cup butter or margarine
1 medium tomato, diced
1 small onion, chopped
1 tablespoon fresh cilantro, chopped fine

1 tablespoon chicken base
1 pound chicken, cooked, boned and diced

Green Chili Sauce:
1 pound tomatillos
1 poblano chili
1 tablespoon fresh cilantro, chopped fine
1/2 cup onion, chopped
Salt to taste
2 cups water
1 medium avocado, diced
1 tablespoon chicken base
1 tablespoon ground cumin

1 tablespoon garlic, granulated
1/2 cup margarine, melted
1/4 cup flour
1/2 cup vegetable oil
10 corn tortillas
1 1/2 cups Monterey Jack cheese, grated
1 1/2 cups Swiss cheese, grated
Sour cream, optional

Chicken Filling: Heat margarine in heavy skillet. Sauté tomato, onion, and cilantro until tender, about 2 minutes. Add chicken base; stir to mix, and diced chicken. Cook at medium heat 10 to 15 minutes. Set aside.

Green Chili Sauce: Soak tomatillos in hot water to cover, about 15 minutes. Peel. Boil tomatillos, pepper, cilantro, onion, and salt in water until tender; this takes about 15 minutes. Drain saving 1 cup liquid. Place drained tomatillo mixture in blender with diced avocado, pulse several times; add remaining ingredients, except butter and flour. Blend until smooth and well blended. Return smooth mixture into saucepan containing reserved 1 cup liquid. Cook on medium heat about 10 minutes. Make a roux with melted butter and flour. Whisk slowly into tomatillo mixture. Cook stirring often, about 5 minutes. Set aside.

To assemble: Heat oil in heavy skillet over medium heat; using tongs, hold a tortilla in hot oil just long enough to make it pliable, about 10 seconds. Drain on paper towels. Place 1 tablespoon chicken mixture, 1 tablespoon Monterey Jack cheese, and 1 tablespoon Swiss cheese in center of each tortilla. Roll and place in ovenproof baking dish, seam side down; repeat with remaining tortillas. Pour desired amount of Green Chili Sauce over rolled tortilla and top with remaining cheese. Bake in preheated oven at 350 degrees for 15 minutes. Top each serving with sour cream, if desired. Serve with Pinto Bean Soup (in cookbook) and fresh fruit and enjoy. Serves 5–10.

JALAPEÑO CHICKEN
Elaine Oliver

This was a recipe my step-mother used to fix. The "hotness" can be adjusted.

¹/₂ cup butter or margarine	¹/₂ pound Velveeta cheese,
1 onion, chopped	cubed
1 frying chicken, cut up	3 jalapeño peppers,
1 15-ounce can tomatoes,	chopped
chopped	2 cups cooked rice

Melt butter in pot. Sauté onion until tender, but not brown. Cook the chicken until lightly browned. Turn heat to simmer and add the tomatoes. Next add the cheese, then the peppers. Cook until the chicken is tender or you can take the meat off the bone and put back in the pot. Pour mixture over hot cooked rice. Serves 4–6.

KING RANCH CHICKEN
Gwen Pickett

1 chicken boiled and cut in	¹/₂ to 1 can chicken broth
bite sized pieces	(should not be too soupy)
1 medium onion, chopped	12 corn tortillas, cut into
1 can cream of chicken soup	strips
1 can cream of mushroom soup	Grated cheese
¹/₂ can Ro-Tel tomatoes and	
green chiles	

Combine broth, Ro-Tel tomatoes and soups, mix well. Layer chicken and

tortillas in 9 x 13 inch pan. Add soup mixture, then onions and cheese. Bake at 325 degrees for 1 hour. Serves 4–6.

LEMON FRIED CHICKEN

Cynthia Smith

1 chicken, cut up   3 to 4 tablespoons oil

Brown chicken slightly in oil but do not cook. Remove chicken and put in a baking dish. Discard the oil.

Sauce:
$^1/_2$ teaspoon salt $^1/_4$ teaspoon dry mustard
$^1/_2$ teaspoon sugar $^1/_8$ teaspoon powdered
$^1/_2$ teaspoon black pepper   garlic
$^1/_3$ cup lemon juice $^1/_4$ cup salad oil

Shake together in a jar and pour over browned and drained chicken. Bake uncovered for 30 minutes at 325 to 350 degrees. Serves 4–6.

LOUISIANA STEWED CHICKEN

Betty Wood

1 fryer chicken, cut up   1 cup onion, chopped
$^2/_3$ cup flour   2 cloves garlic, chopped
$^3/_4$ cup oil or vegetable   Hot water
    shortening   Hot cooked rice
Salt and pepper to taste

Brown chicken in a small amount of vegetable shortening in a heavy iron Dutch oven over medium heat. Remove chicken and set aside. Drain pot. Mix flour and oil in pot. After it is mixed, turn the heat to low, stirring constantly. Stir all over the bottom. As you stir, the roux browns slowly. Do not cook your roux fast, because as it reaches the done point, it will be too hot and burn. When the roux is a rich dark brown, add chicken, onion, garlic and enough hot water to fill pot 1/2 full (do not add cold water as this causes the roux to separate). Bring to a boil; reduce heat and simmer on low for 45 minutes to 1 hour. Gravy should be slightly thickened at this point. Serve over rice. This is all the chicken needs. The roux gives it all the flour it needs. Serves 4–6.

MEXICAN CHICKEN

Olga Zauner

6 chicken breasts, deboned
Flour
2 eggs, beaten
Bread crumbs
6 tablespoons olive oil
3-4 shallots or green onions,
 finely chopped
1 teaspoon basil

2 tablespoons parsley,
 finely chopped
1/2 teaspoon freshly ground
 pepper
1 cup tomato pureé
1 tablespoon tomato paste
2 tablespoons Marsala
Salt to taste

Flatten chicken breasts by pounding, then dip in flour, beaten eggs, then bread crumbs. Sauté shallots in oil, then sauté chicken quickly; cover and cook 15 minutes or so. Remove chicken breast to a hot platter. Add basil, parsley, pepper, and tomato pureé to pan. Stir until well blended. Add tomato paste and Marsala. Salt to taste. Bring to a boil. Serve over chicken breast or in sauce boat on side. Polenta, rice or fried corn meal with cheese can accompany. Serves 6.

CHICKEN ORIENTAL

Flora Cox

This recipe was served at our Teachers' Luncheons many times at the Phillips Independent School which is now consolidated with Plemons and Stinnett. This is the panhandle of Texas.

1 chicken, cooked, boned
 and cut in bite size pieces
1/2 cup celery, chopped
1 green pepper, chopped
1 onion, chopped
3 tablespoons margarine
3 tablespoons flour
1 1/2 cups chicken broth
1 can cream of mushroom
 soup
1 box, 6-ounce, Uncle Ben's
 wild rice

2 1/2 cups chicken broth
1 cup Cheddar cheese,
 grated
1 can water chestnuts, sliced
1 3-ounce can mushrooms,
 sliced
1/4 teaspoon curry powder
1/3 teaspoon cayenne
Pepper to taste
1/2 cup margarine
1 cup cracker crumbs

Sauté celery, green pepper, and onion in margarine. Add flour. Mix broth and soup to the sautéed vegetables. Cook rice in chicken broth. When cooked add to mixture. Mix cheese, chestnuts, mushrooms, curry powder, and cayenne pepper to mixture. Place in casserole. Melt margarine and stir in cracker crumbs. Place over top of casserole. Bake at 350 degrees for 30 minutes. Serves 6–8.

PECAN CHICKEN
Norma Honeycutt

Saw this recipe and since we love Dijon mustard, gave it a try and now it is a favorite.

4 chicken breast halves, skinned and boned
$^{1}/_{4}$ cup honey

$^{1}/_{4}$ cup Dijon mustard
1 cup pecans, finely chopped

Place each piece of chicken between 2 sheets of wax paper; flatten to 1/4-inch thickness, using meat mallet or rolling pin. Set aside. Combine honey and mustard; spread on both sides of chicken and dredge chicken in chopped pecans. Arrange chicken in a shallow baking dish, slightly greased. Bake at 350 degrees for 30 minutes or until tender. Serves 4.

NO PEEKIE CHICKEN
Peggy Arbon

1 package, 6-ounce, Uncle Ben's Wild Rice mix
1 chicken, cut in pieces
$^{1}/_{2}$ package Lipton's Onion soup mix

1 2$^{1}/_{2}$-ounce can mushrooms
1 can cream of celery soup
2 cups water

Sprinkle contents of both packets on bottom of greased casserole. Lay chicken on top of rice. Sprinkle onion soup (dry) on top of the chicken and add mushrooms and canned soup. Add water. Cover with foil and bake at 350 degrees for two hours and No Peekie!!! Serves 6.

POPPY SEED CHICKEN
Heather Bushnell

4 chicken breasts, cooked and diced
2 cans cream of chicken soup

4 ounces sour cream
2 cups crushed Ritz crackers
Poppy seed
$^{1}/_{4}$ cup butter

Boil and dice chicken breasts. Place chicken pieces in a greased casserole dish. Mix soup and sour cream together and spread over chicken pieces. Sprinkle crushed Ritz crackers and poppy seed on top of mixture. Melt butter and pour over crackers and poppy seed. Bake at 350 degrees for 35 minutes. You may prepare this ahead of time and freeze it. Leave the crackers off and after thawing add crackers and bake. Serves 4–6.

HOMEMADE CHICKEN POT PIE
Norma Honeycutt

This recipe was given to me by my mother-in-law. It was and is my husband's favorite; also it was the first recipe my children asked for and mastered when they left home.

2 small potatoes, peeled and diced
1 10-ounce box frozen mixed vegetables
1 chicken or 4 chicken breasts, boiled, boned and diced, save broth

Salt and pepper to taste
Pie dough, enough to line and cover a 13 x 9 x 2-inch dish
3 tablespoons flour
Butter

Cook potatoes about 5 minutes. Do not cook until done or they will be mushy in pie. Add frozen vegetables to boiling water potatoes are in, and stir to thaw. Combine chicken, drained potatoes and vegetables with salt and pepper. Roll pie dough to line baking dish. Pour chicken mixture in dish over crust; sprinkle flour evenly over mixture. Pour chicken broth over mixture until covered; shake dish to mix flour and broth. Cover with top crust and cut slits in crust. Butter top. Cook at 350 degrees about 1 hour 30 minutes; let sit in oven after done, or on top of stove about 20 minutes to set. Serves 8–10.

RITA'S CHICKEN FILÉ GUMBO
Peggy Arbon

In the late 1940's we were stationed in Japan with the Air Force. A new family had recently moved into the adjoining duplex and while I was gardening in the back yard, I was tantalized by a delicious aroma coming from the newcomer's apartment. Being with child, I couldn't control my passion for food, so I marched right over and knocked on the door. The new lady was Rita Ashford, from Baton Rouge, Louisiana, and she told me she was cooking "chicken filé gumbo." Well, needless to say, we became friends, even to this day and consequently our family was completely "hooked" on the authentic Cajun cooking of which Rita is a true master.

1 cup oil	1 gallon water
1 cup all purpose flour	1 large chicken, cut in
1¹/₂ cups white onions,	serving pieces
finely chopped	1 pound Kielbasa sausage,
¹/₂ cup green onions and	cut in 1¹/₂-inch pieces
tops, finely chopped	¹/₂ cup parsley, finely
1 cup celery, finely chopped	chopped
¹/₂ cup bell pepper, finely	¹/₂ cup green onions and
chopped	tops, finely chopped
2 cloves of garlic, pressed	Salt and red pepper to taste
6 cubes chicken bouillon	1 tablespoon gumbo filé

Make a roux by browning the flour and oil over medium heat in a heavy iron skillet. Stir the flour and oil mixture CONSTANTLY until it is darker than a brown paper bag. Be careful not to burn the roux. If this happens discard and begin again. When the roux is the desired color add the vegetables and stir. This will cool the roux and wilt the vegetables. Place the mixture into a deep stock pot. Place over medium heat and add the chicken and bouillon cubes; smother down for about 5 to 10 minutes. Add about a gallon of boiling water. When the mixture has boiled a while, add salt and red pepper to taste. Reduce heat; simmer, uncovered until meat is tender but still in serving pieces. Add parsley and green onion tops. Just before serving stir in the gumbo filé. It is very hard to give you the exact amount of filé as this is a matter of taste. Some people like to sprinkle it over the bowl of gumbo and stir it in just before eating. My family leaves this job to me and I add the filé to the pot just before serving. About 1 tablespoon should be enough for this recipe, or add to your taste. Serve over steamed rice in soup bowls. A bowl of hot gumbo, some garlic bread and a good tossed salad makes a delightful meal. Note: The sausage is optional to the recipe but should you use it; add at the same time you add the chicken. The sausage adds to the flavor. Serves 12–16.

★ ★ ★ ★ ★

HINT:
Veal and chicken breast are interchangeable in recipes.

★ ★ ★ ★ ★

CHICKEN SPAGHETTI   *Beryl Pickle*

Beryl Pickle is the wife of our U.S. Representative, J. J. (Jake) Pickle.

1 stewing chicken, cut up	1 4-ounce can pimientos,
2 quarts water	chopped
2 stalks celery with leaves,	¹/₂ cup margarine
chopped	1 can cream of mushroom
1 onion, quartered	soup
Salt and pepper to taste	1 teaspoon Worcestershire
1 16-ounce package	sauce
spaghetti	¹/₄ cup black olives,
¹/₂ cup onion, chopped	chopped
¹/₂ cup green pepper,	¹/₂ pound Velveeta cheese,
chopped	cubed

Boil chicken covered in water with celery, onion, salt and pepper until tender. Remove chicken and strain broth. Skin and bone cooled chicken and cut into bite size pieces. Return the broth to boiling and slowly add spaghetti. Cook until most of the broth is absorbed. Sauté onion, green pepper and pimientos in margarine; add soup, Worcestershire sauce and olives. Bring soup mixture to a boil, add cheese and stir until cheese is melted. Combine with the spaghetti and the chicken mixture in a casserole. May be frozen. Serves 10–12.

KITTIE CLYDE'S CHICKEN SPAGHETTI   *Kittie Clyde Leonard*

1 hen or large fryer	1 pound cheese, grated
1 green pepper, chopped	³/₄ teaspoon garlic salt
1 onion, chopped	1 small jar pimientos,
³/₄ stalk celery, chopped	chopped
1 can cream of mushroom	2 tablespoons picante sauce
soup	10-ounces spaghetti

Boil chicken, green pepper, onion and celery together. Remove chicken. Cool, bone and chop. Drain broth. Cook spaghetti in broth. Drain if necessary and add chicken, soup, cheese, garlic salt, pimientos and picante sauce. Place in casserole and bake at 350 degrees until heated through, about 30 minutes. Serves 10–12.

RUTH'S SPAGHETTI   *Ruth Teague*

Delicious one dish meal and perfect for the freezer.

1 hen or 2 fryers
1/2 cup margarine
1 cup green pepper,
  chopped
1 cup celery, chopped
1 large onion, chopped
1 cup pimientos, chopped

1 pound spaghetti, cut
2 cups American cheese,
  diced
3 cups chicken broth
1 can cream of mushroom
  soup

Boil hen or fryers until tender. Cool; remove meat from bone and cut into bite size pieces. Save broth. Slowly cook in skillet margarine, green pepper, celery, and onion until tender; add pimientos and continue cooking 2 minutes. Cook spaghetti; drain and add cheese, broth and soup. add chicken, vegetable mixture and salt and pepper to taste. Simmer for 15 minutes. Serve hot. Serves 10–12.

EL RANCHO GRANDE   *Daisy Cox*

1 pound ground turkey
1/4 cup onion, chopped
1 16-ounce can tomatoes,
  chopped and undrained
1/4 cup green pepper,
  chopped

1/4 cup celery, chopped
6 ounces noodles
2 cups water
1/2 cup Mozzarella cheese,
  grated

Brown turkey and onions over low heat in nonstick skillet. Add tomatoes, green pepper and celery. Cook until vegetables are tender, about 10 minutes. Add noodles and water and cook 20 minutes more. Sprinkle cheese evenly over servings. Serves 6.

★   ★   ★   ★   ★

HINT:
Allow 1 pound chicken, bones and all, for 1 serving.

★   ★   ★   ★   ★

Seafood — Fish

FISH AMANDINE
Joycelyn Carter

2 pounds firm fish fillets,
  mild flavored
1/4 cup flour
1 teaspoon seasoned salt
1 teaspoon paprika
1/4 cup butter, melted

1/2 cup almonds, sliced
2 tablespoons lemon juice
5 drops liquid hot pepper
  sauce
1 tablespoon fresh parsley,
  chopped

Cut fillets into serving pieces. Combine flour, salt and paprika. Roll fish in mixture and place in a well greased baking dish, in a single layer. Drizzle 2 tablespoons melted butter over fish; broil about 4 inches from heat for 10 to 15 minutes or until fish flakes easily when tested with a fork. While fish is broiling, sauté almonds in remaining butter until golden, stirring constantly. (I do mine in the microwave on HIGH, stirring every minute until golden). Mix almonds with lemon juice, hot sauce and parsley. Pour over fish and serve at once. Serves 6–8.

EASY BLACKENED FISH
Rita Reiner

4 fresh fish fillets (6 ounces
  each)
1/4 cup butter or margarine

4 teaspoons Blackened Fish
  Seasoning

Spread margarine on both sides of fillets; then sprinkle with seasoning. Heat cast-iron skillet over medium high heat until smoking, 3 to 5 minutes. Add 2 fillets and cook until done, about 2 minutes per side. Keep warm in oven and repeat with remaining fillets. Serves 4.

HINT:
It is important to add shrimp the last in a recipe to prevent over cooking, so that it will be very tender.

HINT:
Baking fish on a bed of celery and onions will keep the fish from sticking as well as add flavor.

STUFFED FLOUNDER
Pauline Spurlock

4 flounder or other whole fish
1¹/₂ pounds shrimp, boiled, peeled, deveined
  and chopped
¹/₂ pound crabmeat, fresh or canned
¹/₂ cup cooking oil
¹/₂ cup celery, chopped
1 cup onions, chopped
4 cloves garlic, minced or use powder
3 stale buns soaked in water
4 eggs, 2 whole eggs and 2 eggs separated
¹/₂ cup cracker meal or bread crumbs
¹/₂ cup green onion tops and parsley, chopped
Salt, black pepper and red pepper to taste

Put oil, celery, onions, and garlic in heavy pot. Cook over medium heat uncovered until onions are wilted. Add shrimp to onion mixture. Then add crabmeat, soaked buns and 2 unbeaten eggs. Mix well. Add 2 egg whites and mix. Then add 2 egg yolks, cracker meal, green onion tops and parsley. Season generously with salt, black pepper and red pepper. Split fish lengthwise, removing bones. Stuff with the prepared mixture. Brush egg yolk across tops of fish and broil 10 minutes on one side; turn over and broil 10 minutes more. Serve with drawn butter or garlic butter. (I do not turn my fish, just test with a fork). Serves 4–8.

SEATTLE SALMON STEAKS
Daisy Cox

6 salmon steaks, 1-inch
  thick
¹/₃ cup butter or margarine
¹/₂ teaspoon salt
¹/₄ teaspoon paprika

1 teaspoon Worcestershire
  sauce
2 tablespoons onion, grated

Place salmon steaks in greased shallow baking pan. Melt butter; add seasonings and Worcestershire sauce, and spread over salmon. Sprinkle 1 teaspoon onion over each steak. Bake in hot oven, 425 degrees, for 30 minutes. Serve with your favorite sauce. Frozen salmon steaks may be used. Serves 6.

CYNTHIA'S CRABMEAT AU GRATIN   *Cynthia Smith*

1 cup onion, chopped finely
1 stalk celery, chopped finely
¹/₄ pound margarine
¹/₄ cup flour
1 13-ounce can evaporated milk
2 egg yolks
1 teaspoon salt
¹/₄ to ¹/₂ teaspoon red pepper
1 pound crab meat
¹/₂ pound Cheddar cheese, grated
Mushrooms, optional
Slivered almonds, optional
Bread crumbs, optional

Sauté onion and celery in margarine. Blend flour in onion mixture. Stir milk in gradually. Add egg yolks, stirring until mixed well. Cook 5 minutes. Add salt and red pepper. Place crabmeat in a greased casserole. Pour cooked sauce over the crabmeat and sprinkle with cheese. Mushrooms, slivered almonds, or bread crumbs may be sprinkled on top. Bake at 375 degrees for 10 to 15 minutes. Serves 6–8.

CRAB FLORENTINE CASSEROLE   *Vanessa Luce*

2 10-ounce packages frozen spinach, cooked and drained well
1 10-ounce can Ro-Tel tomatoes and green chilies
1 cup sour cream
1 cup cheese, grated
1 cup crabmeat, canned, fresh or frozen
¹/₂ teaspoon nutmeg
¹/₂ teaspoon seasoned salt
1 tablespoon onion, grated

Put spinach in greased shallow 2 quart casserole. Mix other ingredients and pour over spinach. Bake at 350 degrees for 25 minutes. Serves 4–6.

CRAB STUFFED MUSHROOMS   *Mariallen Moursund*

12 large fresh mushrooms
1 can crab meat, drained
4 tablespoons butter or margarine
2 tablespoons onion, finely minced
1 to 4 cloves garlic, minced
¹/₄ cup cracker, bread or Italian seasoned crumbs
1 tablespoon parsley, chopped

103

Remove stems and lightly brown topside of mushrooms in skillet. Place caps, top down, in baking dish. Sauté above ingredients in butter and fill mushroom caps. Bake for 8 minutes at 350 degrees. Serves 6. May omit crab, add shrimp or just plain.

ÉTOUFFEÉ Á LA MICROWAVE   *Peggy Arbon*

SANDY'S CRAWFISH . . . My Louisiana friend's daughter, Carla White-head, enjoys cooking Cajun dishes but uses a quicker method. This dish is just as delicious as the older method of cooking.

¹/₂ cup margarine	**2 tablespoons flour**
1 cup onion, chopped	**¹/₄ cup fresh parsley,**
²/₃ cup green pepper, chopped	**chopped or a tablespoon**
¹/₂ cup celery, chopped	**parsley flakes**
1 pod garlic, minced or	**2 tablespoons tomato paste**
powder	**1 cup hot water**
1 pound crawfish tails, with	**Salt and pepper or Tony's**
fat, if desired	**Creole Seasoning to taste**
¹/₄ cup green onions, chopped	

In 2¹/₂-quart, deep casserole put margarine, onion, green pepper, celery and garlic. Microwave on HIGH 10–12 minutes or until tender. Add crawfish tails, fat (if desired) and green onions. Microwave on HIGH 5 minutes covered with lid or plastic wrap. Stir in flour. Add parsley, tomato paste, water and seasonings. Microwave 70% power for 10 minutes uncovered or until thick. Stir once or twice during cooking time. Serve over hot cooked rice. Serves 6–8.

BARBECUED SHRIMP   *Shirley Lawson*

This recipe was given to me by my daughter-in-law's brother, Charlie Haynes.

1¹/₂ to 2 pounds raw large	**1 teaspoon hot pepper sauce**
shrimp	**¹/₂ teaspoon pepper**
1¹/₂ cups butter or	**¹/₈ teaspoon oregano**
margarine, melted	**2 cloves garlic, minced**
1 tablespoon chili sauce	**Juice of 1 lemon**
1 teaspoon paprika	**1 cup white wine**
1 teaspoon salt	

Leave shells and tails on shrimp. Cut down back of shrimp and remove black line. Wash and drain. Mix rest of the ingredients and marinate shrimp in sauce one hour or more. Grill 4 to 6 inches from coals about 5 minutes, turning and basting after each turn. Save remaining sauce for dipping. Serves 6–8.

PAULINE'S (FRIED SHRIMP) BATTER   *Pauline Spurlock*

3 eggs, beaten
Garlic powder to taste
Onion powder to taste
Salt

3 teaspoons baking powder
1 large can evaporated milk
2 to 3 pounds large shrimp,
    shelled and deveined

Mix all ingredients except shrimp together. Marinate shrimp several hours in mixture before frying. Fry shrimp in hot oil until light golden brown. Do not over cook. Serves 6–8.

SHRIMP CREOLE   *Aline Slack*

This recipe came from my daughter's Home Economics teacher in Corpus Christi. I find it very easy to make and very tasty.

3 tablespoons oil
1 onion, chopped
1 bell pepper, chopped
2¹/₂ cups tomatoes, cut up
1 bay leaf
1¹/₂ teaspoon salt
1 teaspoon sugar

¹/₂ teaspoon Worcestershire
    sauce
¹/₂ teaspoon oregano
¹/₄ teaspoon pepper
Dash of thyme
1 pound raw shrimp,
    cleaned and deveined

Sauté onion and bell pepper in oil. Add other ingredients except shrimp and simmer uncovered until sauce is thick. Add shrimp; simmer 10 more minutes. Serve over rice. Serves 4–6.

★   ★   ★   ★   ★

HINT:
Thawed fish should not be held more than a day before cooking; the flavor is better if it is cooked immediately after thawing.

★   ★   ★   ★   ★

SHRIMP ÉTOUFFEÉ (A TOO FAY)   *Peggy Arbon*

My favorite dish.

¹/₂ cup butter	Salt and pepper to taste
2 large onions, chopped	1 to 2 pounds raw shrimp,
2 stalks celery, chopped	peeled and deveined
2 or more cloves garlic,	2 cups chicken broth
minced	¹/₄ cup white wine
1 medium bell pepper,	¹/₄ to ¹/₂ cup green onions,
chopped	chopped
4 tablespoons flour	¹/₄ cup parsley, chopped

Melt butter in large skillet. Sauté onions, celery, garlic, and bell pepper in butter for 30 minutes. Add flour and cook 10 minutes more, stirring constantly. Add the broth, wine and shrimp. Cook until the shrimp turns good and pink, then add the green onion and parsley. Better made a day ahead for flavors to blend. Serve over rice with a green salad and ranch biscuits or French bread. Serves 8.

CAJUN SHRIMP GUMBO Á LA ROBICHAUX   *Cynthia Smith*

¹/₃ cup flour	¹/₄ cup fresh parsley,
¹/₃ cup Crisco	chopped
2 cups onions, chopped	3 bay leaves
1 cup green onions,	1 8-ounce can tomato sauce
chopped	1 can chicken broth
2 cups celery, chopped	2 or 3 cups water
1 cup bell pepper, chopped	Pepper to taste
2 tablespoons Worcestershire	2 pounds raw shrimp,
sauce	peeled and deveined
1 tablespoon thyme	1 pound crabmeat, optional
2 teaspoons garlic salt or 2	
cloves, chopped	

First you make a roux. Heat Crisco in large cast iron kettle or Dutch oven, if possible. When really hot add 1/2 of the flour and keep stirring until it is brown. Add the other 1/2 of the flour and stir until roux is color of a beer bottle. If you see black specks in the roux, you've burned it. Throw away and start over. Add chopped vegetables; stir. Add seasonings, water and chicken broth. I boil the shrimp shells after I have peeled them; strain, add this water at this time. Bring to boil and watch it; it can boil over. Then turn the heat down and simmer for several hours. Add shrimp and cook about 30 minutes. I usually cook it one day, refrigerate it, heat and serve the next day over cooked hot rice. Serves 8.

SHRIMP WITH LEMON BUTTER   *Joycelyn Carter*

1 cup butter or margarine
1 clove garlic, minced
1 teaspoon Worcestershire
  sauce
1/4 teaspoon salt
1/2 teaspoon black pepper,
  coarsely ground

1/4 cup lemon juice
1 teaspoon parsley flakes
1 teaspoon soy sauce
1/4 teaspoon garlic salt
2 pounds large raw shrimp,
  peeled and deveined
Lemon wedges, optional

Melt butter in a large skillet. Add other ingredients except shrimp; bring to a boil. Add shrimp; cook over medium heat 5 minutes, stirring occasionally. Garnish shrimp with lemon wedges, if desired. Serve with rice. Serves 4–6.

JAMBALAYA   *Elaine Oliver*

This is a real old recipe of mine.

2 tablespoons shortening
2 medium green onions,
  chopped
1 bell pepper, chopped
1 cup celery, chopped
2 pounds raw shrimp,
  peeled and deveined or
  use frozen

1 16-ounce can tomatoes or
  8-ounce can tomato sauce
3 cups cooked rice
1/4 cup parsley, chopped
1 clove garlic or garlic salt
Salt to taste
Red pepper to taste

In a Dutch oven, melt shortening; add onions, bell pepper, and celery. When slightly brown add shrimp. Cook slowly. When liquid forms on mixture, add tomatoes or sauce, rice, parsley and seasoning. Simmer about 30 minutes. Serves 8.

FETTUCINE CON FRUITTI DI MARE   *Vanessa Luce*

3 ounces green noodles	2 tablespoons butter
1 tablespoon peanut oil	2 tablespoons white wine
6 shrimp, peeled and deveined	1/2 cup whipping cream
	Juice of 1 lemon
6 scallops, sliced in half	Salt
6 oysters, removed from shells	Pepper
	Parmesan cheese, grated

Cook noodles in salt water. Rinse with cold water and strain. Add one tablespoon of peanut oil to the noodles to prevent them from sticking together. Heat butter in a skillet; stir in seafood and sauté lightly. Add white wine, lemon juice and whipping cream to the seafood mixture and cook over medium heat until the sauce is slightly thickened. Season to taste. Add noodles to seafood and heat. Serve with freshly grated Parmesan cheese. Serves 3–4.

BAKED SEAFOOD CASSEROLE   *Ola Matus*

1 pound crabmeat, canned or fresh, or substitute	1 cup celery, chopped
	1 cup cooked rice
1 pound shrimp, cooked, peeled and deveined	1 cup salad dressing
	1/2 teaspoon salt
1/2 green pepper, chopped	1/8 teaspoon pepper
1/2 cup pimientos, chopped	1 tablespoon Worcestershire sauce
1/2 onion, chopped	
1 4 1/2-ounce can sliced mushrooms	1 cup milk

Place crab, shrimp, green pepper, pimiento, onion, mushrooms, celery and rice in bowl. Mix salad dressing, salt, pepper, Worcestershire sauce and milk well. Pour over fish mixture and combine well. Place in 2-quart casserole, and bake at 375 degrees for about 30 minutes. Serves 4–6.

★   ★   ★   ★   ★

HINT:
When boiling shrimp, add celery to the water. It eliminates the strong odor of shrimp.

★   ★   ★   ★   ★

Game

ARMADILLO STEW

Holly Lawson

My husband, Roger, brought home this recipe after a hunting trip. The guys have a rule in camp "you shoot it, you eat it." Somebody shot it.

1 armadillo, shelled, cleaned and cut into chunks
1 pound dried pinto beans, cleaned and soaked

1 large onion, chopped
Water to cover
Garlic, salt, and pepper to taste

Brown meat in oil. Add beans, onion, water and seasonings to meat. Cook until beans are done. May need to add more water. Serves 8.

DRUNK BIRDS

Joycelyn Carter

My father, who is a Baptist minister, named this when he found out there was wine in the recipe.

8 doves or quail
¹/₂ cup butter
1 clove garlic, chopped
1 small onion, chopped
³/₄ cup celery, chopped

¹/₂ cup boiling water
Salt and pepper to taste
1 cup dry white wine
1 can cream of chicken soup

Clean and wash birds. Melt butter in heavy pot with well-fitting lid. Sauté birds, onions, garlic, celery, salt and pepper until birds are brown. Add boiling water. Cover, and simmer on low heat for 1/2 hour, then add wine. Simmer until birds are tender, about 1 hour. If pan gets dry, add more wine or chicken broth. A few minutes before serving, add soup and stir to blend. Serve with rice. Serves 4.

DOVES OR QUAIL IN FOIL
Betty Wood

12 doves or quail
Salt and pepper
1 onion, chopped

8-ounces whipped butter
12 slices bacon
6 squares of foil, 12 x 12

Clean and wash birds. Salt and pepper. Mix onions and butter together. Fill each cavity with the onion butter mixture. Wrap each bird with a slice of bacon. Place two birds on a foil square. Seal packet by double folding edges of foil leaving air space in packet. Place on cookie sheet or baking pan. Bake in 350 degree oven for 1 hour. Serves 6.

CANADIAN COOKED GOOSE
Cynthia Smith

Probably we each thought at least once in our life, "we've cooked our goose." The following are the literal instructions for cooking the feathered kind.

1 wild goose
Salt and pepper to taste
1 orange, quartered
1 apple, quartered

1 onion, quartered
1 package Lipton's onion
   soup mix
¹/₂ cup butter, melted

Wash and drain cavity well. Sprinkle cavity with salt and pepper. Stuff cavity with orange, apple and onion. Place goose on heavy foil. Brush breast with butter and sprinkle with onion soup mix. Fold foil over and bake 2 hours and 20 minutes at 325 degrees. Makes its own gravy to serve over wild rice. Serves 10–12.

BARBECUED RABBIT
Brad Smith

Rabbit is tender white meat that has fewer calories and is higher in protein than any major meat.

¹/₂ cup onion, finely
   chopped
¹/₄ cup butter or margarine
1 8-ounce can tomato sauce
³/₄ cup pineapple juice
2 tablespoons lemon juice
2 tablespoons brown sugar,
   firmly packed

1 teaspoon salt
¹/₂ teaspoon dry mustard
¹/₄ teaspoon seasoned salt
¹/₄ teaspoon pepper
1 (2–2¹/₂ pound) rabbit,
   cleaned and cut up

Cook onion in butter until tender. Mix in tomato sauce, pineapple juice, lemon juice, brown sugar and seasonings. Cook over low heat 15–20 minutes to blend flavors. Place rabbit in bowl and pour mixture over it. Let stand 1¹/₂ to 2 hours. Place rabbit pieces on grill 7–9 inches from coals. Cook 45 minutes or until tender. Turn about every 10 minutes. Baste frequently with sauce. Salt before serving. Serve with hot mustard sauce if desired. Serves 4.

DRESSED VENISON STEAKS
Holly Lawson

I am always looking for a new way to fix venison because my husband, Roger, and I enjoy hunting and believe in eating what we kill.

**6 to 8 venison steaks, ³/₄-inch thick
1 package Ranch Style Dressing mix, prepared
Salt, pepper and garlic to taste**

Preheat oven to 350 degrees. Pound steaks with mallet to tenderize meat. Put steaks in a oven proof pan. Sprinkle salt, pepper, and garlic over meat. Pour dressing over steaks liberally, getting a little dressing under steaks to prevent sticking. Bake to desired doneness, about 20 minutes for well done. This is a very easy recipe. We really like it. It is different but delicious. Serves 4–8.

Variation: Soak tenderized steaks in buttermilk for at least an hour. Salt and pepper flour. Take steaks out of buttermilk one at a time and roll in flour mixture. Fry in hot oil. Serve with cream gravy. Beef or chicken is also good prepared this way.

ONION VENISON STEAKS
Holly Lawson

This is my favorite way to fix venison steak. It is simple and very good. A tossed salad goes great with it.

**1 large onion, sliced
5 venison steaks, ³/₄-inch
   thick
1 tablespoon Worcestershire
   sauce, more if desired**

**Garlic powder to taste
Pepper to taste
Salt to taste (not as much
   needed with
   Worcestershire sauce)**

Preheat oven to 400 degrees. Sauté onions until wilted. Pound steaks with

111

mallet to tenderize and place in oven proof dish. Add Worcestershire sauce and seasonings. Place onions on top of meat. Cover with foil and bake until done to your taste; 20 minutes and meat is well done. The juice in the pan would make a delicious gravy, but we just use it straight from the pan and spoon it over the meat. Serves 4–5.

ROAST VENISON WITH HERBS   *Elaine Oliver*

An old recipe given to me by my brother's wife. My brother is also a hunter.

1 **clove garlic, grated or 1¹/₂ teaspoon garlic juice**	**¹/₂ teaspoon dried marjoram**
3 **tablespoons salad oil or olive oil**	**Venison roast**
	Salt and pepper to taste

Grate garlic into salad oil, add marjoram and let stand 15 minutes. Wipe roast with damp cloth. Rub on prepared oil mixture. Salt and pepper the roast. Place roast in a covered roasting pan and bake at 350 degrees: 25 minutes per pound for rare; 30 minutes per pound for medium; or 40 minutes for well done. Make brown roast gravy in same manner as for beef roast. Serves 6–8.

VENISON LINK SAUSAGE   *Ronnie Bushnell*

This recipe was shared by an Austin fireman.

25 **pounds pork**	8 **tablespoons ground mustard**
25 **pounds venison or Boston butt roast**	**¹/₂ box mustard seed**
1 **cup salt or to taste**	4 **tablespoons nutmeg**
4-**ounces coarse ground black pepper**	2 **tablespoons sage or garlic to taste**
1 **1.3-ounce box white pepper**	4 **teaspoons paprika**
3 **tablespoons red pepper**	8 **tablespoons MSG**
	2 **cups water**
	Sausage casing

Grind meat as fine as you can get it. Combine all ingredients and mix thoroughly. Stuff into casings and tie securely at both ends. Let hang one day then smoke with hardwood smoke for 2 days — cold smoke. Open windows; let air dry approximately 3 weeks. We do not care for the sage; we omit it and add garlic to taste.

Vegetables and Side Dishes

LYNDON B. JOHNSON
MEMORIAL HOSPITAL BUILDING

The Johnson City Hospital was completed in July 1970. The name was officially changed to Lyndon B. Johnson Memorial Hospital in March 1974, to honor our thirty-sixth President, who was instrumental in obtaining the new building for Blanco County.

The Johnson City Garden Club provided landscaping, as well as grounds maintenance. Throughout the years the hospital functioned as a non-profit organization.

Due to financial problems which many rural hospitals experienced, the doors closed in 1988. However, the lovely building will continue to serve the public, as ownership was transferred to the National Park Service in June 1990.

113

BAKED BEANS   *Rosie Danz*

2¹/₂ cups Pork and Beans   1 tablespoon Worcestershire
³/₄ cup brown sugar, packed   sauce
¹/₄ cup ketchup   1 teaspoon prepared
                                     mustard
                                  Bacon slices

Mix ingredients together except bacon. Place in a baking dish and cover
with bacon. Bake 1 hour at 300 degrees. Serves 4.

FRESH GREEN BEANS AND NEW POTATOES   *Holly Lawson*

*Granny loved to garden and always had fresh vegetables as soon as the weather
would allow. She fixed this when fresh green beans were in season. It was and
still is my favorite, though I remember hers tasting better than mine.*

1 pound fresh green beans,   ¹/₂ pound new potatoes,
   snapped   washed
3 slices bacon, cut up   Butter or margarine,
Salt and pepper to taste   optional

Wash beans and put in large pot with bacon, salt and pepper and cover
with water and start cooking. Wash potatoes and place in pot and cover
with water and bring to a boil. Boil until tender. When potatoes are done,
drain off hot water and add cold water to cool enough to peel. Add potatoes to beans when beans are just about ready, about 10 minutes before
they are fully cooked, and heat thoroughly. A dab of butter may be added
at this time. Serve hot. Serves 4.

GREEN BEAN CASSEROLE   *Mary R. Davis*

A good side dish.

2 10-ounce package frozen   1 16-ounce can bean sprouts
   green beans   1 can cream of mushroom
1 8-ounce can water   soup
   chestnuts, chopped   1 2.8-ounce can French
1 4-ounce can mushrooms,   fried onions
   chopped

Par boil beans for 5 minutes in salted water and drain. Mix all ingredients together except onions. Coat baking dish with butter and place a layer of onions in bottom. Pour mixture into baking dish and top with balance of onions. Bake for 30 minutes at 375 to 400 degrees. Serves 8.

RAY'S SWEET-SOUR BEANS
Ray Sultemeier

2 strips bacon
1 cup onion, minced
1 tablespoon flour
³/₄ cup vegetable liquid
¹/₄ cup vinegar

2 tablespoons sugar
1 teaspoon salt
¹/₄ teaspoon black pepper
2 cups green beans, cooked

Brown bacon until crisp. Cook onion in bacon fat until it turns yellow. Stir in flour; add vegetable liquid, vinegar, sugar, salt, pepper and bring to a boil. Stir in beans. Stir gently until heated through. Serve with crisp bacon sprinkled over the top. Serves 4.

SWEET AND SOUR STRINGED BEANS
Joan Robertson

Good side dish for baked ham or pot roast.

1 pound string beans
3 cups water
1 or 2 tablespoons salt
1 or 2 tablespoons lemon
  juice
1 or 2 tablespoons brown
  sugar

2 tablespoons butter
1¹/₂ tablespoons flour
1¹/₂ cups bean liquid
2 whole cloves
Salt and pepper to taste

Wash beans and cut into 1¹/₂ inch lengths. Mix salt, lemon juice and brown sugar and place into water with beans. Cook for 12 minutes. Drain and keep liquid (keep it hot). Heat the butter in a small saucepan. When bubbling add flour; cook over low heat stirring frequently until the flour is a mellow brown. Pour in the hot liquid from the beans. Add cloves and stir and simmer until smooth. If too thick, add enough bean liquid so it will be smooth. Add all of this to the beans. Add salt and pepper and simmer for 10 minutes. Serves 4–6.

HARVARD BEETS
Jane Mills

This recipe came from my mother-in-law, Alice Mills.

1/2 **cup sugar**	1/3 **cup white vinegar**
1 **tablespoon corn starch**	2 **cups beets, cooked and**
1/2 **teaspoon salt**	**diced**
1/3 **cup boiling water**	2 **tablespoons margarine**

Mix sugar, corn starch, and salt in small saucepan. Add boiling water and vinegar. Cook until sauce is clear. Add beets, cover and keep warm for 30 minutes. Add margarine and serve. Serves 4–6.

BROCCOLI-RICE CASSEROLE
Joy Watson

1/2 **cup onion, chopped**	**4-ounces Cheez Whiz**
1/2 **cup celery, chopped**	1 **can cream of mushroom**
1 **tablespoon margarine**	**soup**
1 **bunch broccoli, steamed**	1 **5-ounce can evaporated**
1 1/2 **to 2 cups rice, uncooked**	**milk**

Sauté onion and celery in margarine. Mix Cheez Whiz, soup, and milk together and stir in rice and broccoli. Place in a baking dish and bake at 350 degrees for 30 minutes or until rice is done. Serves 6–8.

BROCCOLI-RICE SUPREME
Joyce Ellis

2 **bunches broccoli,**	1 **8-ounce jar Cheez Whiz**
chopped	1 **can cream of mushroom**
3 **cups cooked rice**	**soup**
1/2 **cup onions, chopped**	1 **can cream of chicken soup**
1/2 **cup celery, chopped**	1 **5-ounce can evaporated**
1/4 **cup butter**	**milk**
	1/4 **cup almonds, slivered**

Cook broccoli until tender. Cook rice according to directions on package. Layer in 13 x 9 inch oven proof pan; broccoli, rice, onion, celery and butter. Mix cheese, soups and milk and heat. Pour over layered broccoli and rice. Bake at 350 degrees for 35 minutes. Top with almonds. Serves 12. Try the hot Cheez Whiz, it gives a different flavor.

CABBAGE CASSEROLE
Lucia Carbary

This recipe was given to me by Sallye Baker.

1 head cabbage, sliced
1/2 cup milk
1 can cream of chicken soup

1/2 cup American or Cheddar cheese, grated
1/4 to 1/2 cup bread or cracker crumbs

Boil cabbage for 10 minutes. Drain and rinse in cold water twice. Mix milk and soup and add to cabbage. Put in buttered casserole and top with cheese and bread or cracker crumbs. Bake at 350 degrees for 30 minutes. Serves 6.

BAVARIAN CABBAGE
Ray Sultemeier

2 tablespoons butter or margarine
1 medium head cabbage, coarsely shredded
2 tablespoons onion, chopped

1/2 teaspoon salt
1/4 cup water
1 1/2 teaspoons sugar
2 tablespoons vinegar

Melt butter or margarine; add cabbage, onion, salt and water. Cook until barely tender, about 5 minutes. Add sugar and vinegar and blend thoroughly. Cook three minutes longer. Serves 6.

CYNTHIA'S CABBAGE CASSEROLE
Cynthia Smith

We serve this on New Years Day. Cabbage brings you MONEY.

1 head of cabbage, chopped fine
1 large onion, chopped
1/2 cup of margarine
1/2 pound Velveeta cheese, cubed

1 can cream of mushroom soup
3/4 cup seasoned bread crumbs

Boil cabbage until tender. Sauté onion in margarine; add cheese and soup. Drain cooked cabbage and add to mixture. Add bread crumbs. Put in buttered 2 quart casserole; dot with margarine and bake at 350 degrees for 20 minutes. Serves 6–8.

DOLORES' CABBAGE CASSEROLE
Dolores Bowden

2¹/₂ to 3 pound head cabbage
2 heaping tablespoons flour
Bacon drippings

1 cup Velveeta cheese, grated
2 cups milk
1 can cream of mushroom soup

Cut cabbage in chunks and cook in salted water until tender. Drain and place in a large greased casserole dish. Place the flour in large skillet with just enough bacon drippings to wet the flour. (Do not brown flour mixture). Stir in milk, soup and cheese. Cook until thick (may add more milk if mixture becomes too thick). Pour mixture over cabbage and bake in 350 degree oven until it bubbles. Serves 8.

CELERY CASSEROLE
Cynthia Smith

1 quart celery, sliced thin
¹/₄ cup butter or margarine
1 can cream of celery soup
2 tablespoons half and half
2 tablespoons pimientos

¹/₂ cup potato chips, crushed
2 tablespoons butter or margarine

Cook celery in butter 20–25 minutes. Mix soup, half and half, and pimientos and place in casserole. Sprinkle with chips and melted butter. Bake at 350 degrees for 30 minutes. Serves 6.

CORN CASSEROLE
Patty McDonnell

A Sunday School class pot luck dinner years ago in Cincinnati, Ohio was my first time to try this recipe. It's always a hit when I take it to dinners, and it's a delicious reminder of old friends.

¹/₂ cup margarine, melted	1 17-ounce can cream corn
1 box Jiffy cornbread mix	1 17-ounce can whole kernel
1 8-ounce carton sour cream	corn, well drained

Mix all ingredients and bake 1 hour at 350 degrees. Fast, easy, and delicious!! Serves 6–8.

BAKED SCALLOPED CORN
Daisy Cox

1 17-ounce whole kernel corn, drained	1 2-ounce jar pimientos, chopped and drained
1 17-ounce can cream-style corn	¹/₄ teaspoon salt
¹/₄ cup milk	¹/₄ teaspoon pepper
¹/₄ cup round buttery crackers, crushed	2 tablespoons Parmesan cheese, grated
¹/₄ cup onion, chopped	1 tablespoon butter or margarine
2 eggs, beaten	

Combine first 9 ingredients, mixing well. Pour into a greased, 1¹/₂ quart casserole. Sprinkle top with cheese, and dot with butter. Bake, uncovered, at 350 degrees for 40 to 45 minutes or until center is almost set. Let stand 5 minutes before serving. Serves 6.

CHILI CON ELOTE
Thelma Elm

This recipe is from a friend in Minnesota whose grandmother passed it on to her.

2 tablespoons oil	¹/₂ teaspoon salt
1 large onion, chopped	1 11-ounce can whole kernel
1 green pepper, chopped	corn
1 clove garlic, chopped	2 16-ounce cans kidney
1 teaspoon chili powder	beans
1 teaspoon cumin	1 16-ounce can tomato
1 teaspoon oregano	pieces

Sauté onion, green pepper, and garlic in oil; then add seasonings. Add

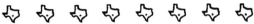

corn, beans, and tomatoes. Simmer uncovered 20 minutes. Serve with cornbread or corn chips. Serves 8.

EGGPLANT AU GRATIN
Norma Honeycutt

If eggplant wasn't fried around our house no one would eat it, so I found this recipe, made it, didn't tell anyone it had eggplant in it and they all loved it. Tastes like dressing.

1 medium-sized eggplant, about 2 pounds, pared and diced
3 medium onions, chopped
³/4 cup cracker crumbs or left over cornbread, crumbled

1 egg, beaten
¹/2 cup Cheddar cheese, grated
3 tablespoons butter or margarine
¹/4 cup cracker crumbs or cornbread

Cook eggplant with onions in small amount of boiling salted water until tender, about 10 minutes. Drain. Add 3/4 cup crumbs or cornbread, egg, and cheese. Mix lightly but thoroughly. Turn into greased 1¹/2 quart casserole. Top with rest of crumbs and dot with butter. Bake 350 degrees for 30 minutes. If you are a cheese lover, about 5 minutes before done add more cheese to top. Serves 4 to 6.

STUFFED MUSHROOMS SUPREME
Vanessa Luce

1 tablespoon butter or margarine
2 medium shallots, chopped
2 cloves garlic, chopped
1 pound frozen spinach, cooked and drained
Pinch of salt, pepper and nutmeg or to taste
24 mushroom caps, can use fine quality canned mushrooms
¹/2 cup Parmesan cheese, grated
4 tablespoons spicy butter (add a dash of tabasco, Worcestershire sauce, salt, pepper and garlic to the butter or margarine)

Melt butter in skillet and sauté shallots and garlic briefly with spinach.

Season to taste with salt, pepper and nutmeg. Break stems off mushroom caps and fill caps with spinach mixture. Arrange in buttered serving dish and sprinkle with cheese. Melt butter and add spices to make spicy butter and pour over mushrooms. Bake at 375 degrees for 15 minutes. Serves 8.

HOMEMADE NOODLES
Helen Mayfield

This is one of my grandmother's recipes she used in 1890. The recipe is given as she wrote it.

Beat 2 eggs. Add a little salt and 2 egg shells of water, flour to make a stiff dough. Roll out as thin as paper, let dry on both sides, then roll up in a roll and cut in thin strips. Separate well. Bring water to a rapid boil, then add noodles, boil until tender. Drain well. These are good with boiled chicken and broth.

ONION CASSEROLE
Joan Robertson

Try it; you will like it.

9 to 10 medium onions,
   sliced thin
1 tablespoon salt
4 to 5 slices buttered toast,
   crust removed
1/2 pound American cheese,
   grated

1 egg, slightly beaten
1 cup milk
1 teaspoon salt
1/4 teaspoon pepper
1 teaspoon celery seed

Butter a flat 2 quart baking dish. Boil onions in salted water to cover until just tender, about 10 minutes. Drain and line baking dish with toast. Cover with a layer of onions and cheese. Repeat layer of toast, onions and cheese. Mix egg, milk, salt, pepper and celery seed and pour over casserole. Bake at 375 degrees for 40 minutes. Serves 8.

★　★　★　★　★

HINT:
If you over salt vegetables add 1 teaspoon vinegar and 1 teaspoon sugar, one at a time until salty taste is gone.

★　★　★　★　★

CAJUN FRENCH FRIED ONION RINGS   *Cynthia Smith*

They are wonderful. Yummy.

1 large onion, sliced thin	1 5-ounce can evaporated
Flour	milk
1 egg, slightly beaten	Dash red pepper

Dust onion slices with flour. This makes the batter stick. Dip onion rings into mixture of egg, evaporated milk and red pepper, (the evaporated milk is the secret, so do not substitute), then back into the flour. You can make these ahead by battering them first and refrigerate and cooking them later in hot oil until golden brown. Serves 3–4.

CREAMY MASHED POTATOES   *Ola Matus*

These potatoes are great for a buffet as they hold the heat so long. This is my daughter-in-law, Leslie's, recipe. She serves them with Rib Roast.

5 pounds potatoes, peeled and quartered	1/2 teaspoon garlic salt
	1/2 teaspoon pepper
2 teaspoons salt, divided	2 cups heavy cream
2 3-ounce packages cream cheese with chives, cubed	2 tablespoons butter or margarine
4 tablespoons butter or margarine	Paprika

Cook potatoes with 1 teaspoon salt in boiling water. Drain. Mash until smooth. Add cream cheese, butter, garlic salt, 1 teaspoon salt and pepper. Mix until smooth and add heavy cream gradually. Spoon in a greased 13 x 9 x 2 dish. Dot top with butter and sprinkle with paprika. At this point you can refrigerate up to a day ahead of time. Bake, uncovered, at 325 degrees for 30 minutes. Increase heat to 375 degrees for 30 more minutes. Serves 10–12.

FLUFFY POTATO CASSEROLE   *Cynthia Smith*

2 cups potatoes, mashed
1 8-ounce package cream
   cheese, softened
1 small onion, finely
   chopped
2 eggs, well beaten

1 tablespoon flour
$1/4$ teaspoon salt
$1/8$ teaspoon pepper
1 3-ounce can French-fried
   onion rings, crushed

Combine all ingredients except onion rings; beat 2 to 3 minutes at medium speed of electric mixer. Pour into a greased $1^1/2$-quart casserole. Spread crushed onions evenly over top. Bake uncovered at 300 degrees for 30–40 minutes. Serves 4.

HASH BROWN POTATO CASSEROLE   *Dolores Bowden*

1 32-ounce package frozen
   hash brown potatoes,
   thawed
1 can cream of chicken soup
1 8-ounce carton sour cream

Salt and pepper to taste
1 medium onion, chopped
$1/2$ cup margarine, melted
2 cups Pepperidge Farm
   cornbread dressing mix

Place hash browns in a large greased casserole dish. Mix soup, sour cream, salt, pepper and onions. Pour over potatoes. Top with the dressing mix that has been mixed with the margarine. Bake at 350 degrees for 45 minutes. Serves 8–12.

HOT GERMAN POTATO SALAD   *Dorothy Uecker*

This is more of a vegetable dish than a salad.

8 potatoes, peeled, sliced, boiled and drained
4 slices bacon, cooked crisp, drained and crumbled

Dressing:

1 egg, beaten (optional)
1 tablespoon flour
$1/2$ cup sugar
$1/2$ cup water

$1/2$ cup vinegar
1 tablespoon bacon grease
$1/2$ teaspoon salt
$1/4$ teaspoon pepper

Boil potatoes in salted water. Drain. If you like mushier potatoes, slice after cooking. Toss lightly with bacon.

Dressing: In same skillet bacon was fried, combine ingredients in order given, stirring after each addition. Simmer until thick. Pour warm dressing over bacon and potatoes. Toss very lightly to avoid mashing potatoes. Serve warm. I omit the egg. Serves 8–12.

NELL'S POTATO CASSEROLE
Cynthia Smith

1 32-ounce sack frozen hash brown potatoes
³/₄ cup butter or margarine, divided
¹/₂ cup chopped onions, white or green
1 can cream of mushroom soup

2 cups sour cream
2 cups Cheddar cheese, grated
2 cups corn flakes, crushed
Paprika

Thaw potatoes. Melt 1/2 cup butter in a 3 quart casserole and add potatoes, onion and toss with butter. Mix soup, sour cream and cheese and stir into casserole. Top with corn flakes mixed with 1/4 cup melted butter. Sprinkle with paprika. Bake, uncovered, at 325 degrees for 1 hour. Serves 10–12.

SMITH RANCH SWEET POTATO CASSEROLE
Mary Smith Amis

A Christmas tradition at the Smith Ranch.

3 cups sweet potatoes, about 4, boiled and mashed
¹/₂ cup sugar
¹/₂ cup butter or margarine

2 eggs, beaten
1 teaspoon vanilla
¹/₃ cup milk

Topping:
¹/₃ cup butter or margarine, melted
1 cup brown sugar

¹/₂ cup flour
1 cup pecans, chopped

Mix potatoes, sugar, butter, eggs, vanilla and milk. Place in a 13 x 9 x 2-

inch baking dish. Topping: melt butter and mix with remaining ingredients. Sprinkle on top of potato mixture. Bake, uncovered, for 25 minutes at 350 degrees. Serves 6–8.

FESTIVE SWEET POTATOES   *Dolores Bowden*

Same recipe as above but uses 1/4 cup milk. Adds 1 cup coconut to topping.

SCALLOPED SWEET POTATOES AND APPLES   *Faye Baird*

Columbus not only discovered America, he also discovered sweet potatoes on some of the islands and took some back as a gift to Queen Isabella of Spain. So the story goes, later, the early colonist brought sweet potatoes from Europe to Virginia and they became a highly prized food in the South.

2 cups sweet potatoes,
   boiled and sliced
1½ tart apples, sliced
½ cup brown sugar

4 tablespoons butter or
   margarine
1 teaspoon salt

Put half the sliced potatoes in a buttered baking dish and cover with half the apple slices. Sprinkle with 1/2 the sugar and dots of butter. Repeat with second layer finishing with sugar and butter. Bake, uncovered, at 350 degrees for 1 hour. Serves 6.

SPINACH CASSEROLE   *Cynthia Smith*

3 10-ounce packages frozen
   chopped spinach, slightly
   cooked and drained
1 cup sour cream

1 package dry onion soup
   mix
1 cup Cheddar cheese,
   grated

Mix all ingredients well. Bake, uncovered, in a 3-quart casserole dish at 350 for 50 minutes. May be made ahead of time and baked just before serving. Serves 8.

CREAMY SPINACH
Daisy Cox

2¹/₄ pounds fresh spinach
¹/₄ cup onion, chopped
3 tablespoons butter or margarine, melted

¹/₂ to 3/4 cup sour cream
1 teaspoon vinegar
Dash of salt

Remove stems from spinach; wash leaves thoroughly. Cook spinach, covered, in a large Dutch oven 3 to 5 minutes (do not add water). Drain spinach well and chop. Sauté onion in butter in a skillet until tender. Add spinach and remaining ingredients; heat thoroughly (do not boil). Serves 4.

SPINACH FLORENTINE
Dolores Bowden

8-ounces mushrooms, sliced
¹/₄ cup butter or margarine, melted
2 10-ounce packages frozen spinach, thawed
1 teaspoon salt

¹/₄ cup onion, chopped
1 tablespoon prepared mustard
1 cup Cheddar cheese, shredded
Garlic salt to taste

Sauté mushrooms in butter until brown. Thaw spinach and drain well. Add salt, onion and mustard to spinach. Pour into a greased shallow casserole dish. Top with 1/2 of cheese. Arrange mushrooms on top, then sprinkle with garlic salt. Add remaining cheese. Bake at 350 degrees for approximately 30 minutes. May prepare early and refrigerate, then bake. Serves 8.

SQUASH MEDLEY
Genevia Bushnell

4 medium summer squash, unpeeled
¹/₂ cup bell pepper, chopped
2–4 ripe tomatoes, peeled and chopped
1¹/₂ cups processed cheese (American or Velveeta), shredded (jalapeño variety, if you like extra zip)

¹/₃ cup onion, chopped
¹/₂ teaspoon salt
¹/₄ teaspoon pepper
Favorite minced herbs or a dash of oregano and dried basil
¹/₂ cup bread crumbs
1 tablespoon butter or margarine

126

Parboil squash whole for 3–5 minutes or until almost tender. Cool and slice thinly. Combine bell pepper, tomatoes, cheese, onion, salt, pepper and herbs and mix well. Place 1/2 of squash in casserole and cover with 1/2 of cheese mixture, repeat, and top with bread crumbs. Place dabs of butter on top. Bake, uncovered, at 375 degrees for 35 minutes. This dish can also be made in the microwave oven: cook on medium about 10–15 minutes until cheese is melted and squash tests tender with a fork. Serves 8.

LUCIA'S SQUASH CASSEROLE

Lucia Carbary

4 cups squash, cooked
1 cup onion, chopped
1/2 cup green pepper, chopped
1 cup Cheddar cheese, grated
1 teaspoon salt

2 eggs, beaten
1 can cream of mushroom soup
3/4 cup bread crumbs
2 tablespoons margarine, melted

Mix all ingredients together and place in a greased casserole. Sprinkle top with extra cheese. Bake at 350 degrees for 45 minutes. Serves 6–8.

MAE'S SQUASH CASSEROLE

Mae Hernlund

This is one squash dish that appeals to men. It freezes well and is great for freezing in individual or small casseroles to enjoy after the garden squash season is over.

1 8 x 8 microwave casserole dish
6 small yellow squash, sliced
1 medium onion, chopped
1 tablespoon of water
Salt and pepper to taste
1 cup Velveeta cheese, cubed

1 2-ounce can sliced mushrooms, drained
1/2 cup green chilies, chopped and drained
Buttered cracker crumbs (Ritz), optional

Microwave squash and onions in water in casserole dish until just tender. Do not overcook. Drain. Season with salt and pepper, if desired. Add cheese, mushrooms and chilies. Cover dish with plastic wrap and microwave until cheese is melted. Buttered cracker crumbs may be used for topping. Ingredients may be adjusted to suit taste. Serves 4.

JOYCE'S SQUASH CASSEROLE *Joyce Ellis*

Even if you don't like squash try this recipe. You won't even know there is squash in it.

4 cups squash, cut in bite size pieces
1 onion, chopped
1/2 green pepper, if desired
2 or 3 eggs, beaten

Salt and pepper to taste
1/4 cup margarine, melted
1 cup cracker crumbs
1/2 to 1 cup cheese, grated

Steam squash, onion and pepper until tender. Mix in the eggs, salt, pepper, margarine and 1/2 cup cracker crumbs. Pour into baking dish. Top with remaining cracker crumbs and cheese. Bake at 350 degrees for 25 to 30 minutes until thick with a nice brown top. Serves 8 to 12.

CREAMY SQUASH CASSEROLE *Lucia Carbary*

4 cups yellow squash, cooked
1 can cream of chicken or mushroom soup
1 8-ounce carton sour cream
1 4-ounce jar pimientos, drained

1 8-ounce can water chestnuts, thinly sliced
2 medium onions, chopped fine
1/2 cup margarine, melted
1 8-ounce package herb stuffing mix

Slice squash and cook in salted water until tender. Drain well. Mix squash and next five ingredients well. Mix stuffing and margarine well and pack into bottom of baking dish. Put squash on top. Garnish with stuffing croutons. Bake at 350 degrees for 30 minutes. Serves 6–8.

★   ★   ★   ★   ★

HINT:
To keep cauliflower white while cooking, add a little milk to the water.

128

SQUASH DRESSING
Cathy Woods

Excellent with chicken or turkey.

¹/₂ cup onion, chopped	2 cups milk
¹/₂ cup green pepper, chopped	2 eggs, beaten
¹/₂ cup celery, chopped	1 teaspoon salt
¹/₂ cup butter or margarine	¹/₄ teaspoon pepper
1 can cream of chicken soup	¹/₄ teaspoon poultry seasoning
2 cans chicken broth	3 cups yellow squash, chopped, cooked, drained
5 cups cornbread, crumbled	

Sauté onion, pepper, and celery in butter until tender. Add broth and soup and blend in blender until smooth. Pour into large mixing bowl; add cornbread and mix well. Stir in remaining ingredients except squash. Mix well. Beat cooked squash and then add to the cornbread mixture. Adding the squash last keeps the eggs from cooking from the heat of the squash. Mix well. Spray casserole dish with Pam and pour in squash mixture. Bake at 400 degrees for 30 to 40 minutes or until lightly browned. Serves 8–10.

BAKED SQUASH
Kittie Clyde Leonard

2 pounds yellow squash, cut up	Black pepper to taste
¹/₂ medium onion, chopped	2 tablespoons butter
4 tablespoons bacon drippings	30 saltine crackers, crushed
2 eggs, beaten	¹/₂ to 1 cup cheese, grated (optional)
1 teaspoon salt	

Cook squash until tender. Drain. Sauté onion in bacon drippings. Combine with squash. Add eggs, seasonings, butter and 3/4 cup crushed crackers. Pour into greased oblong dish and sprinkle remainder of crackers over top. Cover with grated cheese, if desired. Bake at 350 degrees for 45 minutes. Serves 4–6.

MILLS' FAMILY BAKED SQUASH   *Jane Mills*

3 pounds yellow summer
   squash, cut into small
   pieces
1¹/₂ cups onion, chopped
14 saltine crackers, mashed
3 eggs, slightly beaten

1 tablespoon sugar
1 teaspoon salt
¹/₂ teaspoon pepper
¹/₂ cup margarine, melted
   (divided)
8 saltine crackers, mashed

Cook squash, onion and about 2 cups water in 4¹/₂ to 5-quart saucepan, until tender. Drain very well, in strainer. Return to pan and mash with a hand potato masher. Add crackers, eggs, sugar, salt and pepper and ¹/₄ cup butter mixing well. Pour mixture into a large baking dish. Pour remaining margarine over mixture. Sprinkle the 8 mashed crackers over margarine. Bake at 375 degrees for 30 to 45 minutes or until top is lightly browned. Serves 8–10.

SUMMER GARDEN CASSEROLE   *Peggy Arbon*

1 zucchini, 3 inches in diameter, cut in ¹/₂-inch slices
2 tomatoes, 3 inches in diameter, cut in ¹/₂-inch slices
1 large onion, sliced thin
¹/₄ cup Parmesan cheese,
   grated

¹/₄ cup bread crumbs or
   wheat germ
¹/₂ teaspoon fresh basil,
   finely chopped
1 tablespoon butter or
   margarine
Salt and pepper to taste

Place alternating slices in an oiled baking dish. Mix together cheese, crumbs and basil. Sprinkle over vegetables. Dot with butter. Salt and pepper to taste. Bake at 350 degrees for 30 minutes. May be prepared ahead, baked until nearly done and frozen. Serves 4.

ZUCCHINI BOATS WITH FRESH MUSHROOMS   *Joan Robertson*

8 zucchini
1 tablespoon minced onion
1 tablespoon olive oil
1¹/₄ cup fresh mushrooms,
   chopped

¹/₂ cup Parmesan or
   Gruyere cheese, grated
   and divided
¹/₈ teaspoon marjoram, basil
   or thyme
Salt and pepper to taste
8 strips of bacon, halved

130

Wash and trim off ends of unpeeled zucchini. Cut in half lengthwise and scoop out seeds. Drop into boiling water, cover and simmer for 8 minutes. Very carefully remove and drain upside down on wire rack. In skillet, sauté onions in olive oil until tender. Combine mushrooms, onion, 1/4 cup grated cheese, marjoram, salt and pepper. Mix gently. Spoon mixture into each zucchini boat and sprinkle with remaining cheese. Top each boat with a strip of bacon. Place into a well greased baking dish and bake at 350 degrees for 15 minutes or until bacon is done and browned.

ARROZ CLASSICO — CLASSIC RICE
Cynthia Smith

1/3 cup oil
1 onion, chopped
1 cup raw rice
2 cups hot chicken broth
1 1/2 tablespoons parsley, minced

Salt and pepper to taste
1/2 cup Parmesan cheese, grated
Mushrooms (optional)

Wilt onion in oil. Add rice and stir until coated and oil turns yellow. Drain oil and add broth. Cook covered 20 minutes then add cheese, parsley, salt and pepper and mix. May add mushrooms last. Serves 4.

WILD RICE CASSEROLE
Cynthia Smith

This is delicious! It is different and good with fish.

1 package (6-ounce) Uncle Ben's Wild Rice
2 ribs celery, chopped
1/4 pound Velveeta cheese, cubed

1 cup half and half
1 4-ounce can mushrooms, chopped
3 green onions, chopped
1/2 cup butter, cubed

Prepare rice as per box directions. Heat rest of ingredients in pan until cheese and butter melts. Add to rice. Bake in greased casserole at 300 degrees for 30 minutes. Serves 8.

CORNBREAD DRESSING OR STUFFING   *Shirley Lawson*

Shirley's niece, Ann Gatlin, Carol's mother-in-law, Ada Margaret Carroll, always made this special dressing for Christmas.

3 packages cornbread mix	Butter or margarine
2 or 3 slices white bread	Poultry seasoning to taste
3 hard boiled eggs, chopped	Salt and pepper to taste
2 or 3 ribs celery, chopped	Tad of garlic
1 large onion, chopped	4 to 5 cans chicken broth

Prepare cornbread according to directions on package. Need 2 nine-inch skillets of cornbread. Crumble cornbread and white bread into small crumbs. Add eggs and celery. Sauté onion in butter. Add poultry seasoning, salt and pepper to taste. Add chicken broth and mix well. Pour into a 9 x 13 baking pan and bake 350 degrees uncovered until firm in center. Serves 10–12.

ORIGINAL TURKEY DRESSING OR STUFFING   *Amy Poulton*

Ingredients	6–8 pound	12–18 pound	18–26 pounds
Shortening	2/3 cup	1 1/3 cups	2 cups
Onions, chopped	3/4 cup	1 1/2 cups	2 1/4 cups
Celery, chopped	1 cup	2 cups	3 cups
Salt	2 tsp.	4 tsp.	6 tsp.
Black pepper	1/2 tsp.	1 tsp.	1 1/2 tsp.
Poultry seasoning	1 Tbsp.	2 Tbsp.	3 Tbsp.
Chopped parsley	1 1/3 Tbsp.	2 2/3 Tbsp.	4 Tbsp.
Hot water	1 1/2 cups	3 cups	4 1/2 cups
Bread, cubed	16–18 slices	36 slices	48 slices

Melt shortening in a skillet. Add onions and celery; sauté over low heat for 15 minutes. While this is cooking, mix bread cubes, salt, pepper, poultry seasoning and parsley in large bowl. Pour onions and celery over bread cube mixture. Mix well. Add hot water and mix thoroughly. Spoon stuffing into turkey, just enough to fill bird, because stuffing swells during roasting or baking.

★   ★   ★   ★   ★

HINT:
For fluffier mashed potatoes add a pinch of baking soda with milk and butter.

Breads

BLANCO COUNTY JAIL

The Blanco County Jail was constructed in 1894 "of limestone rock, using local labor." The property on which it stands was purchased from W. H. Withers for $100 in the spring of 1894. It is one of only a few jails built before the turn of the century that still meets jail standards.

ANGEL FLAKE BISCUITS
Kittie Clyde Leonard

1 package dry yeast
2 tablespoons warm water
1 cup Crisco
5 cups flour
4 teaspoons sugar

1 teaspoon soda
3 teaspoons baking powder
1 teaspoon salt
2 cups buttermilk
Butter

Dissolve yeast in the warm water. Combine dry ingredients and cut in shortening; add yeast and buttermilk. Knead to dough consistency. Roll out to 1/2-inch thickness. Cut with biscuit cutter. Melt butter. Dip biscuits in melted butter and fold in half. Freeze 12 to a pan. Bake at 350 degrees for 30 minutes or until brown. Do not thaw before baking. Makes 4–5 dozen.

WHOLE WHEAT ANGEL BISCUITS
Jewell Sultemeier

1 package dry yeast
2 tablespoons lukewarm
  water
1¹/₂ cups whole wheat flour
3¹/₂ cups all-purpose flour
3 teaspoons baking powder

1 teaspoon soda
1 teaspoon salt
4 tablespoons sugar
1 cup shortening
2 cups buttermilk plus 2
  tablespoons

Dissolve yeast in water. Sift the dry ingredients and cut in shortening. Add buttermilk and yeast. Knead lightly and quickly. Roll out and cut. The recipe will make 200 small biscuits. At this point, biscuits may be frozen by placing on cookie sheets, top with wax paper, put on another layer of biscuits and continue in this manner until all biscuits are layered on the sheet. After biscuits are frozen take off cookie sheet and place in plastic bag until you are ready to bake them. When ready to bake, take out of freezer and thaw. When double in size bake at 400 degrees for about 10 minutes.

BAKING POWDER BISCUITS
Elaine Oliver

1¹/₄ cups flour
2 teaspoons baking powder
¹/₂ teaspoon salt

3 tablespoons shortening
¹/₂ cup sweet milk

Sift flour, baking powder and salt together. Cut shortening into flour mixture. Slowly mix in milk. Mix together and pour out onto well floured waxed paper. Shape into circle and pat to 1/2-inch thickness. Cut with small biscuit cutter and place in 9-inch round pan. Bake 450 degrees until done, about 15 minutes. Makes 12–16 small biscuits.

BEER BISCUITS
Shirley Lawson

My sister Nell Terry gave me this recipe.

4 cups dry biscuit mix
4 ounces cheddar cheese, grated
1 can beer, room temperature
3 tablespoons sugar

Mix all ingredients. Fill muffin tins 1/2 full. Bake at 400 degrees for 15 minutes. Makes 24 biscuits.

CHEDDAR HERB BISCUITS
Peggy Arbon

1 cup flour
1 teaspoon rosemary
1 teaspoon thyme
1 teaspoon parsley
$^1/_3$ cup butter
1 cup Cheddar cheese, grated
1 tablespoon cold water

Combine the flour and crushed herbs in a large bowl. Cut in the butter with a pastry blender. Add the grated cheese and mix with your hands until the dough holds together. You may add a tablespoon of cold water, if necessary. Form the dough into a ball and roll out to 1/2-inch thickness on a lightly floured board. Cut biscuits with a biscuit cutter or glass. Prick the top with a fork. Place biscuits on an ungreased cookie sheet and bake at 350 degrees for 12 to 15 minutes. Makes 12 biscuits.

YEAST BUTTERMILK BISCUITS
Cynthia Smith

1 package of dry yeast
1 cup buttermilk, warmed
2 cups sifted flour
2 teaspoons baking powder
2 teaspoons sugar
$^1/_8$ teaspoon soda
1 teaspoon salt
3 tablespoons Crisco

Dissolve yeast in warm buttermilk. Sift flour with other dry ingredients. Cut in Crisco. Add yeast and buttermilk mixture and stir. Knead a few minutes on floured board. Make into small biscuits. Let rise about 1 hour. Bake in hot oven 400 degrees until golden brown. Makes 18 small biscuits.

TEXAS SOURDOUGH "STARTER"   *Committee*

Use this with the Sourdough Biscuit "Texas Style" recipe.

4 cups flour
1 package dry yeast
4 cups warm water

3 tablespoons sugar
2 teaspoons salt

Place all ingredients in a crock that has a top. Leave at room temperature covered with only a piece of cheesecloth for 2 or 3 days until mixture begins to ferment. When it foams and bubbles it is ready for use. To increase sourness keep starter in a warm place; to arrest it put it in the refrigerator.

Feeding the Starter:
Equal parts flour and milk   ¹/₃ cup sugar
Pinch of salt

Start the Starter with water but feed it with milk. Add to the Starter and let it sit overnight covered.

SOURDOUGH BISCUITS — "TEXAS STYLE"   *Committee*

This recipe should be made using the Texas Sourdough Starter

2 cups flour
2 teaspoons baking powder
1 husky pinch salt
1 husky pinch soda

¹/₂ cup butter
1 cup starter
¹/₃ cup cold water

Mix the flour, baking powder, salt and soda. Blend in melted butter, then add starter and cold water. Mix this well until heavy, slightly sticky dough results. Pinch off gobs of dough one and a half times the size of a golf ball. If cooked in a Dutch oven biscuits are best baked in a pie tin atop a trivet in the oven. This prevents scorching on the bottom should the coals be-

come enthusiastic. If cooked in a conventional oven, bake for 15–17 minutes at 425 degrees. Makes 12–16 biscuits.

DUMPLINGS
Duke Rumpf

This is my mother's recipe for dumplings. Momma said if it was just us three, 1/2 a chicken was plenty but if company dropped by she could add dumplings and feed a couple more.

2 cups flour, approximately
2 eggs
1/2 teaspoon salt

Walnut-size lard
2 teaspoons baking powder
Cold water

Mix all ingredients well and put on floured board. Roll out and cut into 1-inch squares. Put in boiling liquid and cover loosely. The liquid can be chicken broth, a thin soup or stew. This will thicken up your liquid. Serves 4–6.

DILLY BREAD
Elaine Oliver

1 package dry yeast
1/4 cup warm water
1 cup creamed cottage
   cheese, heated to
   lukewarm
2 tablespoons sugar
1 tablespoon instant minced
   onions

1 tablespoon butter
2 teaspoons dill seed
1/4 teaspoon soda
1 teaspoon salt
1 egg
2 1/4 to 2 1/2 cups flour

Soften yeast in water. To cottage cheese add sugar, onions, butter, dill seed, soda and salt. Combine in mixing bowl cottage cheese mixture with yeast; add egg to this mixture. Add flour to make a stiff dough; beat well after each addition. Let rise in warm place until light and double in size, about 1 hour. Stir dough down and put into round casserole or bread loaf pan. Let rise. Bake at 350 degrees for 40 to 50 minutes. Yield: 1 loaf.

137

LACEY'S TEDDY-BEAR BREAD

Lacey Lawson

I made this bread and entered it in the prepared foods during the 1987 Fair and Rodeo Exhibit when I was 10 years old. I received the Merit Award and was tickled pink.

$^1/_4$ cup milk
3 tablespoons sugar
2 teaspoons salt
3 tablespoons margarine
1 envelope active dry yeast
$1^1/_2$ cups warm water, 110-115 degrees

$6^1/_2$ to 7 cups flour
Oil
8 raisins
1 egg, slightly beaten with 1 tablespoon cold water

Pour milk into saucepan. Heat over medium heat until bubbles form around edge. Remove from heat. Stir in sugar, salt and margarine. Cool to lukewarm. Sprinkle yeast over warm water in a large bowl. Let stand a minute or two, then stir to dissolve. Add milk mixture and 3 cups of the flour. Beat with wooden spoon until smooth. Stir in $3^1/_2$ to 4 cups more flour, or enough to make a stiff dough. Knead dough on floured board for 8 to 10 minutes. Place in bowl greased with oil, grease top lightly. Cover with towel. Let rise for 1 hour. Punch down. Divide dough into four equal pieces. Set two aside for bear bodies. Cut one of the remaining pieces in half for two heads and the other one into fourteen pieces. Shape all pieces of dough into balls. Place large balls on greased baking sheets for bodies. Place medium balls above for heads. Flatten slightly. Then attach small balls for paws, noses and ears. Cover with a towel and let rise about 1 hour. Adjust rack 1/3 up from bottom of oven and turn on oven to 400 degrees. Make indentations for ears, eyes, noses and belly buttons with end of toothpick. Use egg and water mixture and paint over dough. Bake until golden brown. Place on wire rack to cool. Place raisins in indentations for eyes, ears, noses and belly buttons. Spread a little butter over warm golden bread to give a shiny crust. Makes two Teddy Bears.

JOY'S BREAD

Joy Anderson

2 cups boiling water
$^1/_2$ cup butter
$^3/_4$ cup sugar
1 tablespoon salt
2 packages dry yeast

3 teaspoons sugar
$^1/_2$ cup lukewarm water
2 eggs, beaten
Flour

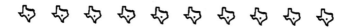

Melt butter in boiling water; add sugar, salt, and set aside to cool to luke-warm. Dissolve yeast and sugar in lukewarm water and add eggs. Combine yeast mixture with liquid mixture and add flour to make a fairly stiff dough. Beat mixture after adding flour to keep dough smooth. Pour on floured board and work until pliable. Place in greased bowl; cover with waxed paper and let rise. Pour on floured board and shape into loaves, rolls etc. Bake loaves at 350 degrees for 30 minutes or until brown. Bake rolls at 400 degrees for 12 to 15 minutes or until lightly browned. Makes 2–3 loaves or 30–36 rolls.

CRACKED WHEAT BREAD

Genevia Bushnell

This recipe came from a 1942 cookbook.

2 cakes Fleischmann's Yeast	3 tablespoons sugar
3/4 cup lukewarm water	1 tablespoon salt
3 cups cracked wheat, cooked	6 cups flour
3 tablespoons melted shortening	

Cook cracked wheat using 1 cup cracked wheat to 3 cups water and cook about 1 hour. Dissolve yeast in lukewarm water; mix lukewarm cracked wheat, shortening, sugar and salt together; add yeast, mix well. Add flour. Turn out on floured board and knead about 10 to 15 minutes until elastic. Place dough in greased bowl; cover and set in warm place, free from draft. Let rise until doubled in bulk, about 1 hour and 15 minutes. When light, divide into equal portions and shape into loaves. Place in greased bread pans. Cover and let rise until light, about 55 minutes. Bake in moderate oven at 400 degrees about 1 hour. Makes two loaves.

GOUDA CHEESE BREAD

Gail Rucker

2 packages active dry yeast	2 tablespoons salad oil
2 cups warm water	1/2 cup powdered milk
2 tablespoons sugar	1 cup Gouda cheese, grated
2 tablespoons salt	5 cups flour, sifted

Dissolve yeast in warm water. Add sugar, salt, oil, powdered milk and 2 cups of the flour. Beat with mixer 1 minute. Add three cups flour and cheese and stir with spoon to mix. Cover with damp cloth and let rise 45 minutes. Then beat 5 strokes and put in bundt pan. Cover with damp towel and let rise 15 minutes. Remove towel and bake 45 minutes at 350 degrees. Yield: 1 bundt pan.

ONION BREAD
Joan Robertson

1 package dry yeast
1 cup water (105–115 degrees)
2 teaspoons sugar
2 teaspoons salt, divided

3¹/₄ cups flour, divided
2 tablespoons butter, melted
¹/₂ cup onion, diced
2 teaspoons paprika

Dissolve yeast in water; add sugar, 1 teaspoon salt, and 2 cups flour. Stir, then beat well. Stir in remaining flour. Put on bread board and knead for 8 to 10 minutes; add more flour if needed. Put into a greased bowl; turn to grease all of the ball of dough, then cover bowl. Let rise for 1 hour. Punch down. Divide dough and place into two well greased loaf pans. Brush with butter, and sprinkle onions on top of loaves. Punch onions down into the dough so it is dented with onions. Let rise for 45 minutes. Sprinkle each loaf with 1/2 teaspoon salt and 1 teaspoon paprika. Bake in 450 degrees oven for 20 minutes. Yield: 2 loaves.

WHOLE WHEAT BAGUETTES
Peggy Arbon

I have used this recipe for over a year now, and we enjoy it very much. It tends to dry out quickly, so try to use a whole loaf at a time.

2¹/₂ to 3 cups unbleached all-purpose flour
2 packages active dry yeast
1 tablespoon sugar
1¹/₂ teaspoons salt

2 cups warm water, 120 to 130 degrees
2 cups whole wheat flour
1 slightly beaten egg white
1 tablespoon water

In a large mixer bowl, stir together 2 cups flour, yeast, sugar and salt. Add warm water. Beat with an electric mixer at low speed for 1/2 minute, scraping sides of bowl constantly. Beat 3 minutes at high speed. Using a spoon, stir in the whole wheat flour and as much of the remaining all-purpose flour as you can. Turn out onto a lightly floured surface. Knead in

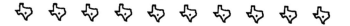

enough of the remaining flour to make a stiff dough that is smooth and elastic, about 8 to 10 minutes. Shape into a ball. Place in a lightly greased bowl; turn once to grease surface. Cover, let rise in a warm place until double, about 1 to 1 hour 15 minutes. Punch dough down, turn out onto a lightly floured surface. Divide dough in thirds. Cover, let rest 10 minutes. Roll each third into a 12 x 10 inch rectangle. Roll up tightly from long side; seal well. Taper ends. Place, seam side down, on a greased baking sheet. Brush with mixture of egg white and water. Cover; let rise until nearly double, about 30 to 45 minutes. With a sharp knife, make 3 diagonal cuts about 1/4-inch deep across tops of loaves. Bake in a 450 degree oven for 15 to 20 minutes or until done. Serve same day or freeze. Makes 3 loaves or 24 servings. Hold one loaf in refrigerator while other two bake if the three loaves do not fit on one large baking sheet in your oven.

How to Raise Dough in Microwave

First test microwave to make sure it is suitable for proofing bread. Place 2 tablespoons cold, stick margarine in microwave for 4 minutes at 10%. If margarine melts the oven has too much power and will kill the yeast before the bread has a chance to rise.

To raise, place ball of dough in a lightly greased microwave safe mixing bowl and turn once to grease the surface. Put 3 cups water into a 4-cup measure. Microwave on high for $6^{1}/_{2}$ to $8^{1}/_{2}$ minutes or until it boils. Move measure with water to the back of the oven. Cover dough with waxed paper. Heat dough and water on 10% power for 13 to 15 minutes or until dough is almost double.

UNCLE BOB'S RAISIN BREAD   *Joyce Penick Ellis*

This Raisin Bread was made, served and sold at Uncle Bob's Cafeteria in Johnson City for all the years it was open. Over 10,000 loaves were made.

1 cup milk, scalded
$^{1}/_{2}$ cup sugar
2 teaspoons salt
$^{1}/_{2}$ cup margarine, melted
4 packages dry yeast
Icing:
2 cups powdered sugar
Milk

$^{1}/_{2}$ cup warm water
4 eggs
8 cups flour
1 cup raisins

1 teaspoon vanilla

To scalded milk add sugar, salt, margarine and stir until sugar is dissolved. Cool to lukewarm. Dissolve yeast in water. Combine eggs, milk mixture, flour, raisins and yeast mixture and mix well. Place into greased bowl and let rise until double, about 1 hour. Divide dough into 5 portions. Let rest 10 minutes. Shape into loaves and place into bread pans. Bake at 350 degrees for 30 minutes or when loaves sound hollow when tapped. Makes 5 loaves.

Icing: Put powdered sugar into mixing bowl, add vanilla and enough milk, a tablespoon at a time, to make a thick but spreadable consistency. Stir in vanilla. Ice bread as soon as cool enough to remove from pans. If bread is too warm icing will melt and run off sides. Cool completely, then place in bags leaving air in bags so bags cannot touch icing.

APPETIZER WHOLE GRAIN BUNS   *Genevia Bushnell*

You will find seven-grain cereal at a health food store.

1 cup boiling water	**1¹/₂ cups whole wheat flour**
³/₄ cup uncooked seven-	**1 package active dry yeast**
grain cereal	**1 egg**
¹/₂ cup milk	**2 to 2¹/₃ cups all-purpose**
3 tablespoons butter or	**flour**
margarine	**Cornmeal**
2 tablespoons sugar	**Butter or margarine, melted**
³/₄ teaspoon salt	

Pour boiling water over cereal; cool 5 minutes. Stir in milk, the 3 tablespoons butter, the sugar, and salt. Stir until butter is almost melted. Combine 1 cup of the whole wheat flour and the yeast. Stir cereal mixture into flour mixture. Add egg; beat well. Using spoon, stir in remaining whole wheat flour and as much all-purpose as you can. Knead in enough remaining all-purpose flour to make a moderately stiff dough that is smooth and elastic, 6 to 8 minutes. Shape into a ball. Place in a greased bowl, turn once to grease surface. Cover and let rise until almost double, about 1¹/₄ hours. Punch down. On lightly floured surface divide dough into 4 equal portions. Divide each portion into 8 pieces. Roll each piece into a ball. Lightly grease baking sheets, sprinkle with cornmeal. Place balls of dough on baking sheets. Cover and let rise until nearly double, about 30 minutes. Bake in a 375 degree oven for 12 to 15 minutes or until done. Remove from baking sheet; cool on wire racks. Brush with melted butter. Makes 32 buns.

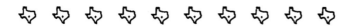

EGG BATTER BUNS

Elaine Oliver

This recipe was given to me by my step-mother Ruth Sines.

1 package active dry yeast	2¹/₄ cups flour
1 cup warm water	1 egg
2 tablespoons sugar	2 tablespoons shortening
1 teaspoon salt	

Sprinkle yeast into warm water in large bowl. Stir in sugar, salt and 1¹/₂ cups flour. Beat until smooth. Add egg and shortening. Beat in rest of flour. Cover bowl and let rise in warm place until doubled in size, about 30 minutes. Stir down. Spoon into 12 greased muffin cups, filling each 1/2 full. Let rise again until doubled in size. Bake at 400 degrees for 15 minutes or until brown. Yield: 12 buns.

GRANDMOTHER'S POTATO ROLLS

Cynthia Smith

These are sure good and a little different since they have potato as one of the ingredients. It makes a very light and delicate roll and they are as delicious when left-over and split open, buttered and toasted in the oven. They are so well liked by my friends that I often make them and give the ready to use dough as a Christmas gift in a nice bowl. The dough will keep covered in the refrigerator for a week to ten days, or you can bake them all at once and freeze the ones not eaten.

1 envelope dry yeast	²/₃ cup shortening
¹/₂ cup potato water, cooled to lukewarm	²/₃ cup sugar
	1 teaspoon salt
1 cup cooked mashed potatoes, unseasoned	2 eggs, beaten
	6 to 8 cups flour
1 cup scalded milk (heat just until skim forms on top)	

Dissolve yeast in potato water and set aside. Mix potatoes with the milk; then add shortening, sugar and salt. Add the dissolved yeast; mix and add well beaten eggs. Stir in enough flour to make stiff dough. Knead on a board then place in a large greased bowl and roll the dough around to grease all sides. Cover with a damp cloth or plastic wrap and let rise until double in bulk; punch down to let air out. It can be refrigerated at this time until you wish to use it or pinch off a ball the size of a softball, roll it on a floured board and knead well; then pinch off a wad the size of a ping pong ball and place it on a greased pan about an inch apart. Let these rise until doubled in size. It could take several hours if cold. Bake in oven at 400 degrees for 15 to 20 minutes or until golden. Yield: 3 to 4 dozen rolls.

QUICK YEAST ROLLS
Lucia Carbary

This recipe is a family favorite. I remember my mother having doughnuts and cinnamon rolls prepared from this recipe when we were children and came in from school. Ummmmm good!

1 package dry yeast	2 tablespoons shortening,
1 cup lukewarm water	melted and cooled
2 tablespoons sugar	1 teaspoon salt
	3¹/₄ cups flour

Dissolve yeast in water and add sugar, shortening, salt and 1 cup flour. Beat at medium speed. Add remaining flour. If sticky, add a little more flour. Let rise. Knead and let rise again. Make into rolls and let rise again. Bake at 400 degrees for 12 to 15 minutes or until golden brown. Yield: 20 to 24 rolls.

NO-KNEAD WHOLE WHEAT ROLLS
Peggy Arbon

These rolls are delicious, but can be improved for healthy heart by substituting Eggbeaters for the whole eggs, and use one of the polyunsaturated oils.

4¹/₄ cups unbleached all-purpose flour	2 eggs
	2 cups warm water (120 to
¹/₃ cup sugar	130 degrees)
2 teaspoons salt	³/₄ cup cooking oil
2 envelopes active dry yeast	2 cups whole wheat flour

In a large mixer bowl combine 3 cups flour, sugar, salt, and yeast. Stir together the eggs, water and oil; add to flour mixture and beat with an electric mixer at low speed for 1/2 minute, scraping bowl. Beat 3 minutes at high speed. Using a spoon, stir in remaining all-purpose flour and all of

144

the whole wheat flour. Transfer dough to a very large greased bowl, turn once. Cover and refrigerate for 2 to 24 hours. Stir dough down. Let dough rest 10 minutes. Spray a 13 x 9 x 2-inch baking pan and a 9 x 9 x 2 baking pan with nonstick spray coating or lightly grease with shortening. On well-floured surface roll dough to 1-inch thickness; cut with a 2¹/₂-inch round floured cutter. Transfer rolls to pans. Form scraps into a ball. Let rest 10 minutes, reroll and cut. Transfer rolls to pans. Cover and let rise in warm place until doubled, about 40 minutes. Bake in 375 degree oven 25 minutes or until golden. Serve warm. Or, use the cooled rolls for sandwiches. Yield: 21 rolls.

SOMETHING DIFFERENT SWEET ROLLS   *Joycelyn Carter*

1 package yellow cake mix
   without pudding
2 packages dry yeast
5 cups flour
2¹/₂ cups warm water

2 tablespoons butter,
   softened
¹/₂ cup sugar
2 teaspoons cinnamon
¹/₂ cup raisins (optional)

Topping:
¹/₂ cup butter
6 tablespoons white corn
   syrup

6 tablespoons brown sugar
¹/₂ cup pecans, chopped

Mix cake mix, yeast and flour well. Stir in warm water. Let rise until doubled in size, about 40 minutes. Roll dough into oblong 9 x 18 inches on a lightly floured board. Mix sugar and cinnamon. Brush dough with butter and sprinkle with sugar and cinnamon mixture. Sprinkle on raisins if desired. Roll up tightly, beginning at wide side. Seal well by pinching ends of roll together. Cut roll into 1 inch slices. Place a little apart in greased 13 x 9-inch pan. Cover and let rise until double. Before baking, melt topping ingredients in sauce pan over low heat; pour over rolls. Bake at 375 degrees for 25 minutes. Yields: 18 rolls.

★   ★   ★   ★   ★

HINT:
Bread stays fresher longer at room temperature or frozen. Do not store bread in the refrigerator.

★   ★   ★   ★   ★

OLIVER FAMILY'S SPECIAL ROLLS

Elaine Oliver

An old Oliver family recipe. Jim's mother and sisters used it and passed it on to me.

1 cup sugar	Favorite biscuit dough
Pickled peach juice from a	1 cup sugar
quart of pickled peaches	Butter
1 tablespoon butter, heaping	Cinnamon

Add sugar to the pickled peach juice and heat until sugar dissolves. Add butter. Make biscuit dough and roll out thin. Sprinkle sugar over dough. Cut small pieces of butter and dot over dough, sprinkle with cinnamon. Roll into a roll and cut into 1 inch pieces. Place rolls in a shallow baking pan. Pour peach juice mixture over all and bake in 350 degree oven until brown. Great served as a breakfast roll, or with vanilla ice cream or whipped cream. Yield: about 12 rolls.

YEAST DOUGHNUTS

Holly Lawson

This recipe is time consuming. It takes about 2¹/₂ to 3 hours, but once you try these a store bought doughnut just won't do. I have fixed these several times for Bible School and the kids really look forward to them. I have also won the Merit Award on these doughnuts in the food preparation booth at the Blanco County Fair.

1 cup milk	2¹/₂ ounce yeast cake or ³/₄
¹/₄ cup sugar	tablespoon dry yeast
¹/₄ cup oil	¹/₄ cup warm water
¹/₈ teaspoon salt	2 eggs
¹/₂ teaspoon vanilla	4 cups flour
	6 cups oil to fry doughnuts

Icing:

6 cups powdered sugar	1 teaspoon vanilla
3 to 4 tablespoons water	
(more if necessary)	

Scald milk. Add sugar, oil, salt and vanilla. Stir to dissolve sugar. Let cool to lukewarm. Dissolve yeast in warm water. Mix milk mixture, yeast and

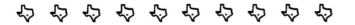

eggs in large mixing bowl. Add flour. Mix well. Place in a greased bowl and cover with a dish towel. Let set and double in size. Punch down and let rise again. When double in size dump dough on floured counter and roll to 1/2-inch thickness. Dip doughnut cutter in flour (to prevent sticking) and cut out doughnuts. Place strips of wax paper on cookie sheet and dust with flour (to prevent sticking) and place doughnuts on wax paper. Any excess dough from around doughnuts, except doughnut holes, can be put together and formed into a ball and covered with a towel and let rise until you are finished with doughnuts and then made into cinnamon rolls. While doughnuts are rising mix the icing ingredients together to make a semi-thick but not runny icing. Too thick and you get too much icing on the doughnuts and too runny and it all runs off. After icing is ready, heat oil to get it hot, about 375 degrees. Use the doughnut holes to test oil. They should rise to the top of the oil in about 1 to 1¹/₂ minutes and turn them over to brown on the other side. They should be a golden brown. Doughnuts should take about 20 minutes to rise until you have a nice large doughnut. Gently lift doughnuts off paper and put in hot oil. Fry until golden brown, then turn over and brown on the other side. Take out and place on a wire rack with a cookie sheet under it to let excess oil drip off and to cool slightly. (I use the stick end of 2 wooden spoons to get doughnuts out of hot grease). When cool and able to pick up with hands, dip in icing, place on another wire rack with cookie sheet under it to let the excess icing drip off. The doughnuts are warm and ready to sample with a glass of cold milk. Yield: 4 dozen doughnuts.

GRANDMOTHER'S CORNBREAD   *Cynthia Smith*

From Pearl Tarver.

¹/₂ cup cornmeal, white
¹/₂ cup flour
1 egg
1 teaspoon salt
2 tablespoons sugar

2 teaspoons baking powder
1 small can Pet milk (do not dilute)
1 tablespoon bacon grease

Mix all ingredients together except bacon grease. Heat bacon grease in baking pan. Pour in cornbread mixture. Bake in hot oven 400 degrees for 20 to 25 minutes. Only evaporated milk will do for this recipe. Yield: 8 servings.

JALAPEÑO CORNBREAD   *Mary Dyer*

Determine amount of jalapeño peppers to use by how hot they are. We first ate this at a friend's house in Arkansas and it was so hot it almost made us smoke.

1½ cups yellow cornmeal
1 heaping tablespoon flour
3 teaspoons salt
½ teaspoon soda
1 cup buttermilk
½ cup oil
2 eggs, beaten
1 16-ounce can cream style corn

3 to 6 jalapeños, chopped
½ cup green peppers, chopped
4 to 5 green onions, chopped, use tops also
1½ cups Cheddar cheese, grated

Mix cornmeal, flour, salt and soda. Add buttermilk, oil, eggs and corn. Mix well. Stir in jalapeños, green pepper and onion. Grease 9 x 14 pan, pour in batter and sprinkle with cheese. Bake 375 degrees for 35 minutes or until done. Serves 12–16.

EAST TEXAS CORNBREAD   *Joycelyn Carter*

When I went off to college, this is the one food I missed the most.

1 cup white cornmeal
¾ teaspoon salt
1 tablespoon bacon grease

¾ cup boiling water
Cooking oil for frying

Mix cornmeal, salt and bacon grease together. Add boiling water and stir. Water must be boiling. Take about a tablespoon of mixture in hand and roll in ball, then flatten in hand using three fingers. Mixture is hot so do this quick. Fry in hot oil until brown turning once. We eat this with butter and a glass of milk. It is also good with fish. Yield: 12 corn cakes.

SQUASH HUSH PUPPIES   *Teet Hobbs*

2 cups yellow squash, cooked and mashed
1 egg, beaten
1 small onion, chopped

¾ cup cornbread mix, any prepared mix
½ cup flour
Oil for frying

148

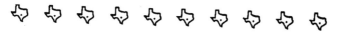

Mix together all ingredients. Drop by 1/2 teaspoonsful into deep fat, hot but not smoking. They will be thin and delicate and will turn over by themselves. Remove when golden brown. Makes 2¹/₂ dozen.

APPLE MUFFINS
Norma Honeycutt

This recipe came from a cookbook out of Blanco, tried it because we needed to find something to do with an over zealous buying spree of apples. Very good for a brunch, and makes your kitchen smell great!

1 egg	¹/₂ cup sugar
¹/₄ cup oil	2 teaspoons baking powder
1 cup milk	¹/₂ teaspoon salt
1 cup apple, grated	¹/₂ teaspoon cinnamon
1¹/₂ cups flour	¹/₂ cup pecans, chopped

Break egg into small bowl, stir with fork. Add oil, milk and apple. Sift together flour, sugar, baking powder, salt and cinnamon. Combine with liquid mixture and add pecans and stir well. Batter will be lumpy. Grease or paper line muffin tins. Fill cups 2/3 full. Bake in 400 degree oven for 20 to 25 minutes. Makes 12 muffins.

APPLESAUCE MUFFINS
Mary Dyer

I use miniature muffin tins for finger size goodies. This is a recipe that my mother-in-law gave to me soon after Eddie and I were married, thirty-eight years ago. This is the only applesauce cake recipe I've ever used.

1 cup sugar	1¹/₂ cups flour
¹/₂ cup shortening	1 teaspoon cinnamon
1 egg, beaten	¹/₄ teaspoon allspice
¹/₂ teaspoon salt	1 teaspoon soda
1 teaspoon vanilla	1 cup pecans, finely
1 cup applesauce	chopped
1 cup dates, chopped	Powdered sugar

Cream sugar and shortening. Add egg, salt, vanilla, applesauce and dates and mix well. Sift flour, spices and soda and add to first mixture. Stir in pecans. Pour into greased and floured loaf pan or muffin tins. Bake in a

350 degree oven until done. Dust with powdered sugar. Makes 12 large or 30–36 miniature muffins.

BRAN MUFFINS   *Jeanne Hardy*

This is an American Cancer Society EAT SMART recipe. I have added the bananas, pecans and yogurt.

1¹/₄ cups whole bran cereal	1 large egg, beaten or low
1 cup skim milk	cholesterol substitute
1 cup whole wheat flour	¹/₄ cup polyunsaturated
¹/₂ cup sugar	vegetable oil
2¹/₂ teaspoons baking	2 tablespoons yogurt
powder	1 teaspoon vanilla
¹/₂ teaspoon baking soda	2 bananas, mashed
1 teaspoon ground	¹/₂ cup raisins
cinnamon	¹/₂ cup pecans, chopped

Preheat oven to 400 degrees. Mix bran with skim milk until bran is moistened; let stand 5 minutes. Combine flour, sugar, baking powder, baking soda and cinnamon; set aside. Add beaten egg, oil, yogurt and vanilla to bran mixture; stir well. Make a well in center of dry ingredients and add bran mixture, stirring just until combined. Do not over mix. Fold in bananas, raisins and nuts. Line muffin pan with paper muffin cups and fill 2/3 full. Bake 20 minutes or until done. Yield: 12 muffins.

THE REVEREND'S BRAN MUFFINS   *Rev. Joe Jones*

Rev. Joe Jones is pastor of the Rocky Creek Church.

4 cups Raisin Bran cereal or	1 cup Crisco
favorite bran cereal	3 cups sugar
2 cups Nabisco 100% Bran	4 eggs
2 teaspoons salt	5 cups flour
2 cups boiling water	5 teaspoons soda
1 quart or 4 cups buttermilk	

Combine Raisin Bran, 100% Bran, salt, and stir into boiling water. Add buttermilk. Set aside. In another bowl, cream Crisco and sugar; add eggs

150

one at a time beating well after each addition. Combine the bran mixture and the egg mixture and fold in the flour and soda. Stir well. Makes 1 gallon of batter and will keep in refrigerator for 4 weeks. Bake at 375 degrees for 20 to 25 minutes. Yield: 6 dozen large or 18 dozen miniature muffins.

SIX WEEK MUFFINS
Patsy Holloway

This is good for breakfast with cereal and skim milk.

15-ounces Raisin Bran
  cereal, Post is good,
  unsweetened
5 cups all purpose flour
5 teaspoons soda
3 cups sugar (may use 2¹/₂
  cups)

2 teaspoons salt
¹/₄ cup raisins (optional)
4 eggs
1 quart or 4 cups buttermilk
1 cup oil

Mix first 6 ingredients. Add eggs, buttermilk, oil, and mix thoroughly. Cover batter and refrigerate. Refrigerate overnight before using. Bake at 400 degrees for 20 minutes or at 350 degrees for 25 minutes. Batter will keep in the refrigerator for 6 weeks. Muffin is equal to one slice of bread. Muffins may be frozen after being baked. I spray my muffin pans with Pam. Yield: 6 dozen large muffins.

CHEESE FILLED BACON MUFFINS
Holly Lawson

I like to make these in a miniature muffin tin and use as an appetizer. Makes 48 small muffins. The cheese will need to be cut smaller.

1 pound bacon
1¹/₂ cups Hungry Jack
  Buttermilk or Extra Light
  Pancake and Waffle Mix
¹/₂ cup milk
¹/₃ cup bacon grease

1 egg
¹/₃ cup green pepper,
  chopped
¹/₃ cup onion, chopped
2-ounces American cheese,
  cut into 12, ¹/₂-inch cubes

Fry bacon until crisp, reserving grease. Crumble bacon and set aside. Preheat oven to 425 degrees. Line muffin pan with paper baking cups or grease. Lightly spoon pancake mix into measuring cup; level off. In large bowl combine pancake mix, milk, bacon grease and egg. Stir until blended. Add bacon, green pepper and onion; mix well. Fill prepared muffin cups 2/3 full. Press a cheese cube in center of batter. Bake at 425 degrees for 15 to 20 minutes or until golden brown. Remove from pan immediately. Serve warm. Makes 12 muffins. They are good at room temperature too.

SMURFBERRY MUFFINS   *Mary Pat Carter*

These are blueberry muffins but the batter is blue and my sons named them. It is one of their favorites.

¹/₂ cup margarine	2 tablespoons baking
¹/₂ cup oil	powder
2¹/₂ cups sugar	1 cup buttermilk
¹/₄ teaspoon salt	1 16-ounce can wild
2 eggs	blueberries and juice
4¹/₂ cups flour	

Mix margarine and oil. Add sugar, salt, eggs, flour and baking powder. Add buttermilk and mix well. Gently fold in blueberries with juice. Grease muffin pan well or use cupcake papers. Bake at 375 to 400 degrees for 15 to 20 minutes. Batter will keep in refrigerator for 6 weeks. Yield: 5 dozen.

SPICY APRICOT BREAD   *Pat Wiedebusch*

This was served at a surprise bridal shower brunch given for Joyce Ellis.

2 cups flour, sifted	6 tablespoons shortening
1 teaspoon baking soda	¹/₂ teaspoon each, cloves,
1¹/₂ cups dried apricots,	cinnamon and salt
diced	¹/₄ teaspoon nutmeg
1 cup water	1 egg, beaten
1 cup sugar	

Preheat oven to 350 degrees. Sift together flour and soda. In a saucepan put the apricots with the remaining ingredients except the egg. Bring to boil and cook over medium heat for 5 minutes. Cool. Blend beaten egg into the apricot mixture. Gradually sift in flour and soda. Pour into well greased loaf pan 9 x 5 inches. Bake 1 hour. Cool 5 minutes and remove from pan onto rack. Yield: 1 loaf.

BANANA NUT BREAD
Addie Paul

This recipe has never been a failure. I double the recipe and make 2 loaves. It can be made ahead and frozen for later use.

¹/₂ **cup shortening or butter**	**1¹/₂ cups flour**
1¹/₂ cups sugar	**1 cup bananas, mashed**
3 eggs	**1 cup nuts, chopped**
1 teaspoon soda in 4	**1 teaspoon vanilla**
tablespoons buttermilk	

Mix all together. Pour in greased oven proof loaf pan. Bake at 350 degrees for approximately 1 hour and 15 minutes. Yield: 1 loaf.

WHOLE WHEAT BANANA BREAD
Jeanne Hardy

¹/₂ **cup margarine**	¹/₂ **teaspoon salt**
1 cup sugar	**1 teaspoon soda**
2 eggs, slightly beaten	**1 cup whole wheat flour**
3 medium-sized bananas or	¹/₃ **cup hot water**
1 cup, mashed	¹/₂ **cup pecans, chopped**
1 cup all-purpose flour, sift	
before measuring	

Melt margarine and blend in sugar. Mix in eggs and bananas, blending until smooth. Sift flour again with salt and soda. Stir in whole wheat flour. Add dry ingredients alternately with hot water. Stir in pecans. Turn into a greased 9 x 5 loaf pan. Bake in a moderately slow oven, 325 degrees, for 1 hour and 10 minutes. Yield: 1 loaf.

BLUEBERRY NUT BREAD
Cathy Woods

2 cups flour	¹/₂ **cup pecans, chopped**
1 cup sugar	**2 eggs, well beaten**
3 teaspoons baking powder	**1 cup milk**
¹/₄ **teaspoon salt**	**3 tablespoons oil**
1 cup blueberries	

Sift together flour, sugar, baking powder and salt. Add berries and nuts. Combine eggs, milk and oil; stir into flour mixture just to moisten. Pour into waxed paper-lined 9 x 5 x 3 inch loaf pan. Let stand 20 minutes. Bake loaf 1 hour in 350 degree oven. Yield: 1 loaf.

BOSTON BROWN BREAD

Elaine Oliver

1 cup white flour
$^1/_2$ cup cornmeal
2 cups whole wheat flour
$^1/_2$ cup sugar
2 teaspoons salt
$1^1/_2$ teaspoons soda
$1^1/_4$ teaspoons baking powder

1 cup molasses
2 cups sour milk
1 cup raisins or 1 cup nuts
or $^1/_2$ cup each
2 tablespoons butter or
shortening, melted

Mix and sift the dry ingredients. Add molasses and milk and stir thoroughly. Wash, dry and flour raisins. Cut nuts coarsely and flour. Add to batter. Then add fat. Pour into 2 well greased 13-ounce coffee cans or baking pans until 2/3 full. Cover the cans with brown paper that has been oiled or a double thickness of foil; tie securely with string. Place cans on a shallow rack in a large, deep kettle; add boiling water to come half way up side of cans. Cover kettle; steam bread 3 to $3^1/_2$ hours over low heat with water boiling constantly or in a slow oven (250–300 degrees). Add more water if necessary. Remove bread from cans; let cool 10 minutes on wire racks. Serve warm. A two quart mold with lid can also be used. Yields: 2 small loaves or 1 large.

CRANBERRY NUT COFFEE CAKE

Kittie Clyde Leonard

$^3/_4$ cup brown sugar
$^1/_2$ cup pecans, chopped
$^1/_4$ teaspoon cinnamon
2 cups Bisquick baking mix
2 teaspoons granulated sugar

1 egg
$^2/_3$ cup water or milk
$^2/_3$ cup whole cranberry
sauce

Icing:
1 cup powdered sugar
$^1/_2$ teaspoon vanilla

1 tablespoon water

Heat oven to 400 degrees. Grease 9 x 12 pan. Mix brown sugar, nuts and

154

cinnamon; set aside. Combine baking mix, sugar, egg and water and beat vigorously 1/2 minute. Spread in pan; sprinkle with nut mixture. Spoon cranberry sauce over top. Bake 20 to 25 minutes. While warm spread with icing. Serves 12.

Icing: Blend ingredients and spread over cake.

IRISH SODA BREAD
Neatta Cade

Good for camping trips.

1 egg, slightly beaten
1 cup sugar
1 teaspoon baking soda
3 teaspoons baking powder
1 pinch salt

2 tablespoons margarine, melted
1 cup raisins
2 cups buttermilk
4 cups flour

Beat egg slightly with fork. Add sugar, soda and baking powder. Add salt to margarine, raisins and buttermilk. Stir in flour. Mix all ingredients together well. Bake in 350 degree oven for about 1 hour in greased iron skillet. When fresh out of the oven, slice and spread with butter.

MONTEREY JACK CHEESE BREAD
Patty Casparis

1 loaf French bread
1 cup mayonnaise or salad dressing

3 cups Monterey Jack cheese, grated
1 7-ounce can green chilies, chopped

Slice bread in half lengthwise (2 long flat-top pieces of bread). Mix dressing, cheese and chilies together. Spread mixture thick on top of bread slices. Cook in 400 degree oven until cheese melts and bread is slightly toasted. Slice into serving pieces, 20 to 24 slices. Too much dressing will make topping slide off bread. Great with Italian food.

★   ★   ★   ★   ★

HINT:
Before slicing fresh bread run a serrated knife under hot water, dry blade and slice.

★   ★   ★   ★   ★

POPPY-SEED CAKE-BREAD   *Cathy Woods*

Bread:

3 cups flour
1¹/₂ teaspoons baking powder
¹/₂ teaspoon salt
2¹/₂ cups sugar
1¹/₂ cups milk
1¹/₃ cups Wesson cooking oil

Glaze:
³/₄ cup powdered sugar
¹/₄ cup orange juice

3 eggs
1¹/₂ tablespoons poppy
  seeds
1¹/₂ teaspoons vanilla
1¹/₂ teaspoons almond
  flavoring

¹/₂ teaspoon almond extract
2 tablespoons butter, melted

Mix all bread ingredients together. Beat for 2 minutes. Pour into greased loaf pans, two large or four regular. Bake at 350 degrees for 50 to 60 minutes. For glaze, mix powdered sugar with liquids until it is well mixed. Let bread cool and then drizzle glaze over the bread.

PUMPKIN BREAD   *Holly Lawson*

Lacey, my daughter, brought this recipe home from school when she was in the second grade. The date on the paper is November 27th. Thanksgiving was being studied and different ways to use the different foods that were eaten on the first Thanksgiving. She later used this recipe in the 4-H food show. With her knowledge of nutrition and the delicious bread to sample, the judges gave her a blue ribbon.

2 cups sugar
1 cup brown sugar
4 eggs
2 cups pumpkin, 16-ounce can
1 cup oil
2 teaspoons soda in ²/₃ cup
  water

2¹/₂ cups flour
1¹/₂ teaspoons salt
1 teaspoon nutmeg
1 teaspoon cinnamon
1 teaspoon cloves

Beat sugars and eggs together. Add pumpkin, oil and soda with water and stir. Add rest of ingredients and stir. Pour into a greased oven proof bread pan. Bake at 350 degrees for 1 hour. Yield: 1 loaf.

SOUR CREAM TEA LOAF

Daisy Cox

1¹/₂ teaspoons baking
  powder
1 teaspoon baking soda
2 cups all-purpose flour
1 cup sugar
¹/₂ cup butter or margarine
1 8-ounce container sour
  cream

3 eggs, beaten
2 teaspoons vanilla
1 cup or 6-ounce package
  dried apricots, chopped
1 cup pecans, chopped

Crumb Topping:
¹/₂ cup flour
¹/₄ cup sugar

¹/₄ cup butter or margarine,
  softened

Preheat oven to 350 degrees. Grease 9 x 5 inch loaf pan. In a large bowl,
mix baking powder, baking soda, flour and sugar. With pastry blender or
two knives used scissor-fashion, cut in butter until mixture resembles
coarse crumbs. Stir in sour cream, eggs and vanilla just until flour is moistened. Stir in apricots and pecans. Spoon batter evenly into pan. In bowl,
combine crumb topping ingredients with hands, until mixture resembles
coarse crumbs. Sprinkle crumb topping evenly over batter. Bake bread 60
to 70 minutes until toothpick inserted in center of bread comes out clean.
Cool bread in pan on wire rack 15 minutes; remove from pan and cool
completely on rack. Yield: 10 servings.

STREUSEL FILLED COFFEECAKE

Mary Gross

1¹/₂ cups flour
3 teaspoons baking powder
¹/₄ teaspoon salt
³/₄ cup sugar

¹/₄ cup shortening
1 egg
¹/₂ cup milk

Filling:
¹/₂ cup brown sugar
2 teaspoons cinnamon
2 tablespoons flour

2 tablespoons butter, melted
¹/₂ cup nuts, chopped

Mix all cake ingredients and set aside. Mix all filling ingredients. In oven
proof dish place 1/2 of cake mixture, then filling mixture, then add rest of
cake mixture. Bake at 375 degrees for 25 to 30 minutes. Yield: 8 servings.

TRASH TREASURE FROM ROSA ROFFE   *Faye Baird*

This is really good buttered and toasted.

2 to 2¹/₂ cups leftover jam or   ¹/₂ teaspoon salt
   jelly   ¹/₂ teaspoon baking soda
2 eggs   ¹/₂ cup nuts, any kind
¹/₂ cup milk, if needed   ¹/₂ cup Grape Nut cereal
¹/₂ cup oil   2 cups self-rising flour

Mix all ingredients together and beat well. Put into 2 greased loaf pans.
Bake at 350 degrees about 45 minutes. Yield: 2 loaves.

ZUCCHINI BREAD   *Jane Mills*

1 cup salad oil   ¹/₄ teaspoon baking powder
3 eggs, slightly beaten   1 teaspoon salt
2 cups sugar   1 teaspoon soda
2 cups zucchini, grated   3 teaspoons ground
2 teaspoons vanilla extract   cinnamon
3 cups all-purpose flour   1 cup pecans, chopped

Combine oil, eggs, sugar, zucchini and vanilla in large bowl. Blend well.
Stir in flour, baking powder, salt, soda and cinnamon. Do not beat. Stir in
pecans. Spoon into 2 well-greased 9 x 5 x 3 inch loaf pans. Bake at 325 degrees for 1 hour and 30 minutes. Yield: 2 loaves.

APPLE UPSIDE DOWN GINGERBREAD   *Mary Gross*

¹/₄ cup butter   1 package gingerbread mix
¹/₂ cup brown sugar   Whipped topping, garnish
1 teaspoon cinnamon   Maraschino cherries,
3 small apples, peeled and   garnish
   cored

Melt butter in bottom of 9-inch square cake pan. Combine brown sugar
and cinnamon. Sprinkle in bottom of pan. Cut apples in rings. Arrange on
brown sugar mixture. Prepare gingerbread mix as directed on package.

Pour over apples. Bake as directed on package. Invert on serving plate. Garnish with whipped topping and maraschino cherries. Cut into squares. Yield: 9 squares.

GERMAN GINGERBREAD

Helen Mayfield

There is no ginger in this bread.

1 pound box light brown sugar	1 teaspoon cinnamon
2 cups flour	1 teaspoon nutmeg
1¹/₂ cups margarine	2 eggs, beaten
1 teaspoon baking soda	1 cup buttermilk

Mix brown sugar, flour and margarine until it resembles course meal. Set aside 1 cup of this mixture, to be sprinkled on top before baking. To remainder, add baking soda, cinnamon, nutmeg, eggs, buttermilk and mix well. Place in a greased and floured 9 x 13 inch pan. Sprinkle on the 1 cup of mixture that was reserved at this time. Bake at 350 degrees for 25 minutes. Yield: 12 squares.

DAVID'S PANCAKES

Sallye Baker

¹/₂ cup flour	¹/₂ teaspoon vanilla
¹/₂ cup milk	¹/₄ cup butter
2 eggs, lightly beaten	2 tablespoons sugar
Pinch of nutmeg	Juice of half a lemon

Preheat oven to 425 degrees. Combine flour, milk, eggs, nutmeg and vanilla in a bowl, beating lightly. Batter should be slightly lumpy. Melt butter in a 12-inch oven-proof skillet. When very hot, pour in batter and bake in oven 15 to 20 minutes or until golden brown. Sprinkle with sugar and return to oven, briefly. Sprinkle with lemon juice, then serve with jam or marmalade. Enough for two hungry people or four otherwise.

★ ★ ★ ★ ★

HINT:
Next time you fix pancakes try a hint of vanilla, approximately 1/2 teaspoon.

★ ★ ★ ★ ★

159

Eggs

EASY FRENCH TOAST FOR TWO *Joycelyn Carter*

(MICROWAVE) . . . Recipe can be doubled and an electric skillet can be used instead of the microwave.

2 eggs, lightly beaten
1/4 cup milk
1 teaspoon sugar
1/8 teaspoon salt

1/4 teaspoon vanilla
1/2 teaspoon butter or
   margarine
4 slices of bread

Combine first 5 ingredients in a large bowl; beat well. Set aside. Place a browning grill in microwave oven; preheat on HIGH for 4 to 5 minutes. Add butter to hot grill, tilting to coat surface. Dip bread slices in egg mixture, coating both sides. Place slices on grill; microwave on HIGH for 1 minute. Turn slices over; microwave on HIGH for 1 minute. Serve with your favorite syrup. Serves 2.

BREAKFAST MIGAS FROM ROSA ROFFE *Faye Baird*

4 slices bacon
4 corn tortillas
1/2 cup onion, chopped
1/4 cup cilantro, chopped

To taste, jalapeño, chopped
1 tomato, chopped
4 eggs, beaten

Fry bacon crisp, drain and crumble. Break tortillas into small pieces (migas) and toast in bacon grease. Drain on paper towels. Mix together onion, cilantro, jalapeño and tomato and cook in same pan. While cooking add eggs to tomato mixture along with tortillas and crumbled bacon. Scramble all together and serve when eggs are done. Season if desired. Serves 2–3.

★   ★   ★   ★   ★

HINT:
Buy eggs from a refrigerated case, and refrigerate them as soon as possible.

★   ★   ★   ★   ★

BREAKFAST STRATA
Vanessa Luce

1 tablespoon butter
16 ¹/₂-inch slices crusty
  French or Italian bread
4 large eggs
2 cups milk
¹/₂ cup Parmesan cheese,
  grated
2 teaspoons Dijon mustard

¹/₄ teaspoon salt
¹/₄ teaspoon pepper, freshly
  ground
4 scallions, thinly sliced
4 ounces sliced bacon,
  cooked crisp, crumbled
1 ripe medium tomato,
  cored, seeded, chopped

Butter 1¹/₂ quart shallow baking dish; then arrange bread slices in bottom of dish. Whisk eggs, milk, Parmesan cheese, mustard, salt and pepper in mixing bowl until smooth. Pour egg mixture over bread and press bread into mixture. Let stand 15 minutes or refrigerate covered overnight. Heat oven to 350 degrees. Sprinkle scallions over top of bread. Bake 25 minutes. Scatter bacon and tomato over scallions and continue baking until puffed and edges are golden, about 10 minutes. Let stand 5 minutes before serving. Serves 6.

HAM OMELET
Daisy Cox

¹/₂ cup diced ham
1 cup mashed potatoes
2 tablespoons milk
¹/₂ teaspoon salt

¹/₈ teaspoon pepper
1 teaspoon baking powder
4 egg yolks, well-beaten
4 egg whites, stiff-beaten

Fry ham in heavy skillet; remove and pour off excess grease, if any. Combine mashed potatoes, milk, seasonings, baking powder, and egg yolks; fold in egg whites. Pour into skillet; sprinkle ham over top; cook over low heat until puffed and brown. Fold over; garnish with parsley. Serves 4.

MICROWAVE SCRAMBLED EGGS
Daisy Cox

4 eggs
¹/₄ cup whipping cream
1 tablespoon margarine, cut up

¹/₈ teaspoon salt
Dash of pepper

Beat eggs in 1-quart casserole. Stir in whipping cream and margarine. Microwave on HIGH a total of 3 minutes, or until egg curds are just past the runny stage. Cook 1 minute and stir. Stir 3 times during remaining cooking time. Stir in seasonings, cover and let stand 1 to 2 minutes. Serves 2.

Variation: Cheese and bacon: When you remove casserole of scrambled eggs from oven, lightly stir in 1/2 cup shredded cheddar cheese. Sprinkle with 2 slices crumbled cooked bacon. Cover and let stand 2 minutes.

BROCCOLI AND SWISS CHEESE QUICHE   *Genevia Bushnell*

Even frozen broccoli is good in this one.

1 pound broccoli	4 eggs, beaten
1 medium yellow onion, peeled, sliced	³/₄ cup cream
2 tablespoons butter	1¹/₄ cups milk
1 quiche crust (recipe follows) baked and cooled	Salt and pepper to taste
	¹/₂ pound Swiss cheese, grated into coarse pieces

Clean the broccoli, and cut into flowerets. Sauté the onion and the broccoli in the butter until tender but not soft. Place the vegetables in the bottom of the quiche crust. Mix the eggs, cream, milk, salt and pepper. Fill the shell, and top with the Swiss cheese. Bake at 375 degrees for 30 to 40 minutes, or until a knife inserted in the center of the pie comes out dry. Cool for 10 minutes before cutting. Can also be served at room temperature. Serves 6.

Variation: Substitute 1/2 pound cooked crab or cooked shrimp for the broccoli. If you can afford more than 1/2 pound of seafood for this one, go ahead. It will be heaven! Serves 6.

QUICHE CRUST   *Genevia Bushnell*

Note that there is no salt or animal fat in this crust. If you need salt, add it sparingly.

2 cups flour	¹/₂ cup vegetable oil
2 teaspoons baking powder	¹/₄ cup milk
Salt (optional)	

Mix the flour and the baking powder together. Add salt if you wish. Mix the oil and milk together, and then pour into the flour. Stir only until mixed. The mixture will be rather coarse and granular, but it will roll out well. Do not over mix. Mold into two balls, and wrap with plastic. Allow to sit for 15 minutes. Each ball will make one 9-inch piecrust. If you are using a larger French quiche pan, then use a bit more of the dough. Roll out between two sheets of wax paper. Place the pastry in the quiche pan or pie plate, and prick the bottom with a kitchen fork. Line the inside with wax paper or aluminum foil. Put two cups of dry beans into the piecrust, and bake at 400 degrees for 12 minutes. Save the beans for the next piecrust session. The shell is now ready for filling and cooking. Makes 2, 9-inch crusts or 1 larger crust.

SMOKED SALMON QUICHE
Mary A. Thurlkill

Good as appetizer or entree.

1/2 cup mayonnaise
2 tablespoons flour
2 eggs, beaten
1 5 or 7-ounce can smoked salmon, do not overdo the fish

8 ounces Swiss cheese, chopped
1/2 cup green onions, chopped
1 unbaked pie shell

Combine all ingredients except pie shell. Pour into the pie shell and bake at 350 degrees for 40 to 45 minutes. Serve hot or cold. Serves 4.

QUICHE SUPREME
Vanessa Luce

1 small package frozen broccoli, spinach, cauliflower or asparagus
1 small stick Pepperoni or sausage, diced
1 onion, diced
1 green pepper, diced
Small package fresh mushrooms, sliced

New York sharp cheddar cheese, shredded, use 3/4 in mixture and 1/4 on top
4 to 6 eggs, beaten
1/2 pint heavy whipping cream
2 Mrs. Smith's 9⁵/₈ pie crusts

Mix first 8 ingredients together and pour into pie shells. Bake in 350 degree oven for 30 to 40 minutes and about 10 minutes before done top with rest of cheese. Serves 8–12.

Cheese

CHEESE SOUFFLÉ   *Daisy Cox*

1 tablespoon quick-cooking   3 egg yolks, well beaten
  tapioca   ¹/₈ teaspoon Worcestershire
1 teaspoon salt   sauce
1 cup milk   3 egg whites, stiff-beaten
1 cup American cheese,
  grated

Combine tapioca, salt and milk; cook in double boiler 10 minutes; stir frequently. Add cheese; cook until cheese melts. Add a little hot mixture to egg yolks; stir into remaining hot mixture. Add Worcestershire sauce. Cool slightly; fold into egg whites. Bake in ungreased casserole in slow oven, 325 degrees, for 1 hour and 15 minutes, or until mixture doesn't adhere to knife. Serves 6.

★   ★   ★   ★   ★

HINT:
To grate soft cheese, such as Velveeta, freeze first.

★   ★   ★   ★   ★

HINT:
Grate dried cheese or small pieces of cheese; place in freezer bag and freeze to use for casseroles or other dishes.

Sweets, Cakes, Pies, Cookies, Candy, Ice Cream

CITY PARK

Life Magazine *donated "The old W. E. Withers" place to the community to be used as a City Park. It was given on President Lyndon Baines Johnson's fifty-seventh birthday, August 27, 1965, in recognition of his and Mrs. Johnson's efforts in behalf of beautification.*

The Gazebo was a 1976 Bicentennial Project of the Johnson City Art Guild assisted by the Johnson City Lions Club and local citizens. In 1988, the bird bath was placed in the park by the Community Garden Club of Johnson City.

FRIED APPLES

Duke Rumpf

3 medium to large Rome or Jonathan apples	1 egg
2 cups flour	$^3/_4$ cup evaporated milk
$^1/_8$ teaspoon baking powder	$^1/_4$ cup sugar
	1 cup margarine

Peel, core and slice apples. Stir together flour, baking powder, egg, milk and sugar to make thick batter. Dip apple slices in batter and fry in margarine over medium heat. Serves 6.

CHERRY CHEWBILEES

Elaine Carpenter

Crust:

$1^1/_4$ cups flour	$^1/_2$ cup Butter Flavor Crisco
$^1/_2$ cup brown sugar, firmly packed	$^1/_2$ cup pecans, chopped fine
	$^1/_2$ cup flake coconut

Filling:

2 8-ounce packages cream cheese, softened	1 21-ounce can cherry pie filling
$^2/_3$ cup granulated sugar	$^1/_2$ cup pecans, coarsely chopped
2 eggs	
2 teaspoons vanilla	

Preheat oven to 350 degrees. Grease 13 x 9 x 2-inch pan. Set aside. For crust, combine flour and brown sugar. Cut in Crisco until fine crumbs form. Add finely chopped pecans and coconut. Mix well. Remove 1/2 cup. Set aside. Press remaining crumbs in bottom of pan. Bake for 12 to 15 minutes, until edges are lightly brown. For filling, beat cream cheese, granulated sugar, eggs and vanilla in small bowl at medium speed of electric mixer until smooth. Spread over hot baked crust. Return to oven. Bake 15 minutes longer. Spread cherry pie filling over cheese layer. Combine pecans and reserved crumbs. Sprinkle evenly over cherries. Return to oven. Bake 15 minutes longer. Cool. Refrigerate several hours. Cut into bars, about 2 x $1^1/_2$-inches. Makes 36 bars.

166

QUICK BANANA PUDDING   *Dolores Bowden*

1 7-ounce box vanilla
   instant pudding
2¹/₂ cups milk
1 14-ounce can sweetened
   condensed milk

1 8-ounce carton whipped
   topping
1 16-ounce box Vanilla
   Wafers
3 large bananas

Mix pudding mix and milk; add sweetened condensed milk and whipped topping. In serving container layer pudding mixture, bananas and wafers, ending with cookies on top. Serves 6–8.

RAISIN BREAD PUDDING   *Aline Slack*

This is a fast and easy way to make bread pudding.

1 pound raisin bread
1 quart milk
3 eggs, beaten

2 cups sugar
2 tablespoons vanilla

Tear up bread and soak in milk. Add beaten eggs, sugar and vanilla. Place in shallow dish set in pan with 1-inch of water. Bake in 350 degrees oven for 1 hour. Serves 6–8.

DIRT PUDDING   *Daisy Cox*

1¹/₄ pounds (large bag) Oreo
   cookies, crushed (crush 3
   or 4 at a time in a blender)
¹/₂ cup margarine
1 8-ounce package cream
   cheese

1 cup powdered sugar
3¹/₂ cups cold milk
2 packages instant French
   Vanilla pudding mix
1 16-ounce carton Cool
   Whip

Crush cookies. Cream together margarine, cream cheese and powdered sugar. Set aside. Mix milk, pudding mix and Cool Whip. Add to creamed mixture and mix well. Layer pudding and Oreos in clean flower pot lined with foil (two 6-inch pots or one 8-inch pot with some left over). In layering, be sure Oreos end up on top. Place artificial flowers in center of pud-

ding (cover stems with foil) for an attractive and delicious pudding or cake. Serves 10–12.

Variation: Dolores Bowden makes a Dirt Cake. She uses 1/2 cup sugar instead of powdered sugar and no pudding mix or milk.

FEDERATION CHRISTMAS PUDDING *Helen O'Bryant*

This pudding is made weeks before Christmas in Australia.

Pudding:

¹/₂ kilogram raisins	245 grams plain flour
130 grams currants	5 level teaspoons mixed spice
240 grams mixed peel	
240 grams dates	2 level teaspoons nutmeg
¹/₂ kilogram sultanas (golden raisins)	¹/₂ level teaspoon bicarbonate of soda
350 grams butter	¹/₄ level teaspoon salt
240 grams brown sugar	240 grams breadcrumbs
5 eggs	³/₄ cup brandy

Chop all fruits into a bowl. Cream butter and brown sugar together until light and fluffy. Add eggs one at a time, beating well after each. Fold in prepared fruits, sifted dry ingredients and breadcrumbs. Lastly add brandy. Mix until all ingredients are combined. Place in a scalded and flavoured pudding cloth (or pudding steamer) and tie securely with string. Lower into large saucepan of boiling water, or in a steamer over boiling water. Steam 7–7¹/₂ hours. The flavours of this pudding are improved if kept at least a few days before eating. To re-heat, steam a further 2 hours. Serve with Rum Butter. Serves 10–12.

Rum Butter:

¹/₂ kilogram butter	1 teaspoon cinnamon
1 kilogram castor sugar	1 teaspoon nutmeg
¹/₂–³/₄ cup rum	

Cream butter and sugar together until smooth. Add other ingredients, mixing well. Serve over pudding.

MOTHER'S LEFTOVERS PUDDING   *Norma Honeycutt*

When I was a kid my Mother always fixed dessert every night, and it always amazed me how she could make something so good out of leftovers. Rice pudding is still my favorite followed closely by bread pudding.

1 cup cooked rice	2 cups milk
³/₄ cup sugar	Dash of nutmeg
2 eggs, beaten	1 teaspoon vanilla

Crumble rice in baking dish; mix sugar, eggs, milk, nutmeg and vanilla, and pour over rice. Bake at 350 degrees until brown and set, about 1 hour. Serves 4.

RICE PUDDING   *Daisy Cox*

2 large eggs, beaten slightly	2 cups cooked rice
¹/₂ cup sugar	¹/₂ cup seedless raisins
¹/₄ teaspoon salt	Nutmeg for flavoring
2 cups milk	

Beat eggs slightly and add sugar and salt. Scald milk and when slightly cooled, pour into egg mixture. Fold in rice and raisins. Pour into 1-quart casserole and set in pan of water, 1-inch deep. Sprinkle with nutmeg. Bake in a 350 degrees oven for 1 hour and 15 minutes. Serves 6.

ELENA'S FLAN   *Mary A. Thurlkill*

This recipe is a favorite in the home of my friend, Sra. Esperanza Enriquez of Cd. Guzman, Jal., Mexico and has been passed down to her by her mother, Elena.

¹/₂ cup sugar	2 teaspoons vanilla or to
4 eggs	taste
2 14-ounce cans sweetened condensed milk	2 to 3 tablespoons cognac or brandy
2 cups milk	¹/₂ cup pecans, chopped

Put sugar in a 9-inch round cake pan; place over medium heat. Using

oven mitts, carefully caramelize the sugar by shaking pan over the heat until sugar melts and turns a light golden brown. Tilt pan to cover sides with sugar. Cool. Mixture may crack as it cools. Beat eggs until fluffy; add remaining ingredients. Stir until all is well mixed. Pour over caramelized sugar; cover pan with aluminum foil, and place in a large shallow pan. Pour in hot water, about one-inch deep. Bake at 350 degrees for 55 minutes or until knife inserted in center comes out clean. Very carefully remove pan from hot water. Let cool. Loosen edges and invert flan on serving plate. If desired, may be refrigerated until serving time. Serves 6–8.

KAHLÚA JELLY
Mary A. Thurlkill

This recipe is good made a day in advance. It is especially good after a heavy Mexican meal, for it is cool and light. The recipe was given to me by a Japanese lady who was living at that time in Mexico City.

2 envelopes unflavored gelatin
3 cups hot, strong coffee
³/₄ cup sugar
1 heaping teaspoon powdered cocoa

¹/₂ cup Kahlúa or other coffee liqueur
1 pinch salt
Whipped or heavy cream

Dissolve gelatin in hot coffee. Let cool and add all other ingredients and stir until clear. (This is important or cocoa powder may not dissolve). Pour into 8 separate molds or wine glasses. To serve, top with whipped cream or simply pour on heavy cream. Serves 8.

FRUIT PIZZA
Patsy Holloway

Crust:
¹/₂ cup margarine
¹/₄ cup brown sugar, firmly packed

1 cup flour
¹/₄ cup quick-cooking oats
¹/₄ cup pecans, chopped fine

Filling:
1 8-ounce package cream cheese, softened
1 cup powdered sugar

1 teaspoon vanilla
1 tablespoon lemon juice
Fruit

For crust: beat margarine and sugar until fluffy, mix in remaining ingre-

170

dients. Press onto lightly oiled 12-inch pizza pan, forming a rim. Prick with fork. Bake at 375 degrees for 10 to 12 minutes or until golden brown. Cool. **For filling:** beat cream cheese until fluffy. Beat in sugar, vanilla and lemon juice. Spread over cooled crust up to the rim. Arrange desired fruits in pretty circles on top. Serves 4.

SUGGESTED FRUITS: Mandarin oranges, canned pineapple, kiwi fruit, seedless grapes, strawberries, bananas or anything you would like.

PASTEL DESSERT
Sallye Baker

A favorite among children!

1 3-ounce package Jello, any flavor	1 cup cold water
1 cup boiling water	1 pint vanilla ice cream

Dissolve gelatin in boiling water; add cold water. Spoon in ice cream, stirring until melted and smooth. Chill until slightly thickened; stir and pour into small dishes. Chill until set, about 1 hour. Makes 7 servings.

GERMAN MILK RICE
Ray Sultemeier

1 cup regular rice	1/2 cup sugar
4 cups water	1 tablespoon butter
1 pint rich milk	Cinnamon and sugar

Boil rice until tender, drain off water; add milk, sugar and butter. While hot put in dish and sprinkle liberally with cinnamon and sugar. Serves 6.

PEGGY'S FRESH PEACH ROLL
Ola Matus

Charles and I helped Tammy and Adlai Weiershausen move to Knox City. Tammy's mother, Peggy Grindstaff, prepared dinner for us that night and the dessert was this Fresh Peach Roll which I thought was delicious. It is worth the extra effort it takes to prepare.

½ cup margarine
2 cups sugar
2 cups water
1 teaspoon vanilla
1 cup flour
1 teaspoon baking powder
¼ teaspoon salt
⅓ cup shortening
⅓ cup milk
3 cups fresh peaches, peeled
and sliced
Cinnamon

Melt margarine in 9 x 13-inch dish. Bring sugar and water to boil; add vanilla. Prepare dough from flour, baking powder, salt, shortening and milk. Roll thin, using lots of flour, and place peaches on the dough, then sprinkle with cinnamon. Roll up and slice thick and place slices in baking dish. Pour boiling mixture over rolled dough and peaches. Bake at 350 degrees for 1 hour. Do not use canned peaches. Also good with fresh apples, pears and apricots. Makes 12 rolls.

TRIFLE
Fran Toms

4 large boxes instant
chocolate pudding
4 quarts half and half
2 Angel food cakes, cubed
2 16-ounce cartons Cool
Whip
2 21-ounce cans cherry pie
filling
1 package Oreo cookies,
broken
1 package Chocolate Chip
cookies, broken
1 package (6) Butter
Fingers, crushed
1 package (6) Heath bars,
broken
1 package (6) Hershey bars,
broken
Chopped nuts

Mix pudding with half and half as directed on package. Layer in very large bowl cherries, cake, pudding, cookies, candies, Cool Whip, nuts, and repeat until all used. Be sure to end with Cool Whip and nuts on top. This makes enough for a very large crowd. Recipe can be halved. Serves 30–40.

★　★　★　★　★

HINT:
Whipped cream will keep a day or two if you add 1 teaspoon light Karo for each 1/2 pint of cream.

★　★　★　★　★

Cakes

ALMOND LEGEND CAKE

Holly Lawson

This cake brightens any occasion. The legend is whoever finds the whole almond is insured good luck.

¹/₂ cup almonds, chopped
1 package yellow cake mix
   with pudding
¹/₂ cup orange juice
¹/₂ cup water

¹/₃ cup oil
¹/₂ teaspoon almond extract
3 eggs
1 whole almond

Glaze:
¹/₃ cup apricot preserves

2 to 3 teaspoons orange juice

Preheat oven to 350 degrees. Grease 12 cup fluted tube pan. Gently press almonds in bottom and half way up sides of pan. In large bowl, combine cake mix, orange juice, water, oil, almond extract and eggs at low speed until moistened; beat 2 minutes at high speed. Stir in whole almond. Carefully pour batter in pan. Bake for 35 to 45 minutes or until toothpick comes out clean. Cool in pan 10 minutes. Invert onto serving plate. In small bowl, combine glaze ingredients; blend well. Spoon over warm cake. Cool completely. Makes 16 servings.

APPLESAUCE CAKE

Leonard B. Talburt

I grew up in the country where life was hard, times were lean, but the food was hearty and simple. My mother, an excellent Missouri cook, always provided delicious and filling snacks that delighted any growing boy, or girl. This was one of my favorites.

1 cup sugar
¹/₂ cup shortening
1³/₄ cups flour
1 cup warm applesauce
1 teaspoon soda

¹/₂ teaspoon orange extract
1 teaspoon cinnamon
¹/₂ teaspoon ginger
1 cup raisins
¹/₂ cup nuts, chopped

Cream the sugar and shortening together; add flour and the warm apple sauce in which the soda has been dissolved; add orange extract, spices, nuts and raisins which have been dredged in flour. Bake in a 9 x 13-inch greased and floured pan at 350 degrees for 35 to 45 minutes. Serves 8. (Not including hungry boys).

GOLDEN APRICOT CAKE

Lucille Newman

Cake:

1 package yellow cake mix with pudding
1 cup apricot nectar
1/3 cup oil

1/4 cup honey
3 eggs
1 10-ounce jar apricot preserves (2/3 of jar)

Frosting:

1 3-ounce package cream cheese
1/4 cup margarine or butter, softened

2 to 2 1/2 cups powdered sugar
1/3 cup apricot preserves
1/3 cup pecans, chopped

Heat oven to 350 degrees. Grease and flour two 8 or 9-inch round cake pans. In large bowl, beat cake mix, apricot nectar, oil, honey and eggs at low speed until moistened. Beat 2 minutes at highest speed. Pour batter into prepared pans. Bake for 25 to 35 minutes or until toothpick inserted in center comes out clean. Cool 10 minutes. Remove from pans. Cool completely. To assemble cake, place one cake layer on serving plate. Spread with 2/3 of preserves; save remaining for frosting. Place second layer over first layer. In small bowl, blend cream cheese and margarine. Add powdered sugar and beat until smooth. Heat reserved preserves until warm. Add enough preserves to cream cheese mixture for desired frosting consistency. Stir in pecans. Frost side and top of cake. Refrigerate before serving. Store in refrigerator. Serves 12.

BANANA CAKE SUPREME

Cora Byars

This cake is very rich and doesn't last long.

1 package Duncan Hines Banana Cake Supreme
1 package vanilla pie and pudding mix, not instant
1 1/2 cups milk

1 cup whipped cream or Cool Whip
1 cup miniature marshmallows
3 medium ripe bananas, sliced
Fruit Fresh

Preheat oven to 350 degrees. Grease and flour two 9-inch round pans. Prepare cake mix and bake according to box instructions. Cook pudding with 1¹/₂ cups of milk. Put this mixture in refrigerator until it is cold, with waxed paper on top of it to prevent skim from forming. Beat cream until stiff or use Cool Whip and fold into pudding with the marshmallows. When cake is done and slightly cooled, slice through the middle of each layer, making 4 round thin layers. Place one layer on plate and spread 1/4 of filling and add next layer of cake, filling until you have 4 layers with filling between layer and on top. Sprinkle Fruit Fresh on sliced bananas to keep them from discoloring and then use the sliced bananas to decorate the top of the cake. Keep this cake stored in the refrigerator. Serves 12.

BANANA NUT CAKE

Amy Poulton

This cake will make 2 small loaf cakes or one large bundt cake. It is so moist, it needs no icing.

1 cup shortening	**¹/₂ cup concentrated orange**
4 cups sugar	**juice**
4 eggs, beaten	**2 tablespoons orange peel,**
4 cups flour	**grated**
2 teaspoons soda	**6 to 7 overripe bananas,**
4 teaspoons baking powder	**mashed**
¹/₂ cup buttermilk	**1¹/₂ cups pecans, chopped**

Mix shortening and sugar, one cup of sugar at a time. Add eggs to sugar mixture. Sift and add dry ingredients alternately with milk and orange juice and peel. Add bananas and nuts and mix well. Pour into greased and floured bundt pan or two loaf pans. Bake at 350 degrees for 90 minutes or until done. It freezes well. Serves 16.

Genevia Bushnell's day care children loved this cake as well as her own children. Variation is the baking powder, orange juice and orange peel is omitted.

★   ★   ★   ★   ★

HINT:
To prevent cake from sticking to your cake pan or plate, sprinkle the surface with powdered sugar.

★   ★   ★   ★   ★

BANANA SPLIT CAKE   *Mavis Lemons*

2 cups graham cracker crumbs
1¹/₂ cups margarine, divided
2 cups powdered sugar
2 eggs

4 bananas, thinly sliced
2 cups crushed pineapple
1 9-ounce carton Cool Whip
1 cup pecans, chopped
Maraschino cherries

Mix crumbs and 1/2 cup of margarine; press into bottom of 9 x 13-inch glass baking dish. In a mixing bowl, combine the remaining 1 cup margarine, powdered sugar, and eggs. Mix with electric mixer for 15 minutes. Spread mixture over crumbs. Place sliced bananas on top and spread pineapple over bananas. Spread whipped topping over pineapple. Top with nuts and maraschino cherries. Chill 2 to 3 hours or overnight. Cut into squares. Serves 12.

DELUXE BANANA SPLIT CAKE   *Aline Slack*

First tried this recipe in the 1970's. It has been passed along in our family since then.

2 cups graham cracker crumbs
¹/₂ cup margarine
5 bananas
2 cups powdered sugar
1 8-ounce package cream cheese

1 20-ounce can crushed pineapple, drained
1 9-ounce carton whipped topping
Crushed nuts
Maraschino cherries

Put graham cracker crumbs in a 9 x 13-inch pan. Melt margarine and pour over crumbs; mix and spread crumbs over bottom of pan. Slice bananas lengthwise and arrange over crumbs. Beat together powdered sugar and cream cheese. Spread over bananas. Drain pineapple and spread over cheese mixture. Cover pineapple with whipped topping. Garnish with crushed nuts and cherries. Chill 2 to 3 hours. Serves 12.

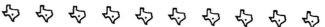

CARROT CAKE

Gracie Wittkohl

This is my favorite carrot cake recipe.

3 eggs
2 cups sugar
1¹/₂ cups salad oil
3 cups flour
2 teaspoons soda
¹/₄ teaspoon salt

1 teaspoon cinnamon
1 teaspoon vanilla
1 20-ounce can crushed
 pineapple, drained
2 cups raw carrots, grated
1 cup pecans, chopped

Beat eggs, sugar and oil until fluffy. Sift dry ingredients and add to sugar mixture. Add vanilla, pineapple and carrots. Add nuts. Pour into greased, floured tube pan and bake at 350 degrees for 60 to 75 minutes or bake in a 9 x 13-inch cake pan for 40 to 45 minutes. Serves 12–16.

CHERRY-PINEAPPLE NUT CAKE

Robyn Henderson

This recipe is from Thelma Lively, my grandmother, and my favorite recipes have come from her. I learned the basics of cooking from my mother, but Granny's kitchen is where I sat sometimes for hours. Watching her cook and listening to her talk, have been an inspiration to me. Granny's kitchen is always filled with love. The way food is thought of today is very different than in Granny's day so this recipe has all the calories and all the love Granny put into it. I'll remember her cooking and her kitchen, always.

1 20-ounce can crushed
 pineapple in heavy syrup
1 21-ounce can cherry pie
 filling

1 package yellow cake mix
 for 2 layer cake
1 3-ounce can pecans or 1
 cup pecans, chopped
¹/₂ cup margarine or butter

Preheat oven to 350 degrees and grease 9 x 13-inch baking dish or pan. Spread pineapple with its syrup evenly in baking dish. Spoon cherry pie filling over pineapple. Sprinkle DRY cake mix over fruit, then pecans. Cut margarine into thin slices over ingredients in pan. Bake 50 minutes or until golden. Serve warm. Serves 12.

177

CINNAMON CHOCOLATE CAKE

Cathy Woods

If you do not have buttermilk, add 2 teaspoons of white vinegar to each 1/2 cup of milk, let stand a few minutes to curdle.

2 cups flour
2 cups sugar
1 teaspoon cinnamon
1 cup water
1/2 cup margarine
1/2 cup Crisco shortening

4 tablespoons cocoa
1/2 cup buttermilk
1 teaspoon soda
2 eggs, beaten
1 teaspoon vanilla

Frosting:
1/2 cup margarine
6 tablespoons milk
4 tablespoons cocoa
1 teaspoon vanilla

1 box powdered sugar (3 cups)
1 cup nuts, chopped

Sift flour, sugar and cinnamon together and set aside. Bring to boil water, margarine, Crisco and cocoa until melted; mix with flour mixture. Add buttermilk, soda, eggs and vanilla and mix well. Pour into a greased and floured 9 x 13 x 2-inch cake pan. Bake at 400 degrees for 15 minutes or until done. Test center of cake with toothpick. Leave in pan to frost.

Frosting: Bring to boil margarine, milk and cocoa. Remove from heat and add vanilla. Stir in powdered sugar. Stir until smooth. Add pecans. Mix well and spread on cake while hot. Serves 12–16.

Variation: Joycelyn Carter's AUNT ONIE'S CHOCOLATE CAKE is the same as above except cinnamon is omitted and cooked in a 11 x 16-inch Pyrex pan. Mix only by hand. Serves 16.

CHOCOLATE CAKE WITH NEVER FAIL ICING

Ray Sultemeier

1/2 cup shortening
2 cups sugar
2 squares bitter chocolate
1/2 cup hot water
1 teaspoon soda

1 cup buttermilk
2 cups flour
1 teaspoon vanilla
2 eggs

178

Icing:

2 cups sugar
1/2 cup milk
1/2 cup butter
4 tablespoons cocoa

2 tablespoons white Karo syrup
1 teaspoon vanilla
1/2 cup pecans, chopped if desired

Cream shortening and sugar. Melt chocolate in water on stove and add to creamed mixture. Add soda to buttermilk. Then add flour and milk alternately to chocolate mixture. Add vanilla, then eggs and mix. Bake in 8-inch square or 9-inch round layers or 9 x 13-inch sheet cake pan at 350 degrees for 25 minutes. May be baked as cupcakes also.

Icing: Mix together all ingredients except vanilla and nuts in sauce pan. Cook for one minute after it starts to boil. Cool slightly; add vanilla and beat. Add nuts. Spread on cake. Serves 12.

CHOCOLATE DATE CAKE

Mary Dyer

This recipe was given to me by a long-time friend in Sherman, Texas. When I read it over, I didn't think it sounded good at all, but it is an exceptionally moist rich cake.

1 cup dates, chopped
1 cup boiling water
2 cups shortening
1 cup sugar
1 teaspoon vanilla
2 eggs
1 3/4 cups flour

2 tablespoons cocoa
1 teaspoon soda
1/2 teaspoon salt
1 6-ounce package semi-sweet chocolate chips
1 cup pecans, chopped

Combine dates with boiling water. Set aside. Cream shortening, sugar, vanilla, eggs (add one at a time). Beat well. Add dates and water. Sift flour, cocoa, soda and salt. Mix well. Pour batter in a 9 x 13-inch greased pan. Sprinkle with chocolate chips and pecans. Bake at 350 degrees for 40 to 45 minutes. Serves 12.

CHOCOLATE ECLAIR CAKE   *Joy Anderson*

¹/₂ to 1 pound whole graham crackers
2 packages French vanilla instant pudding
1 8-ounce carton Cool Whip

Frosting:

2 squares (2-ounces) semi-   2 tablespoons corn syrup
   sweet chocolate   1¹/₂ cups sifted powdered
6 tablespoons margarine   sugar
2 teaspoons vanilla   3 tablespoons milk or more

Use 9 x 13 shallow pan. Line pan with whole crackers. Prepare pudding according to instructions; mix with Cool Whip and spread half of mixture on crackers in pan. Layer more crackers, remainder of pudding mix, ending with third layer of crackers. Place chocolate, margarine and syrup in sauce pan over low heat to melt chocolate. Remove from heat, add vanilla and stir in powdered sugar. Add milk one tablespoon at a time until of spreading consistency. Spread on top of last layer of graham crackers. Refrigerate 12 hours before serving. Serves 12 to 24.

CHOCOLATE ITALIAN CREAM CAKE   *Daisy Cox*

¹/₂ cup butter or margarine   1 teaspoon soda
¹/₂ cup shortening   1 cup buttermilk
2 cups sugar   1 teaspoon vanilla
5 eggs, separated   1 cup coconut
2 cups sifted flour   1 cup pecans, chopped
¹/₄ cup cocoa

Frosting:

1 8-ounce cream cheese   1 pound box powdered sugar
¹/₂ cup margarine   ¹/₄ cup cocoa
1 teaspoon vanilla   1 cup pecans, chopped

Cream both the margarine and shortening and the sugar. Add egg yolks one at a time, beating well after each addition. Sift flour, cocoa and soda together. Add alternately with buttermilk, beginning and ending with dry ingredients. Stir in vanilla, coconut and nuts. Fold in stiffly beaten egg whites. Bake in 3 greased and floured 8-inch cake pans at 325 degrees for 25 to 30 minutes. Serves 12.

Frosting: Cream softened cream cheese and margarine. Add vanilla. Sift sugar and cocoa together and beat in gradually. Add pecans. Use to frost layers and side of cake.

CHOCOLATE PUDDING CAKE   *Margaret Bergman*

1 package 8-ounce cream cheese, softened
1 cup powdered sugar
1 cup Cool Whip (from 9-ounce carton)
2 cups cold milk

1 package instant chocolate pudding
1 package instant vanilla pudding
Pecans, chopped

Crust:
½ cup margarine, melted
1 cup pecans, chopped

1 cup flour

Mix ingredients for crust. Press into an oblong Pyrex dish. Bake 20–25 minutes at 350 degrees until golden brown, let cool. Mix cream cheese, powdered sugar, and 1 cup Cool Whip and spread over crust. Whip milk and puddings until slightly thickened and spread over cream cheese layer. Spread remaining Cool Whip on pudding layer; sprinkle with chopped pecans.

Holly Lawson also submitted this recipe except she omitted the vanilla pudding mix. She wrote: This recipe is well liked in our home. My niece, Karen, fixed it for us the first time. Everyone has loved it. The chocolate pudding can be changed to any pudding you desire. I have tried lemon and pistachio and both are excellent. Serves 12.

GRANDMA'S CHOCOLATE CAKE   *Genevia Bushnell*

Grandma used to very carefully cream, mix and stir this cake with the greatest of pains and it is excellent. Then one day she allowed her oldest grandson, seven-year-old David, to help her. Grandma turned around and David had dumped everything in the bowl at once. Grandma was beside herself but she let David continue. To Grandma's surprise the cake was as good as ever and from that day on the cake makings have all been dumped together all at once and stirred.

2 cups of sugar
¹/₂ cup shortening
1 egg
2 cups sour milk, buttermilk
  or part yogurt and milk

2 teaspoons of soda mixed
  in milk
2¹/₂ cups flour
4 tablespoons cocoa
1 teaspoon vanilla

Frosting:
¹/₄ cup shortening
¹/₂ teaspoon salt
2 teaspoons vanilla
3 cups powdered sugar

3 tablespoons cocoa mixed
  with sugar
¹/₄ cup milk
1 cup nuts, chopped

Mix all of cake ingredients together in one bowl. Pour into a greased and floured 9 x 13 pan. Bake at 350 degrees for 30 minutes. Serves 12.

Frosting: Cream shortening, salt, vanilla, and 1/3 of sugar. Alternate milk with the rest of sugar. Put the frosting on the cake while still warm and the cake is more moist.

MAHOGANY CAKE

Sallye Baker

My mother started housekeeping with this recipe. It was and continues to be a favorite with my family.

2 1-ounce chocolate squares
5 tablespoons boiling water
¹/₂ cup butter or margarine
1¹/₂ cups sugar
4 egg yolks

¹/₂ cup milk
2 cups flour
2 rounded teaspoons baking
  powder
4 egg whites, well beaten

Filling:
3 cups powdered sugar
¹/₂ cup butter
1 egg yolk
2 teaspoons vanilla

2 tablespoons cream
2 tablespoons cocoa
5 tablespoons strong coffee

Dissolve chocolate in boiling water. Cool. Cream butter, sugar and add to this the beaten egg yolks and cooled chocolate. Then add the milk, flour, baking powder and egg whites. Bake in 3, 9-inch round cake pans at 350 degrees for 25 to 30 minutes. Serves 12.

Filling: Beat all ingredients in filling until smooth and light. Spread filling between layers of each cake.

COCONUT CAKE

Neatta Cade

2 cups flour
1½ cups sugar
3 teaspoons baking powder
½ teaspoon salt

½ cup vegetable shortening
  or margarine
1 cup milk
2 teaspoons vanilla
2 eggs

Icing:
2 egg whites
1½ cups sugar
¼ teaspoon cream of tartar
⅓ cup water

1 teaspoon vanilla
1 cup crushed pineapple,
  drained
1 7-ounce can coconut

Preheat oven at 350 degrees. Grease and flour two 9-inch cake pans. Mix flour, sugar, baking powder and salt; add margarine, milk and vanilla; beat one minute at moderate speed. Add eggs and beat just enough to mix. Pour into pans. Bake for 30 minutes. Cool layers on racks 10 minutes. Turn out and cool completely. Serves 12.

Icing: Place egg whites, sugar, cream of tartar and water in top of very large double boiler. Put over simmering, not boiling, water and beat with rotary hand beater for 6 to 7 minutes until frosting increases in volume and forms peaks. Beat in vanilla.

To assemble cake: Slice each cake layer in half horizontally to make 4 layers. Combine 1½ cups frosting with well drained pineapple. Fill between layers. Cover completely with plain icing and sprinkle with coconut.

CREOLE CAKE

Moline Lorenz

This recipe was given to me by Paulene Strawn of Temple, Texas.

2 eggs, well beaten
2 cups sugar
½ cup Wesson oil
2 cups flour
2 tablespoons cocoa
½ teaspoon salt

½ cup buttermilk
1 teaspoon vanilla
1 teaspoon butter flavoring
1 cup boiling water
1 teaspoon soda, added to
  boiling water

Topping:
6 tablespoons margarine   1 small can angel flake
1 cup brown sugar   coconut
¹/₂ teaspoon vanilla   ¹/₂ cup pecans, chopped
¹/₂ cup evaporated milk

Mix eggs, sugar and oil well. Sift flour, cocoa and salt and add to first mixture. Add buttermilk, vanilla and butter flavoring and mix well. Add all at once, boiling water and soda mixture. Mix well, then pour into well greased and floured 9 x 13-inch pan. Bake at 350 degrees for 40 minutes. Topping: Cream butter and sugar; add vanilla and milk and mix well. Stir in coconut and pecans. Spread topping on hot cake and place in broiler until slightly brown. Serves 12.

STELLAR'S CUPCAKES OR FUNERAL CAKE   *Cynthia Smith*

This recipe and story is printed in the Southern Living Cake Book. The recipe and story were submitted by me. My husband's grandmother, Mrs. Estelle Holland of Bremond, Texas, had a housekeeper/cook named Stellar and on the occasion of a death in the small community, Mrs. Holland would issue the order for Stellar to make some of those cupcakes to send after the funeral. Thus they just became "Stellar's Funeral Cakes." They are light and delicious and a welcome gift on any occasion and as a child, a favorite of my husband's.

1¹/₂ cups sugar   A hen egg sized hunk of
1¹/₂ cups flour   Crisco
2 eggs   A skimpy cup of sweet milk
2 teaspoons baking powder

Mix all ingredients by hand or with electric beater, a few minutes. Pour into cupcake pans. Fill half full, as they rise mightily. Bake at 350 degrees for 15 minutes. They are delicate; don't slam the door on the oven, and if you peek, they will fall, never to rise again. Stellar always sprinkled powdered sugar on top. They are just as good plain. I asked Stellar just what is a "skimpy" cup? She said "Oh honey, just short of a cup." Makes 12 cupcakes.

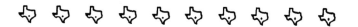

FRUIT CAKE
Lucia Carbary

This was my grandmother, Hilda Hitzfeld Danz's fruit cake recipe. I can remember her baking it well before Christmas time and sometimes adding more brandy after it was baked to keep it moist.

1 pound raisins	1 teaspoon soda
1 pound currants	6 eggs
1/2 pound citron	3 cups brown sugar
2 cups pecans, chopped	2 teaspoons butter
4 cups flour, divided	1/2 cup sour milk
1 teaspoon nutmeg	1/2 cup molasses
1 teaspoon cinnamon	1 wine glass of brandy
1 teaspoon cloves	

Combine raisins, currants, citron and pecans; dredge in 1 cup flour, stirring to coat evenly. Set aside. Combine 3 cups flour, nutmeg, cinnamon, cloves and soda. Set aside. Beat eggs, gradually adding sugar, mixing well. Add butter, milk, molasses, brandy and flour mixture, mixing well. Stir in fruit mixture and blend well. Spoon batter into a greased, floured, and waxed paper-lined 10-inch tube pan. Bake at 300 degrees for 2 hours or until wooden pick comes out clean. Serves 16–20.

GERTIE'S FRUIT CAKE
Ima Hobbs

1 pound dates, chopped	2 cups coconut
1/2 pound candied pineapple, chopped	3 cups pecans, chopped
	1 cup flour
1 pound candied cherries, halved	1 14-ounce can sweetened condensed milk

Mix fruits and nuts in bowl and cover with flour. Pour Eagle Brand milk over fruit mixture and mix well. Spoon batter into a greased and floured tube pan. Place a pan of boiling water on lower oven rack. Bake at 350 degrees for 1 hour. Cool in pan 10 minutes; remove and cool completely. Serves 16–20.

GERMAN CHOCOLATE POUND CAKE

Cathy Woods

Merit Award winner at the Blanco County Fair.

2 cups sugar
1 cup shortening
4 eggs
2 teaspoons vanilla
2 teaspoons butter flavoring (optional)

1 cup buttermilk
3 cups flour, sifted
$^1/_2$ teaspoon soda
1 teaspoon salt
4 ounces German sweet chocolate

Cream sugar and shortening. Add eggs, vanilla, butter flavoring and buttermilk. Sift together flour, soda, and salt. Add to other mixture and mix well. Add German chocolate that has been softened in warm oven, double boiler or microwave. Blend together well. Bake in 9-inch stem pan or 10-inch bundt pan, that has been well greased and dusted with flour. Bake in 300 degree oven about 1 hour or until toothpick inserted in the center comes out clean. Remove cake from pan while still hot and place under a tight fitting cake cover and leave covered until the cake is cold. Serves 12.

HUMMINGBIRD CAKE

Cynthia Smith

This cake was decorated with silk flowers and one tiny hummingbird and was auctioned. Sold for $275 to the local bank. The cake is quite heavy, about seven pounds, so the price per pound was about $38. The money went for a good cause. This cake was also blue ribbon and Award of Merit at Blanco County Fair in 1988.

3 cups flour
2 cups sugar
1 teaspoon salt
1 teaspoon soda
1 teaspoon cinnamon
3 eggs
1 cup vegetable oil

$1^1/_2$ teaspoon vanilla
1 8-ounce can crushed pineapple
2 bananas, mashed
1 cup pecans, chopped (optional)

Icing:
1 8-ounce package cream cheese
1 cup butter, softened

1 box powdered sugar (3 cups)
2 teaspoons vanilla
1 cup pecans, chopped

186

Grease and flour three, 8-inch cake pans. Combine flour, sugar, salt, soda and cinnamon; add eggs and oil. Stir until moist. Stir in vanilla, pineapple and bananas. Add pecans, if desired (I put pecans in the icing rather than in the cake, because it is easier to cut and prettier). Bake at 350 degrees for 25 to 35 minutes. Cool before frosting. Serves 12.

Icing: Cream butter and cream cheese until smooth. Add powdered sugar slowly and beat until fluffy; add vanilla and pecans. Put between layers and on top and sides.

Variations: Ola Matus makes this same cake but uses 2 cups chopped bananas in the cake and 1/2 cup butter and 1 teaspoon vanilla in the frosting.

KRAUT CAKE
Pat Rumpf

2¹/₂ cups flour
1 teaspoon soda
1 teaspoon baking powder
1¹/₂ cups sugar
²/₃ cup shortening
3 eggs

1¹/₄ teaspoons vanilla
¹/₂ teaspoon salt
¹/₂ cup cocoa
1 cup water
¹/₂ cup sauerkraut, chopped
   and drained

Sift together flour, soda and baking powder. Set aside. Cream sugar and shortening; add eggs. Mix well. Add vanilla, salt and cocoa. Mix well. Alternately add flour mixture and water. Add kraut. Grease a 8 x 8-inch pan. Pour batter in and bake at 375 degrees for 25 to 30 minutes. Serves 6–8.

MIMI'S MOUNTAIN CAKE
Lorraine Lanham

This is an old family recipe handed down from my grandmother who baked it on an old wood burning stove in the mountains of West Virginia. The frosting has been added in recent years since grandmother never heard of cream cheese. Also some people use pineapple instead of apples, also pears can be used. The original cake was cooked in an iron skillet and no frosting was added. It was just handed out hot from the stove to anyone in reach.

3 cups flour
1 teaspoon salt
2 cups sugar
1¹/₂ teaspoons cinnamon
1 teaspoon soda
3 eggs, beaten

1¹/₂ cups oil
1¹/₂ teaspoons vanilla
2 cups bananas, chopped
2 cups apples, peeled and
   chopped
1 cup walnuts, chopped

187

Frosting:
1 8-ounce package cream cheese
¹/₂ cup margarine, softened

1 box powdered sugar (3 cups)
1 cup walnuts, chopped
1 tablespoon vanilla

Combine dry ingredients in a large bowl. Beat eggs and oil together; add to dry ingredients. Stir until just moist. Do not beat. Stir in vanilla, bananas, apples and nuts. Spoon batter into three well greased and floured 9-inch cake pans. Bake at 350 degrees for 25 to 30 minutes or until done. **Frosting:** Cream margarine and cream cheese. Add powdered sugar and vanilla and mix until creamy. Serves 12.

To assemble: Place first layer of cake on cake plate and frost. Repeat with next two layers. Frost entire cake and sprinkle top of cake with chopped nuts.

NOTE: The hill country is noted for it's pecans and we substitute pecans for walnuts. Committee

NEIMAN MARCUS CAKE

Holly Lawson

Pat Wiedebusch served this at a Sunday School luncheon. She is a very good cook. You will understand the name after you taste this delicious cake. One weekend I fixed this cake for my in-laws. They loved it, but my sister-in-law became very hyper because it is so rich, so beware.

1 box German chocolate cake mix
¹/₂ cup butter or margarine

2 eggs
¹/₂ cup pecans, chopped (optional)

Icing:
1 8-ounce package cream cheese
1 box powdered sugar (3 cups)

2 eggs, beaten
1 teaspoon vanilla
¹/₂ cup pecans, chopped (optional)

Mix cake mix, butter, eggs and pecans and pat into a 9 x 13-inch greased pan. Mix cream cheese, powdered sugar, eggs, vanilla and pecans and spread over cake mixture. Bake at 350 degrees for 30 minutes. Serves 12.

FRESH PEAR CAKE

Moline Lorenz

Elaine Oliver of Johnson City, Texas gave me this recipe.

1¹/₂ cups Wesson oil
3 eggs
2 cups sugar
3 cups flour, sifted
1 teaspoon salt
1 teaspoon cloves
1 teaspoon nutmeg
1 teaspoon cinnamon

1 teaspoon allspice
1¹/₂ teaspoons soda
1 teaspoon vanilla
1 cup raisins
1 cup pecans, chopped
3 cups fresh pears, peeled
and cut into small cubes
(apples can be used)

Beat eggs, sugar and oil together. Sift flour and save 1/2 cup to mix with raisins and nuts. Sift flour, spices and soda together and add to batter slowly, about a cup at a time. Add vanilla. Mix 1/2 cup flour with raisins and nuts; add to batter. Add pears or apples and mix well by hand. Bake in a tube or bundt pan that has been greased and floured for 1 hour and 15 minutes at 350 degrees. Cool 15 minutes in pan. Serves 12.

PIÑA COLADA CAKE

Helen Mayfield

Evelyn Fuelberg, a very dear friend of mine, gave this recipe to me. Hope you enjoy it as I have.

1 box white cake mix
3¹/₂ ounces coconut
1 teaspoon vanilla

1 15-ounce can Coco-Lopez
Cream of Coconut
1 9-ounce carton Cool Whip
3¹/₂ ounces coconut

Prepare cake mix according to directions on box but add coconut and vanilla. Bake in a 9 x 13 x 2-inch pan. I use a pyrex pan. Bake at 350 degrees for 25 to 30 minutes. When done cool for 10 minutes in pan, then punch holes in cake and pour on cream of coconut. Top with Cool Whip mixed with coconut. Place in refrigerator until ready to serve. Cut and serve from pan. I use a 7-ounce can of coconut and divide it. Serves 12.

GRANDMOTHER TARVER'S NUT CAKE   *Cynthia Smith*

This is a cake we always had at Christmas.

2 cups brown sugar
¹/₂ cup butter, not
   margarine
¹/₂ cup pecans, chopped

2 cups flour, sifted
2 teaspoons baking powder
2 teaspoons vanilla
Maraschino cherries

Mix well all ingredients except cherries. Batter will be stiff. Pour into a greased and floured 9 x 12-inch shallow pan; it may not cover but will get into edges as it gets hot. Bake at 350 degrees for 20 minutes. Sometimes grandmother put maraschino cherries on top. It is soft but then gets firm after cooling. Serves 12.

PINEAPPLE CREAM CAKE   *Joyce Ellis*

This is a delicious cake. It needs to be refrigerated immediately if not served. This recipe is from a friend of my niece, Sandra Rutherford.

1 Duncan Hines yellow cake
   mix
4 eggs
¹/₄ cup oil

¹/₂ cup butter
1 can mandarin oranges,
   undrained

Frosting:
1 8-ounce carton Cool Whip
1 15-ounce can crushed
   pineapple, undrained

1 3¹/₂-ounce package vanilla
   instant pudding mix

Mix cake mix, eggs, oil, butter and mandarin oranges and pour into three greased 8-inch round cake pans and bake at 350 degrees for 25 to 30 minutes. When done let cool and invert onto racks. Place 1 layer on serving plate. Mix frosting ingredients and spread between layers and on top. Serves 12.

SWEDISH PINEAPPLE CAKE   *Kittie Clyde Leonard*

2 cups sugar
1 20-ounce can crushed
   pineapple with juice
1 teaspoon soda

1 teaspoon vanilla
2 cups flour
1 cup pecans, chopped

Icing:

8-ounces cream cheese,
  softened
½ cup margarine, melted

¾ cup powdered sugar
½ cup pecans, chopped

Mix by hand in order listed. Pour into ungreased 9 x 13-inch pan. Bake 30 minutes at 350 degrees. Combine all ingredients for icing and mix well. Pour over hot cake in pan. Serves 12.

PINEAPPLE UPSIDE-DOWN CAKE
Elaine Oliver

1 tablespoon butter or
  margarine
¼ cup brown sugar
6 pineapple slices
8 maraschino cherries or
  more
¼ cup shortening plus 1
  tablespoon
¼ cup brown sugar

¾ cup sugar
1 egg, beaten
1¼ cups cake flour, sifted
1½ teaspoons baking
  powder
¼ teaspoon salt
½ cup milk or pineapple
  juice
1 teaspoon vanilla

Melt butter in round cast iron skillet. Stir in brown sugar. Add pineapple slices in a pattern with cherries. In bowl work shortening with a spoon until fluffy and creamy. Add sugar gradually, while continuing to work with spoon until light. Add egg and beat well. Add sifted dry ingredients alternately in thirds with milk and vanilla in halves, beating with spoon until smooth after each addition. Pour over fruit and spread. Bake in a moderate oven of 350 degrees for 40 minutes. After cooling for awhile turn out on a serving plate, fruit side up. Serve warm or cold with or without whipped cream. Serves 8.

POOR MAN'S CAKE
Gracie Wittkohl

This recipe was passed to me by my mother-in-law, Augusta Wittkohl, the first year Ott and I married, May 28, 1946. It was her favorite. I have baked this cake each year as part of holiday cooking. It is nice to remember her through the years.

2 cups sugar
2 cups water
2 tablespoons shortening
2 teaspoons cinnamon
¹/₂ teaspoon salt

1 pound raisins (1 box)
3 cups flour, sifted
1 teaspoon soda
1 cup pecans, chopped

Place sugar, water, shortening, cinnamon, salt and raisins in a sauce pan and boil together for 5 minutes. Let cool. Stir flour and soda into cooled ingredients. Add pecans. Pour into greased tube pan or 2 loaf pans. Bake slowly 1 hour at 350 degrees or until toothpick comes out clean, when stuck into cake to test it. Serves 12.

MOTHER'S PRUNE CAKE   *Gwen Pickett*

This cake was always baked for special occasions.

1 cup Wesson oil
1¹/₂ cups sugar
3 eggs, unbeaten
2 cups flour
1 teaspoon baking powder
1 teaspoon soda
1 teaspoon salt
³/₄ teaspoon cinnamon

¹/₄ teaspoon nutmeg
¹/₄ teaspoon allspice
¹/₄ teaspoon cloves
1 cup buttermilk
1 cup prunes, cooked,
 drained and chopped
1 teaspoon vanilla
1 cup nuts, chopped

Frosting:
2 egg whites, unbeaten
1 cup brown sugar
¹/₂ cup white sugar
¹/₈ teaspoon salt
6 tablespoons prune juice

6 to 7 prunes, cooked,
 drained and chopped
1 cup pecans, chopped
1 teaspoon vanilla

Mix together sugar, oil and eggs. Sift together the dry ingredients. Add flour alternately with buttermilk. Stir in prunes, vanilla and nuts. Pour into a greased and floured 8 or 9-inch pan. Bake at 350 degrees for 35 minutes. Frosting: Mix well in double boiler, egg whites, sugars, salt, prune juice and prunes. Place over rapidly boiling water, beat with egg beater until mixture will hold peaks, about 14 minutes. Remove from hot water and add pecans and vanilla. Spread over cooled cake. Serves 12.

CALIFORNIA PRUNE CAKE

Elaine Oliver

This recipe was given to me by my sister-in-law, Frances Oliver Lotto.

2¹/₂ cups flour
3 teaspoons baking powder
1 teaspoon soda
1 teaspoon allspice
1 teaspoon cinnamon
1 teaspoon nutmeg

³/₄ cup shortening
³/₄ cup sugar
3 eggs
1 cup prune pulp
¹/₄ cup sour cream
³/₄ cup prune juice

Icing:
1 16-ounce box brown sugar
¹/₂ cup margarine
1 cup milk

1 16-ounce box powdered sugar
1 teaspoon vanilla

Sift flour; then measure and add baking powder, soda, and spices. Sift again. Cream shortening. Add sugar, cream until light and fluffy. Add eggs and beat thoroughly. Add prune pulp; then add dry ingredients with sour cream and prune juice. Bake in two greased and floured 9-inch layer cake pans or three, 8-inch layer pans, at 350 degrees for about 30 minutes. Serves 12.

Icing: Cook brown sugar, margarine and milk until thick. Pour over powdered sugar. Add vanilla. Beat until right consistency to spread. If too thick add small amount of milk.

UGLY DUCKLING PUDDING CAKE

Suzanne Law

Dad's Favorite . . .

1 box yellow cake mix
1 3¹/₂-ounce lemon flavor, instant pudding and pie mix
1 16-ounce can fruit cocktail, including syrup

1 cup coconut
4 eggs
¹/₄ cup oil
¹/₂ cup brown sugar
¹/₂ cup nuts, chopped

Glaze:
¹/₂ cup butter
¹/₂ cup sugar

¹/₂ cup evaporated milk
1¹/₃ cups coconut

Blend all ingredients except brown sugar and nuts in large mixer bowl.

Beat 4 minutes at medium speed. Pour into greased 9 x 13-inch pan. Sprinkle with brown sugar and nuts. Bake at 325 degrees for 45 minutes or until done. Do not underbake. Cool 15 minutes. Serves 12.

Glaze: Combine butter, sugar and evaporated milk in saucepan. Boil 2 minutes. Stir in coconut. Spoon hot glaze over warm cake.

PUMPKIN CHEESECAKE   *Peggy Arbon*

I use this every time I need an excuse to make a dessert.

Crust:
3/4 cup graham cracker
   crumbs
1/2 cup pecans, chopped fine
1/4 cup dark brown sugar,
   packed

1/4 cup granulated sugar
1/4 cup butter, melted and
   cooled

Filling:
1 cup canned pumpkin
3 large eggs, room
   temperature
1 1/2 teaspoons cinnamon
1/2 teaspoon ginger
1/2 teaspoon nutmeg
1/2 teaspoon salt

1 cup plus 2 tablespoons
   sugar
1 1/2 pounds cream cheese,
   softened
2 tablespoons heavy cream
1 tablespoon cornstarch
1 teaspoon vanilla

Topping:
Whipped cream
Cinnamon-sugar

Toffee candy, crushed
(optional)

To make crust: In a bowl combine the crumbs, pecans, brown sugar, granulated sugar and butter. Press the mixture onto the bottom of a 10-inch springform pan. Freeze the crust for 15 minutes.

To make filling: In a bowl whisk together the pumpkin, eggs, cinnamon, ginger, nutmeg, salt and 3/4 cup of the sugar. In another bowl with an electric mixer, cream together the cream cheese and the remaining 6 tablespoon granulated sugar. Beat in the cream, cornstarch and the vanilla. Beat in the pumpkin mixture. Pour the filling into the crust and bake in a preheated oven at 350 degrees for 40 to 45 minutes or until the center is set. Let it cool in the pan on a rack and chill it, covered loosely, overnight. Run a knife around the edge of the pan and remove the side of the pan. Top

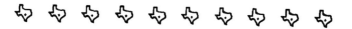

with the whipped cream, the cinnamon-sugar and the candy. Serves 12.

SPICE TOMATO SOUP CAKE
Wanda Clark

1 tablespoon sugar
2 eggs, beaten
2 tablespoons water

Spice cake mix
1 can tomato soup

Sauce:
1 cup sour cream
$^1/_4$ cup brown sugar

1 teaspoon vanilla

Grease bundt pan and sprinkle with 1 tablespoon sugar. Mix eggs, water, cake mix and tomato soup. Pour into bundt pan and bake at 325 degrees for 1 hour or until cake springs back with a touch. Serves 12–16.

Sauce: Mix sauce ingredients and drizzle over hot cake.

SPONGE CAKE
Jewell Sultemeier

I have served this cake for years on Easter Sunday for my family with fresh strawberries and whipped cream. They love it and look forward to the dessert. It's important to have all ingredients at room temperature.

$1^1/_4$ cups flour, sifted
1 cup sugar
$^1/_2$ teaspoon salt
$^1/_2$ teaspoon baking powder
6 egg whites

1 teaspoon cream of tartar
$^1/_2$ cup sugar
6 egg yolks
$^1/_4$ cup water
1 teaspoon vanilla

Sift flour, sugar, salt and baking powder. In a mixing bowl beat egg whites until frothy; add cream of tartar. Gradually add sugar, a little at a time; beat until stiff but not dry. In a small bowl combine egg yolks, water, vanilla and dry ingredients. Fold mixture gently into beaten egg whites. Turn into an ungreased 10-inch tube pan or sheet cake pan. Bake at 350 degrees for 45 minutes. Invert pan to cool. Serves 12–16.

STRAWBERRY CAKE
Mary Dyer

1 3-ounce box strawberry Jello
1/2 cup water
1 box white cake mix
1/2 cup oil

4 eggs, beaten
2/3 package (10-ounce) frozen strawberries, thawed

Icing:
1 16-ounce box powdered sugar
1/2 cup margarine

1/3 package frozen strawberries, thawed

Combine Jello and water and mix with cake mix. To this mixture add oil, eggs and strawberries. Beat well. Bake in three 8-inch layers or 9 x 13-inch sheet cake pan at 300 degrees for 30 minutes. Cool. Mix all icing ingredients together and frost cake. Serves 12.

STRAWBERRY-CARROT CAKE
Daisy Cox

2 1/2 cups all purpose flour
1 1/4 cups brown sugar, packed
1 cup carrots, finely shredded
1/2 cup vegetable oil
1/2 cup low-fat plain yogurt
1/3 cup water
1/2 cup pecans, chopped

2 teaspoons baking powder
1/2 teaspoon baking soda
1/2 teaspoon salt
1 teaspoon ground cinnamon
1 teaspoon ground nutmeg
2 eggs
1 cup strawberries, finely chopped

Strawberry-Cream Cheese Glaze:
2 ounces light cream cheese, softened
1 tablespoon strawberries, mashed

1/2 teaspoon vanilla
3/4 cup powdered sugar

Preheat oven to 350 degrees. Grease and flour 12-cup bundt cake pan. Beat all ingredients except strawberries and glaze in large bowl on low speed 45 seconds, scraping bowl constantly. Beat on medium speed 2 minutes, scraping bowl occasionally. Fold in strawberries; pour into pan.

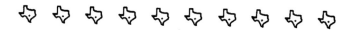

Bake 45 to 55 minutes or until wooden pick inserted in center comes out clean. Cool 5 minutes; remove from pan. Cool completely. Prepare glaze; spoon onto cake. Refrigerate any remaining cake. Serves 12.

STRAWBERRY PEACH SHORTCAKE   *Joyce Ellis*

There are no strawberries in this recipe but I have always called it this. In the summer we have an abundance of ripe peaches that we have to use. That is how this recipe came about. It is so good there is never any leftover.

1 yellow cake mix
12 cups peaches, peeled and sliced

3 cups sugar, more or less
1 12-ounce container Cool Whip

Mix cake according to directions on box and bake in a greased 9 x 13-inch pan. While cake is baking peel and slice peaches; add sugar and use potato masher or hands and mash peaches and sugar together. Let set awhile and stir occasionally to make sure sugar is dissolved. When cake is done, cool for 10 minutes. Then remove from pan. Slice cake lengthwise and place one layer back in cake pan that it was baked in. Place 1/2 of the peach mixture evenly on first layer of cake. Add second layer and add remaining peaches. Let set 30 minutes to one hour. Cut and dish up in individual servings. Add a dollop of Cool Whip to each serving and enjoy. Serves 12.

BOILED RAISIN CAKE   *Ruth Teague*

One of my mother's old fashioned recipes. Simple, good and what a wonderful aroma in the kitchen.

1 cup sugar
1/2 cup butter
1 teaspoon cinnamon
1 teaspoon soda
1 cup raisins

1 cup warm water
1/2 teaspoon cloves
2 cups flour
2 teaspoons baking powder

Mix sugar, butter, cinnamon, soda, raisins, cloves and water well. Bring to a full boil. Let cool and add flour and baking powder. Mix well with minimum amount of stirring. Bake in a greased and floured loaf pan 350 degree oven for 25 to 30 minutes. Serves 8–10.

DEEP SOUTH CAKE

Mary Gross

This is my mother-in-law's favorite recipe.

2 cups sugar	1¹/₂ teaspoons allspice
1 cup butter	1 cup pecans, chopped
5 eggs	1¹/₂ cups coconut
1 cup buttermilk	1 cup blackberry jam
3 cups flour, sifted	1 cup raisins
1 teaspoon soda	

Icing:
1 cup sour cream   2 cups powdered sugar

Cream sugar and butter. Add eggs. Add buttermilk and dry ingredients. Then add fruits, nuts and jam. Bake in three greased 9-inch pans at 350 degrees until done. Mix icing ingredients and spread over each layer and on top. Serves 12.

QUICK YELLOW CAKE

Jewell Sultemeier

1 cup sugar	1¹/₂ cups flour
¹/₂ cup butter	1 teaspoon baking powder
1 teaspoon vanilla	¹/₂ cup water
2 eggs	

Have all ingredients at room temperature. Place all ingredients in large bowl, mixing at low speed until all ingredients are wet. Then beat on high for 1 minute. This makes a finely textured yellow cake. It may be used as cup cakes, layer, loaf or sheet cake. Serves 10.

UPSIDE DOWN CAKE

Jewell Sultemeier

1 yellow cake, recipe above	1 cup brown sugar, firmly packed
1 20-ounce can sliced pineapple	Maraschino cherries, if desired
¹/₄ cup butter	Nuts, if desired

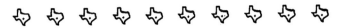

Melt butter in 12 x 12-inch deep pan. Add brown sugar and mix well. Cover evenly over bottom of pan. Cover with pineapple slices, nuts and cherries. Top with cake mixture and bake at 350 degrees for 35 to 40 minutes. Turn out on platter or plate while warm. Serves 9.

WACKY CAKE

Joy Anderson

This recipe comes from a community cookbook of Gravette, Arkansas, dated 1951. It is great for unexpected guests.

¹/₂ cup flour	6 tablespoons oil
1 cup sugar	1 tablespoon vinegar
3 tablespoons cocoa	1 teaspoon vanilla
1 teaspoon soda	1 cup cold water
¹/₂ teaspoon salt	

Sift flour, sugar, cocoa, soda and salt into ungreased 8 x 8-inch baking pan. Punch three holes in mixture; in largest hole pour oil; in medium size hole pour vinegar; and in smallest hole pour vanilla. Cover with cold water, stir well with fork and bake 25 minutes at 350 degrees. When cake is cool, frost with your favorite chocolate icing in baking dish or dust with powdered sugar. Cut in squares and serve. Serves 9.

WALDORF ASTORIA CAKE

Pat Rumpf

2 cups flour	4 tablespoons cocoa
1 cup sugar	1 cup Miracle Whip
1¹/₂ teaspoons soda	1 cup cold water
1¹/₂ teaspoons baking powder	2 teaspoons vanilla

Icing:

1 cup sugar	¹/₄ cup milk
¹/₄ cup cocoa	¹/₄ cup margarine

Mix dry ingredients. Then add Miracle Whip, water and vanilla and beat 2 minutes. Pour into two, 8-inch cake pans that have been greased and co-coaed. Bake at 350 degrees for 35 minutes. Cool. Serves 8.

Icing: Mix all ingredients and bring over heat, to a boil and continue

199

cooking for one minute or until a drop in cold water makes a soft boil. Spread icing between layers and on top of cake.

YUM YUM CAKE
Mary Foster

1 cup sugar
1 egg
¹/₂ cup margarine
1 teaspoon vanilla
2 cups flour
1 teaspoon baking powder
¹/₄ teaspoon soda
¹/₄ teaspoon salt
³/₄ cup buttermilk

3 ounces miniature marshmallows
3 ounces semi-sweet chocolate chips
¹/₄ cup packed brown sugar
2 tablespoons margarine, softened
¹/₂ cup pecans, chopped

Mix sugar, eggs, margarine, vanilla, flour, baking powder, soda, salt and buttermilk. Mix well. Mix marshmallows and chips in batter. Pour into greased 9 x 13-inch cake pan. Mix brown sugar, margarine and pecans and sprinkle over top. Bake at 325 degrees for about 30 minutes or until done. Serves 12.

ZUCCHINI FUDGE CAKE
Elva Shoemake

I make bars instead of layers. A powdered sugar frosting may be used if desired, but I do not frost mine.

4 eggs
2¹/₄ cups sugar
2 teaspoons vanilla
³/₄ cup butter, softened
3 cups flour
¹/₂ cup cocoa

2 teaspoons baking powder
1 teaspoon soda
³/₄ teaspoon salt
1 cup buttermilk
3 cups zucchini, shredded
1 cup pecans, chopped

Beat eggs well; add sugar and beat until thick. Add vanilla and butter. Mix dry ingredients and stir into egg mixture. Add buttermilk and mix well. Fold in zucchini and nuts. Makes 3 large layers or 4 small layers or cook in a 9 x 13-inch greased and floured pan. Bake at 350 degrees until top springs back when lightly touched, about 25 to 35 minutes. Serves 12–16.

COCONUT-PECAN FROSTING

Ruth Teague

Sounds like it takes a lot of time and effort doesn't it? Just wait until you take your first bite; you'll think it was worth it.

1 cup evaporated milk
1 cup sugar
3 egg yolks
1/2 cup butter

1 teaspoon vanilla
1 7-ounce can flaked coconut
1 cup pecans, chopped

Combine milk, sugar, egg yolks, butter and vanilla. Cook mixture over medium heat until thickened, about 10–12 minutes, stirring occasionally. Add coconut and pecans. Remove from heat and beat 2 or 3 minutes until thick enough to spread. Makes 3 cups.

LEMON CAKE FILLING

Dena Heider

2 cups sugar
4 tablespoons flour
2 tablespoons cornstarch
2 eggs, beaten
1 cup cold water

1 cup lemon juice
2 tablespoons margarine
2 teaspoons lemon extract
1 8-ounce Cool Whip

In a 2-quart double boiler, mix sugar, flour and cornstarch. Slowly stir in eggs, water and lemon juice. Cook and stir until thick. Stir in margarine and lemon extract. Cover and chill before icing cake. Top with Cool Whip and refrigerate. Makes 3–3 1/2 cups.

FRESH ORANGE ICING

Ray Sultemeier

3 cups powdered sugar, sifted
1/3 cup Crisco

3 tablespoons orange juice
1/2 tablespoon orange rind, grated

Blend sugar and Crisco and stir in orange juice and orange rind. Ices a

three layer cake or a sheet cake. Makes $2^1/_2$–3 cups.

WHIPPED CREAM FROSTING
Ray Sultemeier

1$^1/_2$ cups heavy cream   2 tablespoons cocoa
$^1/_4$ cup sugar $^1/_2$ teaspoon vanilla

Mix all ingredients in a bowl; do not whip. Set in refrigerator to chill for 2 hours. Then beat until it holds in peaks. Makes $2^1/_2$ cups.

WHITE MOUNTAIN ICING
Cynthia Smith

My grandmother always made an Angel Food Cake and iced the cake with this cooked icing. When she made it for me, she filled the "hole" of the cake with the icing also. This was always a special birthday cake.

2 egg whites   2 tablespoons water
$^1/_2$ cup sugar $^1/_2$ teaspoon vanilla
$^1/_4$ cup white Karo syrup

Beat egg whites until stiff enough to hold a peak and have ready. In a small sauce pan, mix sugar, Karo and water and stir well. Boil quickly until mixture spins a 2–3-inch long thread from a fork. Pour syrup slowly in a thin, steady stream into beaten egg whites, beating constantly with electric beater until it stands in stiff peaks. Blend in vanilla. Will frost a large cake. Makes $2^1/_2$ cups.

SWEET CREAM SAUCE
Norma Honeycutt

This is my Mother's recipe; it was our family's favorite. It is so good on plain pound cake, and keeps well in the refrigerator.

1 cup sugar $^1/_4$ cup margarine
3 tablespoons flour $^1/_2$ teaspoon vanilla
2 cups milk

Mix sugar and flour in saucepan; add milk gradually. Heat slowly. Add margarine; boil 2 minutes, stirring constantly; cool and add vanilla. Serve warm or cold over cake. Makes $2^1/_2$ cups.

Pies

GRANDMOTHER'S EASY PIE CRUST
Cynthia Smith

My grandmother took pity on me and shared an easy or "no fail" pie crust because it was a proven fact I couldn't do pie crust. My crusts were grey looking, tough concoctions that kept sticking to the rolling pin. This recipe requires no rolling.

1 cup flour, sifted
1/2 cup margarine, softened but not melted

2 tablespoons powdered sugar
Dash of salt

Press together with hands to form a ball. Place in pie plate and mash out and up the sides. Bake in moderate oven about 12 minutes until golden. Don't over brown. Makes 1, 9-inch pie crust.

Hint: Sprinkle a little salt in unbaked shell. Prick several times with fork so crust will not bubble.

FRIED PIE PASTRY
Neatta Cade

1/3 cup shortening
2 cups flour
1/2 teaspoon baking powder
1/4 teaspoon salt

1/2 teaspoon sugar
1 egg, beaten
1 5-ounce can evaporated milk

Mix shortening, flour, baking powder, salt and sugar. Beat egg and mix with milk. Combine all together and mix well. Let chill in refrigerator 4 or 5 hours or overnight. Roll thin and fill with fruit. Fry until brown. Makes pastry for about 8 fried pies.

20 PIE CRUSTS
Janette Hoppe

5 pounds flour
21/2 teaspoons salt

3 pounds Crisco
2–21/2 cups Sprite

Mix flour and salt, cut in shortening until it looks like small peas. Add Sprite gradually; will be slightly sticky. Let rest one hour then form into 20 balls or 16 balls for large crusts and freeze. Thaw one hour before needed.

IMPOSSIBLE FRENCH APPLE PIE
Daisy Cox

6 cups tart apples, pared
1¹/₄ teaspoons cinnamon
¹/₄ teaspoon nutmeg
1 cup sugar

³/₄ cup milk
¹/₂ cup Bisquick
2 eggs
2 tablespoons margarine, softened

Streusel:
1 cup Bisquick
¹/₂ cup nuts, chopped
¹/₃ cup brown sugar, packed

3 tablespoons margarine, firm

Preheat oven to 325 degrees. Grease pie pan, 10 x 1¹/₂-inch. Mix apples and spices. Turn into pie plate. Beat remaining ingredients except streusel, until smooth, 15 seconds in blender on high or 1 minute with hand beater. Pour into pie plate. Sprinkle with streusel. Bake until knife come out clean, 55 to 60 minutes. Makes 1, 10-inch pie.

Streusel: Mix Bisquick, sugar, and nuts with margarine until crumbly.

NOTE: Pears are also good baked this way. Committee.

ETHEL'S FRIED PIES
Helen Mayfield

Dried apples
Water
1¹/₂ cups sugar to 1 pound of apples

3 tablespoons Minute tapioca
Canned biscuits
Crisco oil

Soak apples in water; they take up a lot of water. Put on to cook, slow; don't scorch. When done and juice has cooked down, you don't want much juice on them. Mash apples with sugar. Add tapioca and stir until tapioca dissolves. Roll out biscuits pretty thin. Put apples on biscuit and fold over and crimp edges. Put one-inch of oil in frying pan and let oil get hot. Then cut down on heat; don't burn. Fry pies on one side; turn to other side. Drain. Makes 8 pies.

BROWN BEAN PIE

Ava Johnson Cox

The filling can be made up and kept in the refrigerator about 5 days. It is very similar to pumpkin pie.

2 cups pinto beans, cooked
  and mashed real good
3 eggs, beaten until foamy
$^1/_2$ cup dark Karo syrup
$1^1/_2$ cups sugar

1 tablespoon butter
$^1/_4$ teaspoon nutmeg
$^1/_4$ teaspoon cinnamon
Unbaked pie shell

Mix all ingredients except pie shell and pour into pie shell. Bake at 350 degrees for 30 minutes or until done. Coconut, nuts or dried peaches may be added. Makes 1, 9-inch pie.

BLUEBERRY PIE

Elaine Oliver

This is not an old family recipe but I have used it for thirty years.

8-inch baked pastry crust or
  chilled crumb crust
$3^1/_3$-ounce package vanilla
  pudding and pie filling
15-ounce can blueberries,
  drain and reserve juice
$^1/_4$ cup sugar

2 tablespoons cornstarch
1 tablespoon margarine or
 butter
1 tablespoon lemon juice
Whipped cream or Cool
 Whip

Prepare crust. Prepare pudding mix and cool. Pour into crust and chill. Drain blueberries, reserving liquid. Mix sugar and cornstarch in small saucepan. Stir in liquid gradually until smooth. Cook and stir over medium heat until thick and clear, about one minute. Stir in margarine, lemon juice, and berries. Cool. Spread over pudding. Chill until firm. Top with whipped cream or Cool Whip. Makes 1, 8-inch pie.

NOTE: I use nutmeg and cinnamon to flavor blueberries and add sliced bananas on top of pie before adding whipped cream.

BUTTERMILK PIE
Shirley Lawson

I got this recipe from LBJ's cookbook many years ago. It is different from the one in the Ranch Road One chapter.

1¹/₂ cups sugar
2 tablespoons flour
4 eggs
¹/₂ cup buttermilk

1 teaspoon vanilla
¹/₂ cup margarine, melted
9-inch unbaked pie shell

Mix sugar and flour. Add eggs and mix well. Add buttermilk, vanilla and margarine. Mix well. Add to unbaked pie shell and bake in 375 degree oven for 35 to 45 minutes. Makes 1, 9-inch pie.

CARAMEL NUT CREAM PIE
Lucia Carbary

This recipe comes from a dear friend and former classmate, Ruth Tatsch Wunderlich. While visiting in her home shortly after I married, she served this for dessert. It has become one of my favorite recipes.

2 eggs, separated
2 cups milk
1¹/₂ cups sugar, in ¹/₂ cup portions
2 tablespoons cornstarch
2 heaping tablespoons flour

1 teaspoon vanilla
²/₃ cup pecans, chopped
Cool Whip
¹/₃ cup pecans, chopped for topping
9-inch baked pie shell

Beat egg yolks lightly; add milk. Mix 1/2 cup sugar with cornstarch and flour and add to egg mixture. Place in double boiler. Caramelize 1/2 cup sugar and add to ingredients in double boiler and cook until thick. Beat egg whites until stiff and gradually add remaining 1/2 cup sugar. Add vanilla to first mixture and pour over egg whites and fold in. Add 2/3 cup pecans and pour into a baked pie shell. Cover with Cool Whip and top with 1/3 cup pecans. Makes 1, 9-inch pie.

NOTE: To caramelize sugar put in heavy pan or skillet over low heat, stirring constantly until golden brown.

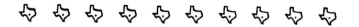

NO MIX CHERRY SUPREME

Shirley Lawson

¹/₂ cup butter	¹/₄ teaspoon salt
¹/₂ cup flour	¹/₂ cup milk
¹/₂ cup sugar	1 20-ounce can cherry pie
1 teaspoon baking powder	filling

Melt butter in bottom of 1¹/₂-quart casserole dish. Mix flour, sugar, baking powder, salt and milk. Pour over butter. Do not mix. Pour cherry pie filling over flour mixture. Do not mix. Cook in 325 degree oven for 45 to 50 minutes or until brown on top. Serves 8.

AUNT LUCILLE'S GREEN GRAPE COBBLER

Liz Carpenter

Gather grapes while seed is still soft and grapes in green stage. Line pie pan with pie crust. Cook 2 cups green grapes with 4 cups sugar until grapes are just about to pop a little. Add grapes; then top with another pie crust. Sprinkle with sugar, 1/2 pound margarine — slice and spread. Bake in 325 degree oven. Serves 8.

As a vice-presidential aide to Lyndon B. Johnson and press secretary to Lady Bird, Liz Carpenter is a true sweetheart! She proved this once again when I, Peggy Arbon, called her to ask her permission to use the recipes from her book, *Getting Better All The Time* for our Garden Club cookbook. Without hesitation she immediately consented, for which we are most appreciative. Liz expressed her wishes for our complete success, and with encouragement like her's, how can we miss?

OLD-FASHION COBBLER

Sadie Sharp

I like this, as it is so easy to make.

¹/₂ cup margarine	3 teaspoons baking powder
1 large can sliced peaches or other fruit	¹/₂ teaspoon salt
1 cup water	1 cup milk
1 cup flour	1 cup brown sugar
1 cup sugar	1 teaspoon allspice or other spices
¹/₂ teaspoon salt	

207

Melt margarine in large baking dish. Add peaches and water. Mix flour, sugar, baking powder and salt with milk. Pour over peaches. Sprinkle brown sugar and spice over peaches. Bake in 350 degrees oven until crust is golden brown. May be served with whipped cream, ice cream or whipped topping. Serves 12.

PEACH COBBLER AND CRUST

Cynthia Smith

Grandmother's . . .

Prepare filling a day ahead.

Crust:
1 cup Crisco
2¼ cups flour, sifted

1 teaspoon salt
¼ cup water

Filling:
8 cups fresh peaches, peeled
   and sliced

2 cups sugar
2 tablespoons flour

Topping:
Dots of butter
1 tablespoon sugar

1 tablespoon cinnamon

Crust: Sift flour and salt into bowl. Take out 1/3 cup of the mixture. Cut Crisco into remaining flour until pieces are size of small peas. Mix water with the reserved flour to make paste. Add flour paste to Crisco flour mix. Mix and shape into ball. Divide ball into 2 pieces. Dust pastry board with flour and roll out dough with short strokes. Make 12-inch diameter piece. Roll out other ball to make top. Cut into strips. Serves 12.

Filling: Combine peaches, sugar and flour in a large bowl. Place covered in the refrigerator for 12 hours. The next day make crust and line a cobbler dish or 9 x 12 x 2-inch pan. Place peaches in saucepan and cook for 10 minutes or until bubbly. Do not scorch. Pour into unbaked pie crust. Put strips of crust across. Dot with butter and sprinkle with cinnamon and sugar. Bake at 400 degrees for 15 minutes or until golden.

COCONUT PIE

Rosie Danz

1 cup sugar
2 heaping tablespoons flour
   or cornstarch
2½ cups milk
4 egg yolks

2 tablespoons butter
1 teaspoon vanilla
1 cup coconut
1 9-inch baked pie shell

Meringue:
4 egg whites
1/4 teaspoon cream of tartar

6 tablespoons sugar
1/4 cup coconut, optional

Mix sugar and cornstarch; add milk. Separate eggs and add beaten egg yolks; reserve egg whites for meringue. Cook stirring constantly until thick. Remove from heat and add butter, vanilla and coconut. Pour into 9-inch baked pie shell. Cover with meringue and bake at 400 degrees until a delicate brown, about 8 to 10 minutes. Makes 1, 9-inch pie.

Meringue: Beat whites with cream of tartar until frothy. Gradually beat in sugar, a little at a time. Continue beating until stiff and glossy. Coconut may be added if desired.

COCONUT BLENDER PIE   *Daisy Cox*

1 13-ounce can evaporated milk
3 eggs
1 cup sugar
3 tablespoons vegetable oil

3 tablespoons flour
1 cup flaked coconut
1/2 teaspoon vanilla
Nutmeg to taste

Combine all ingredients except nutmeg in container of electric blender. Process until well mixed. Pour into a greased and floured 10-inch pie pan. Mixture will be thin. Sprinkle with nutmeg; bake at 325 degrees for 40 minutes or until set. Let pie stand 10 minutes before serving. Makes 1, 10-inch pie.

PEARL TARVER'S CHOCOLATE PIE   *Cynthia Smith*

1 1-ounce square of choco-late or 4 tablespoons cocoa
1 cup boiling water
1 cup sugar
2 tablespoons cornstarch or flour

3 eggs yolks, beaten
2 tablespoons butter
1 teaspoon vanilla
1 pie crust, baked

Meringue:
3 egg whites
6 tablespoons sugar

1/2 teaspoon cream of tartar

Melt chocolate in one cup boiling water. Add sugar and corn starch and cook for 10 minutes. Add egg yolks, butter and vanilla and pour into cooled baked pie crust. Makes 1, 9-inch pie.

Meringue: Beat egg whites adding sugar and cream of tartar slowly until stiff. Bake pie in 350 degree oven until meringue is golden.

COCOA PIE

June Dahmann

1 cup sugar	3 egg yolks
2 tablespoons flour	1 tablespoon margarine
1 cup milk	1 9-inch baked pie crust
3 tablespoons cocoa	

Mix sugar, flour, milk, cocoa and yolks well. Cook on medium heat until thick. Add margarine and pour into baked crust. Top with meringue or Cool Whip. Makes 1, 9-inch pie.

Shirley Lawson also makes a similar pie. She uses 1/3 cup cornstarch for flour, adds 1/8 teaspoon salt, 2 tablespoons cocoa, 2 cups milk, and adds 2 teaspoon vanilla after it is thick.

GERMAN CHOCOLATE PIE

Betty Wood

1/2 cup margarine	1/2 cup flour
1/2 bar German's Sweet Chocolate	1/2 cup nuts, chopped (optional)
3 eggs, beaten	1 teaspoon vanilla
1 cup sugar	Dream Whip topping

Melt margarine and chocolate in top of double boiler. Add sugar and flour to eggs. Mix. Pour margarine and chocolate mixture into egg mixture. Add nuts and vanilla. Pour into buttered pie plate. Bake 35 to 45 minutes at 325 degrees. Pie will form an odd-looking crusty top and be gooey inside. May serve plain or with a Dream Whip topping. Makes 1, 9-inch pie.

GRAPEFRUIT PIE
Helen Mayfield

1 cup water
1/4 cup grapefruit juice
1 cup sugar
3 teaspoons cornstarch or flour
1 3-ounce box of strawberry
   gelatin

2 grapefruit, peeled and
   sectioned
Cool Whip or ice cream
9-inch pie crust, baked

Combine water, juice, sugar and cornstarch in sauce pan and cook until thick. Add gelatin. Line bottom of baked pie crust with half of filling. Then add sections of grapefruit. Put remaining filling over grapefruit. Spread with Cool Whip or ice cream on top. Place in refrigerator until serving time. Makes 1, 9-inch pie.

JELLO ICE CREAM PIE
Lucille Newman

1 3-ounce package lime Jello
1 cup boiling water
1 pint vanilla ice cream, 2 cups

1 8-ounce can crushed
   pineapple
1 graham cracker pie shell

Mix Jello and water; fold in ice cream and pineapple and pour into pie shell. Refrigerate. For variation you may use strawberry Jello and frozen strawberries. Makes 1 pie.

LEMON CHIFFON PIE
Jewell Sultemeier

This is Viris Klappenbach's recipe. She always brought two of these pies to a covered dish meal at church or at Oakcrest Housing. She was faithful and died so suddenly.

3 eggs yolks
1/2 cup sugar
1 teaspoon lemon rind
3 tablespoons water
1/8 teaspoon salt

3 tablespoons lemon juice
3 egg whites
1/3 cup sugar
Pinch of salt
1 9-inch unbaked pie shell

Separate eggs. Cook egg yolks, sugar and water in double boiler, place over hot water. Cook stirring until thickened. Remove from fire. Cool. Add lemon juice and rind. Beat egg whites gradually adding 1/3 cup sugar

and salt. Continue beating until mixture stiffens. Fold into lemon mixture, then into 9-inch pie shell. Bake in moderate oven at 350 degrees for 25 or 30 minutes or until delicately browned. Makes 1, 9-inch pie.

MAMMY'S DREAM PIE
Mary A. Thurlkill

This recipe is an old family favorite from my husband's family. His mother, Betty Sue Thurlkill, always made this at Christmas.

1 cup butter	1 cup pecans, chopped
2 cups sugar	1 tablespoon vinegar
4 egg yolks	4 egg whites, beaten
1 cup raisins	1 9-inch unbaked pie shell

Cream butter and sugar; add egg yolks and mix well. Add raisins, nuts and vinegar. Fold into this mixture the stiffly beaten egg whites. Pour into one 9-inch unbaked pie shell, and bake in 450 degree oven for 10 minutes. Turn down to 325 degrees and cook until filling is set, about 25 minutes. Makes 1, 9-inch pie.

FROZEN MARGARITA PIE
Cynthia Smith

Crust:
> 1/2 cup plus 2 tablespoons margarine
> 5-ounces thin salted pretzels, crushed fine, 1 1/4 cups
> 1/2 cup sugar

Filling:
> 1 can sweetened condensed milk
> 1 1/2 tablespoons lime juice
> 1 1/2 tablespoons Tequila
> 1 tablespoon plus 1 teaspoon Triple Sec
> 1 drop green food coloring
> 2 1/2 cups whipped cream

Crust: Grease 9-inch pie plate. Melt butter, stir in crushed pretzels and sugar. Blend. Press into pie plate.

Filling: Mix milk, lime juice, Tequila, Triple Sec and food coloring in small bowl. In large bowl beat whipping cream until soft peaks form. Fold in milk mixture until blended. Pour into crust and freeze, about 6 hours. Then wrap the entire pie in Saran Wrap, airtight, and freeze 2 more hours; a total of 8 hours until you can serve it. To omit Tequila, increase lime juice to 2/3 cup. I serve this frozen and get 12 slices out of each pie. I sprinkle pretzel crumbs on top. Very rich.

GRANNY'S MINCEMEAT PIE
Joycelyn Carter

This is my mother-in-law, Ruth Read's recipe and our favorite pie. She makes it by a pinch of this and a handful of that so I put a measuring cup under her hand and measured it out as she went.

1 package mincemeat	$^1/_3$ cup flour
2 cups water	$^1/_2$ teaspoon cinnamon
2 cups sugar	$^1/_4$ teaspoon cloves

Break up mincemeat; add water and simmer. Mix together in a bowl the sugar, flour, cinnamon and cloves; add to simmering mincemeat, stir until thick. Pour into 2, 8-inch pie crusts or 1, 10-inch pie crust. Bake at 425 degrees for 30 minutes.

OSGOOD PIE
Mae Hernlund

A delicious pie for special occasions used by my family since 1900 in Ellis and Navarro Counties.

$^1/_2$ cup butter	$^1/_2$ cup pecans, chopped
1 cup sugar	$^1/_2$ cup raisins
2 egg yolks, well-beaten	$1^1/_2$ teaspoons vinegar
$^1/_2$ teaspoon allspice	2 egg whites, beaten
$^1/_2$ teaspoon cloves	1 9-inch unbaked pie shell

Mix butter and sugar until creamy. Add egg yolks, allspice, cloves, pecans, raisins and vinegar and mix well. Fold in egg whites that have been beaten until stiff. Bake 300–325 degrees for about 45 minutes. Test with toothpick in center, should be clean when pie is done. Makes 1, 9-inch pie.

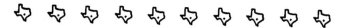
PEANUT BUTTER PIE

Juanita (Teet) Hobbs

This pie can be frozen on the off chance that you might have left-overs or if you want to make it ahead of time.

1 cup crunchy peanut butter	1 teaspoon vanilla
1 cup sugar	2 teaspoons butter, melted
1 8-ounce package cream cheese	1 8-ounce package frozen whipped topping, thawed

Mix peanut butter, sugar, cream cheese, vanilla, and butter thoroughly until creamy; fold in whipped topping. Pour in graham cracker crust. Refrigerate overnight. Makes 1 pie.

NO ORDINARY PECAN PIE

Gwen Pickett

Try it, you'll love it!

1 cup pecans, chopped	1 cup sugar
1 cup graham cracker crumbs	1 teaspoon vanilla
4 egg whites	Whipped cream or Cool Whip
1/4 teaspoon salt	

Combine nuts and cracker crumbs. Beat egg whites until foamy. Add salt; then add sugar gradually, beating until stiff peaks form. Add vanilla. Fold egg white mixture into crumb mixture. Pour in greased 9-inch pie pan. Bake at 350 for 30 minutes. Serve with whipped cream or Cool Whip. Makes 1, 9-inch pie.

MY MOTHER'S PECAN PIE

Janette Hoppe

This is a favorite recipe of my family. My mother, Sofie Marie Odiorne, made pecan pies at Christmas and we all enjoyed them.

3/4 cup granulated sugar	1 1/2 teaspoons vanilla
1/2 cup white Karo	3 eggs, slightly beaten
1/2 cup dark Karo	1 cup pecans, chopped
1/8 teaspoon salt	1 9-inch unbaked pie shell

Mix sugar, white and dark Karo, salt and vanilla; then add eggs which have been slightly beaten. Mix well and add pecans. Pour into unbaked pie shell. Cook at 400 degrees for 5 minutes then at 350 degrees for 25 to 30 minutes or until pie is firm to touch. Makes 1, 9-inch pie.

DELICIOUS PECAN PIE   *Beryl Pickle*

1 cup pecans, whole
1 9-inch unbaked pie shell
3 eggs, slightly beaten
³/₄ cup sugar

³/₄ cup light Karo syrup
¹/₄ cup molasses
¹/₄ teaspoon salt
1 teaspoon vanilla

Spread pecans over pie shell. Mix together next six ingredients and pour over pecans. Bake about 40 minutes at 350 degrees. May freeze. Makes 1, 9-inch pie.

PINEAPPLE COCONUT CHESS PIE   *Moline Lorenz*

This recipe was given to me by Julie Jackson of Waco, Texas.

2 cups sugar
4 eggs, beaten
¹/₂ cup margarine, melted
1 heaping teaspoon flour
1 heaping teaspoon cornmeal

2 cups coconut
1 cup crushed pineapple, drained
2 8-inch or 1, 10-inch unbaked pie shell

Mix sugar and eggs; add margarine, flour, cornmeal, coconut and pineapple and mix well. Pour into 2, 8-inch or 1, 10-inch unbaked pie shell. Bake at 350 degrees for one hour.

PINEAPPLE ICE BOX PIE   *Mavis Lemons*

2 baked 9-inch pie shells
1 can Eagle Brand milk
Juice of ¹/₂ lemon

8-ounce carton Cool Whip
1 20-ounce can crushed pineapple with juice

Blend together and pour into pie shells. Chill for several hours. Serves 12.

PUMPKIN PIE
Amy Poulton

Even if you never liked pumpkin pie, you must try this one.

1½ cups cooked pumpkin
1 cup evaporated milk
1 cup sugar
2 eggs, slightly beaten
¼ teaspoon salt
¼ teaspoon nutmeg
¼ teaspoon cinnamon
1 tablespoon butter
1 unbaked 10-inch pie shell
Cool Whip

Combine all ingredients. Mix thoroughly. Pour into unbaked pie shell. Bake in hot oven 425 degrees about 45 minutes or until an inserted knife comes out clean. Serve with whipped cream topping. Makes 1, 10-inch pie.

HARVEST PUMPKIN PIE
Gracie Wittkohl

Here is a great recipe given to me by my sister-in-law, Meta Gipson.

1½ cups milk
1 6-ounce package instant
vanilla pudding mix
1 cup canned pumpkin
1 teaspoon pumpkin pie
spice
1 cup Cool Whip, thawed
1 baked 9-inch pie shell,
cooled
Cool Whip
Pecans, chopped

Combine milk, pudding mix, pumpkin, spice, and Cool Whip in a bowl. Beat at low speed for 1 minute. Pour into cooled pie shell. Chill in refrigerator until set, about 2 hours. Put additional Cool Whip on top of pie and chopped pecans can be added. Makes 1, 9-inch pie.

FAVORITE RAISIN PIE
Sadie Sharp

2 cups Sun-Maid raisins
1 cup orange juice
1 cup water
½ cup sugar
2 tablespoons cornstarch or
flour
1 teaspoon allspice
1 tablespoon lemon juice
Pastry for double crust 9-
inch pie
1 egg, beaten
Sugar
Whipped cream or ice cream

216

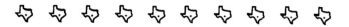

In saucepan combine raisins, orange juice and water and bring to a boil; reduce heat. Simmer 5 minutes. Combine sugar, cornstarch and allspice; stir into raisin mixture. Cook and stir over medium heat until thickened about one minute. Remove from heat; stir in lemon juice. Cool 10 minutes. Pour into pastry lined pie pan. Cover with top crust or lattice strips. Seal and flute edges. Brush top with beaten egg; sprinkle sugar over egg. Bake in preheated oven 425 degrees for 25 to 30 minutes. Cool one-half hour before serving with ice cream or whipped cream. Makes 1, 9-inch pie.

RITZ CRACKER PIE   *Norma Honeycutt*

This is a very rich pie, but I love it because it makes it's own crust and I never was very good at pretty pie crusts.

3 egg whites
1/2 teaspoon baking powder
1 cup sugar
20 Ritz crackers, crumbled

3/4 cup pecans, chopped
1 teaspoon vanilla
Whipped cream or Cool
    Whip

Beat egg whites and baking powder until foamy; add sugar and beat until like divinity. Add Ritz crackers, pecans, vanilla and mix well. Pour into buttered 9-inch pie plate. Bake 30 minutes at 325 degrees. Let cool. Put in refrigerator to chill. To serve, put whipped cream or Cool Whip over pie, slice and enjoy. Makes 1, 9-inch pie.

TOLL HOUSE PIE   *Vanessa Luce*

2 eggs
1/2 cup flour
1/2 cup sugar
1/2 cup brown sugar
1 cup butter, melted and
    cooled

1 cup semi-sweet chocolate
    morsels or chips
1 cup nuts, chopped
1 9-inch unbaked pie shell
1 pint whipped cream

Beat eggs; add flour and sugars. Blend in butter. Stir in chips and nuts. Pour into pie shell. Bake one hour at 325 degrees. Garnish with whipped cream. Makes 1, 9-inch pie.

217

VINEGAR PIE
Jewell Sultemeier

3 egg yolks
1 cup sugar
4 tablespoons flour
1/3 teaspoon salt
2 cups boiling water

1/4 cup cider vinegar
1/2 teaspoon yellow food
 coloring, if desired
1 9-inch baked pastry shell

Meringue:
3 egg whites
3 tablespoons sugar

1 teaspoon lemon extract
1/3 teaspoon salt

Beat egg yolks until thick; add sugar, flour and salt. Mix thoroughly. Then add boiling water gradually. Pour in vinegar and cook in double boiler until thickened. Add food coloring and then pour into baked pastry shell. Meringue: Beat egg whites with sugar; add extract and salt. Cover pie with meringue and bake at 325 degree for 20 minutes. Makes 1, 9-inch pie.

Cookies,
Bars and Squares

GWEN'S BROWNIES
Gwen Pickett

1 cup oil
4 eggs, slightly beaten
2 cups sugar
6 tablespoons cocoa
2 tablespoons white Karo
 syrup

1 teaspoon vanilla
1 1/2 cups flour
1 teaspoon baking powder
1 teaspoon salt
1 cup pecans, chopped

Stir oil, eggs, sugar, cocoa, syrup and vanilla together. Add flour, baking powder and salt. Stir in nuts. Pour into greased 9 x 13-inch pan. Bake at 350 degrees for 35 minutes. Makes about 16–24 squares.

RAY'S BROWNIES
Ray Sultemeier

4 1-ounce squares
  unsweetened chocolate
²/₃ cup shortening
2 cups sugar
4 eggs

1¹/₂ cups flour
1 teaspoon baking powder
1 teaspoon salt
1 cup nuts, broken

Melt chocolate and shortening in double boiler. Beat in sugar and eggs. Sift together flour, baking powder and salt and stir into chocolate mixture. Mix in nuts. Bake in a greased 9 x 13-inch pan at 350 degrees for 30 to 35 minutes. Do not overbake. Makes 16–24 squares.

QUICK AND EASY BROWNIES
Shirley Lawson

Make your own Brownie Mix . . . Fran Lawson, my daughter-in-law, gave me this recipe. It is a lot cheaper than the store bought mix and it is very delicious. So easy my granddaughters can mix it.

4 cups flour
1 tablespoon plus 1
  teaspoon salt

8 cups sugar
2¹/₂ cups cocoa
2 cups shortening

Combine flour, salt, sugar and cocoa and stir well. Cut in shortening with a pastry blender until resembles coarse meal. Store in cool dry airtight container or refrigerator up to 6 weeks. To use:

3 cups brownie mix
3 eggs, beaten
1¹/₂ teaspoons vanilla

¹/₂ cup pecans, chopped
  (optional)

Combine all ingredients and stir well. Pour into greased and floured 8-inch square pan. Bake at 350 degrees for 35 to 40 minutes. Makes 12 squares.

BUTTER BRICKLE BARS
Dena Heider

1 box yellow cake mix
¹/₃ cup butter, melted
1 egg
1 6-ounce package butter
  brickle chips

1 cup pecans, chopped
1 can sweetened condensed
  milk

Mix by hand cake mix, butter and egg. Press onto a large cookie sheet with sides. Spread with butter brickle chips and pecans; then drizzle sweetened condensed milk over all. Bake at 350 degrees for 25 minutes. Cut into squares. Makes 24–36 squares.

CHESS SQUARES

Kittie Clyde Leonard

$^1/_2$ cup margarine, melted
1 egg, slightly beaten
1 package yellow cake mix
1 8-ounce package cream
  cheese

3 eggs
1 box powdered sugar
1 teaspoon vanilla

Mix by hand, margarine and slightly beaten egg with cake mix. Pat into bottom of a greased 9 x 13-inch pan. Beat with mixer, cream cheese, 3 eggs, sugar and vanilla. Pour over cake mixture. Bake at 350 degrees for 45 minutes. Cut into squares. Makes 24 squares.

Variation: Use lemon cake mix for crust. For filling: 1 can lemon frosting (save 1/2 cup for icing) cream cheese and 2 eggs. Pour over crust and bake. Ice with remaining 1/2 cup of frosting.

COCONUT SQUARES

Olga Zauner

$^1/_4$ cup butter
$^1/_4$ cup sugar, white or
  brown
1 cup flour
2 eggs, slightly beaten
$^1/_4$ cup flour

$^1/_2$ teaspoon baking powder
$^3/_4$ teaspoon salt
1 cup brown sugar
$^1/_2$ teaspoon vanilla
$1^1/_2$ cups coconut
1 cup nuts, chopped

Preheat oven to 325 degrees. Blend together butter, sugar (1/4 cup) and flour. Pat into a 9 x 9-inch square greased pan. Bake 10 to 15 minutes. Mix together rest of ingredients and put on top of baked crust. Bake 20 minutes more. Cool slightly and cut into squares. Makes 12 squares.

GRAHAM CRACKER BARS

Cathy Woods

1 box graham crackers, divided
1 egg, beaten
1 cup sugar
1 tablespoon flour
1/2 cup evaporated milk

1/2 cup margarine
2 teaspoons vanilla
1 cup pecans, chopped
1 cup graham crackers, crushed

Icing:
1 cup powdered sugar

2 tablespoons milk

Crush graham crackers to equal 1 cup, set aside. Line jelly roll pan with 1/2 of the remaining crackers. In a saucepan mix together egg, sugar, flour, milk and margarine. Bring to boil over low heat, stirring constantly. Boil one minute. Stir in vanilla, nuts and crushed crackers. Spread filling over layer of crackers. Top with more crackers and press down. Makes 24–36 squares.

Icing: Mix powdered sugar and milk until all sugar is dissolved and ice bars. Cut into squares.

MIZ' GREEN'S HONEY BARS

Cynthia Smith

1 cup sugar
3/4 cup oil
1 egg
2 cups flour
1/4 cup honey

1/4 teaspoon salt
1 teaspoon soda
1 teaspoon cinnamon
1 cup pecans, chopped

Glaze:
1 cup powdered sugar
1/2 teaspoon vanilla

Water to thin

Mix all ingredients, except glaze ingredients, together and press into a greased and floured 9 x 13-inch pan. Bake at 350 degrees for 20 minutes. Mix glaze ingredients and drizzle over bars while hot. Cut into 16–24 squares.

OH HENRY BARS

Dolores Bowden

3 cups oatmeal
$^1/_2$ cup white Karo syrup

$^3/_4$ cup margarine
$^3/_4$ cup brown sugar

Topping:
1 6-ounce bag semi-sweet
   chocolate chips

$^1/_2$ cup peanut butter

Mix together the oatmeal, syrup, margarine and brown sugar. Press in well buttered long cake pan. Bake 15 minutes at 350 degrees or until sides bubble. When cake is cool, melt chocolate chips and peanut butter. Spread on cake. Cool and cut into 16–24 bars.

HELEN'S PUMPKIN SQUARES

Helen Mayfield

1 cup salad oil
2 cups sugar
1 can pumpkin
4 eggs
2 cups flour
2 teaspoons baking powder

1 teaspoon soda
$^1/_2$ teaspoon salt
2 teaspoons cinnamon
$^1/_2$ teaspoon ginger
$^1/_2$ teaspoon cloves
$^1/_2$ teaspoon nutmeg

Cream Cheese Frosting:
1 3-ounce package cream
   cheese
$^1/_4$ cup butter

1 box powdered sugar (3 cups)
2 tablespoons milk
1 teaspoon vanilla

Cream oil and sugar. Stir in pumpkin and eggs until smooth. Add flour, baking powder, soda, salt and spices and mix well. Pour into a greased and floured 9 x 13 x 2-inch pan. Bake at 350 degrees for 25 to 30 minutes. Frost when cool. Frosting: Mix cream cheese and butter; add milk and vanilla. Add powdered sugar gradually, mixing until mixed well. Frost and store in refrigerator until served. Cut into 16–24 squares.

★　★　★　★　★

HINT:
An economical substitute for chopped nuts in cookie recipes is quick-cooking oats, browned in a small amount of butter or margarine.

★　★　★　★　★

Drop Cookies

CHRISTMAS ROCKS
Agnes Stevenson

4 eggs
2 cups sugar
1 teaspoon cinnamon
2 teaspoons ground cloves
1 to 2 pounds pecans,
   chopped

1 pound dates, chopped
1 pound raisins
1^1/$_2$ cups butter, melted
2 teaspoons baking soda
3 cups flour

Beat eggs, sugar and spices; add nuts, fruits, butter and soda and mix well. Stir in flour. Drop on ungreased cookie sheets and bake at 250 degrees for 25 to 30 minutes or 350 degrees for 13 to 15 minutes. Makes a lot of cookies! Keeps in a tight container for a long time. 8–10 dozen.

DROP BROWNIES
Cathy Woods

1^3/$_4$ cups sugar
1 cup margarine
^{2}/$_3$ cup light Karo syrup
2 eggs
4 1-ounce squares unsweetened chocolate, melted

2 teaspoons vanilla
3^1/$_2$ cups flour, sifted
1 teaspoon baking powder
Dash of salt
^{1}/$_2$ to 1 cup pecans, chopped
   or coconut

Mix sugar, margarine, Karo, eggs and melted chocolate. Stir in other ingredients and mix well. Nuts and coconut may be added. Drop by teaspoonsful 2 inches apart onto greased cookie sheets. Bake at 350 degrees for 10 minutes or until set. Cool slightly on cookie sheets; remove to wire racks. About 4 dozen.

★　★　★　★　★

HINT:
Return cookies to 350 degree oven for 2 minutes if they cool in pan and stick. This will loosen the cookies. Remove from pan immediately.

★　★　★　★　★

223

MRS. FIELD'S COOKIES — SAN FRANCISCO

Flora Cox

Takes a large bowl and makes a lot of cookies.

2 cups margarine or butter
2 cups white sugar
2 cups brown sugar
4 eggs
1 teaspoon vanilla
5 cups Quick or Old-Fashioned oats
4 cups flour
2 teaspoons baking powder
2 teaspoons soda

1 teaspoon salt
1 12-ounce bag semi-sweet chocolate chips
1 12-ounce Peanut Butter Reeses or butterscotch chips
3 cups moist coconut
3 cups almonds, pecans or other nuts, chopped

Cream butter, white and brown sugar; add eggs and vanilla; beat. In blender, blend oats and add to butter mixture. Sift flour, baking powder, soda and salt and add to mixture. Mix well. To this mixture add chocolate chips, Reese chips, coconut and nuts. Mix well. Drop by teaspoonsful on ungreased cookie sheets. Bake at 375 degrees for 6–10 minutes. Do not allow to brown too much. Makes 10–12 dozen.

MEXICAN WEDDING COOKIES

Mimi Fincher

When Wince Fincher was a young man he was with the Forest Rangers in New Mexico. This recipe came from there.

1 cup butter or margarine, softened
1/2 cup powdered sugar
1 teaspoon vanilla

1/4 teaspoon salt
2 cups flour
Powdered sugar

Cream butter, sugar, vanilla and salt until fluffy. Stir in flour until well blended. Chill 30 minutes or until firm enough to handle. Shape into 1-inch balls. Place on ungreased cookie sheet 1-inch apart. Bake at 375 degrees until light golden brown. Sift hot cookies with powdered sugar. Makes 2–3 dozen.

Variation by Cynthia Smith: Use 1 cup powdered sugar, 2 teaspoons Mexican vanilla (if possible), 1 tablespoon water and 1 cup pecans, chopped fine. Form into crescents. Bake 350 degrees for 30 minutes. Cool on paper sack.

OATMEAL COOKIES

Mavis Lemons

1 cup seedless raisins
1 cup shortening
1 cup sugar
3 beaten eggs
2 cups flour
1/2 teaspoon salt
1/2 teaspoon soda

1 teaspoon cinnamon
1/2 teaspoon allspice
1/2 teaspoon cloves
2 cups oatmeal
6 tablespoons raisin liquid
1/2 cup dates, chopped
1 cup pecans, broken

Cover raisins with boiling water and cook 5 minutes. Drain, reserving 6 tablespoons of juice. Cream shortening and sugar thoroughly; add eggs and beat until smooth. Sift flour with salt, soda and spices; mix with oatmeal and add to first mixture alternately with raisin liquid. Add fruits and nut meats. Drop on greased baking sheets and bake in moderately hot oven, 375 degrees, 10–12 minutes. Makes 4 dozen.

OATMEAL CHOCOLATE CHIP COOKIES

Olga Zauner

1 cup shortening
3/4 cup brown sugar
3/4 cup sugar
1 teaspoon vanilla
2 eggs
1 teaspoon baking powder
1 teaspoon baking soda

1 teaspoon salt
1 1/2 cups flour
2 cups oatmeal
1 cup raisins
1 cup nuts, chopped
1 16-ounce package semi-
  sweet chocolate chips

Preheat oven to 350 degrees. Mix in a large bowl shortening, sugar, vanilla and eggs. Set aside. Sift together baking powder, soda, salt and flour and add to first mixture and mix well. Add oatmeal, nuts, raisins and chips. Drop by teaspoonsful on greased cookie sheets. Bake 8 to 10 minutes until firm. Makes about 4 dozen.

OATMEAL CRISP COOKIES

Janette Hoppe

1 cup sugar
1 cup brown sugar
1 cup Wesson oil
2 eggs, well beaten
1 teaspoon vanilla
1 cup flour

1 teaspoon salt
1 teaspoon soda
1 cup pecans, chopped
1 cup coconut
3¹/₂ cups Quick Quaker Oats

Mix in the order given. Drop by teaspoonsful on greased cookie sheets. Bake at 350 degrees for 10 minutes. Makes 5–6 dozen.

OLD FASHIONED OATMEAL COOKIES

Cynthia Smith

Circa 1920 . . . Use as much nuts and raisins as you would like. These are chewy.

1 cup shortening
2 cups brown sugar
2 large eggs, beaten
¹/₂ can of Pet milk (5-ounce size)
2 teaspoons vanilla

1 cup flour
¹/₂ teaspoon salt
3 cups oatmeal
¹/₂ to 1 cup nuts, chopped
¹/₂ to 1 cup raisins

Cream shortening and sugar; add eggs, milk and vanilla and mix well. Sift together flour and salt and mix with creamed mixture. Stir in oatmeal. Add raisins and nuts if desired. Drop by teaspoonsful on greased cookie sheets and bake at 350 degrees until done, 10 to 15 minutes. Makes 5 dozen.

SOUTHERN OATMEAL COOKIES

Margaret Withers

1 cup shortening
1 cup sugar
1 cup brown sugar
2 eggs
2 teaspoons vanilla

1¹/₂ cups flour, sifted
1 teaspoon salt
1 teaspoon soda
3 cups old fashion oats
1 cup pecans, chopped fine

Cream shortening and sugars; add eggs and vanilla. Sift flour, salt and soda; add to creamed mixture. Stir in nuts and oats. This isn't easy. It is best to chill the dough then roll into walnut size balls and place on greased cookie sheets. Bake at 350 degrees for 10 minutes. Adjust time for crisp or soft cookies. Makes 5 dozen.

Variation: Omit soda and salt and add 1 teaspoon of the vanilla. Add 1/2 pound of Spanish salted peanuts in place of the pecans.

PERSIMMON COOKIES   *Helen Mayfield*

³/₄ cup shortening or margarine	2 cups flour
1 cup sugar	2 teaspoons baking powder
1 egg	¹/₄ teaspoon salt
¹/₄ teaspoon soda	1 teaspoon vanilla
1 cup persimmons, peeled, seeded and mashed	³/₄ cup pecans, chopped
	³/₄ cup coconut

Cream shortening and sugar until light and fluffy; add egg and beat well. Stir soda into persimmons and add to creamed mixture. Sift flour, baking powder and salt and add to mixture; add vanilla, nuts and coconut. Drop by teaspoonsful on greased cookie sheets. Bake at 375 degrees for 12 to 15 minutes. These cookies are good to freeze. Yield: 4–5 dozen.

SESAME SEED COOKIES   *Jewell Sultemeier*

I got this recipe from an extension homemaker in Mississippi, as we stopped at the visitors center on our way to Nashville in 1990. Flo Velchoff and other extension ladies served cookies and cold drinks to all visitors. I have baked these cookies twice and they are delicious.

¹/₂ cup margarine or butter	¹/₄ teaspoon soda
1¹/₂ cups light brown sugar	¹/₄ teaspoon salt
1 egg	1 cup sesame seeds
1¹/₂ cups flour	

Cream margarine and sugar; add slightly beaten egg and beat. Add flour, soda, salt and sesame seeds. Drop small amounts, 1/4 teaspoonsful, on cookie sheets lined with foil. Bake at 350 degrees for 10 to 12 minutes or until slightly brown. Yield: 5 to 6 dozen.

Molded Cookies

DATE COCONUT PORCUPINES
Lucia Carbary

While in Junior High School we would have a class party for every occasion we could think of. We would always assign Jane Grote Hunt to bring "porcupines" because all of the class liked them so well. It is still a favorite!

³/₄ **cup sugar**	**1 cup nuts, chopped**
1 cup dates, chopped	**2 cups Rice Krispie cereal**
2 eggs, well beaten	**1¹/₂ cups coconut**
1 teaspoon vanilla	

Combine sugar, dates and eggs in skillet. Cook over medium heat, stirring constantly until mixture pulls away from sides (about 5 minutes). Remove from heat and stir in vanilla and nuts. Carefully stir in Rice Krispies. Cool slightly. Moisten hands and shape into small balls and roll in coconut. Chill and store in refrigerator. Yield: 4–5 dozen.

DRUNKEN WOMBATS
Helen O'Bryant

From our Australian member.

250 grams almond meal	**Chocolate sponge cake**
60 grams castor sugar	**¹/₂ cup sherry**
60 grams icing sugar, sifted	**120 grams glace cherries or**
Almond essence	**apricots**
Vanilla essence	**200 grams chocolate, grated**
Brandy	**Apricot jam**
1 egg	

Almond Paste: Mix almond meal with castor sugar and icing sugar. Flavor with essences and brandy. Add 1 egg yolk to bind mixture. (Egg white can also be added if required). Knead mixture on floured board. Crumble sponge cake moistened with sherry. Take two equal teaspoons of each mixture, cake and almond paste, and place an apricot or cherry between. Shape into a ball and leave to dry slightly. Coat the balls with thin almond paste. Paint with heated apricot jam then roll in grated chocolate. Yield: 4 dozen.

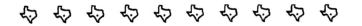

GOOF BALLS

Joy Anderson

1 bag large marshmallows
2 packages caramel candy
1 cup butter or margarine
1 14-ounce can sweetened condensed milk
1 10-ounce box Rice Krispies cereal

Cut marshmallows in half and freeze. Melt caramels, butter, and milk in double boiler. Dip marshmallows in caramel mixture and roll in Rice Krispies cereal. Refrigerate to set. Yield: 4–5 dozen.

MARTHA WASHINGTON'S COOKIES

Jewell Sultemeier

This is Martha Washington's original recipe that she served as First Lady. We were served these delicious Ginger cookies in the Commanders House which we toured in May 1984. Our grandson, Chris Sultemeier was graduating from West Point, New York. We, Felix and Jewell Sultemeier, George and Jean Sultemeier, and Harriet Odiorne attended and were entertained with many events and tours.

2 eggs
3/4 cup butter
3/4 cup Crisco
2 3/4 cups sugar
1/2 cup dark molasses
4 cups flour, white or wheat
2 teaspoons baking powder
2 teaspoons ground cloves
2 teaspoons ginger
2 teaspoons cinnamon
Sugar

Mix eggs, butter, Crisco, sugar and molasses and set aside. Sift flour, baking powder, cloves, ginger and cinnamon and add to first mixture slowly. Chill dough. Roll into 1-inch balls and then roll in sugar. (Coat hands in oil for easy rolling). Place on greased cookie sheet. Bake at 350 degrees for 9 to 10 minutes. May look a trifle underdone but will harden if overcooked. Yield: about 10 dozen.

★ ★ ★ ★ ★

HINT:
Stale cake or cookies can be crumbled up and used as a topping for ice cream or puddings.

MARY'S ORANGE BALLS

Mary Smith Amis

We used to have this at Christmas and it's easy for children to make.

1 box powdered sugar
1 12-ounce package vanilla
   wafers, crushed
1 cup pecans, chopped

1 6-ounce can frozen orange
   juice, thawed
1 7-ounce can coconut

Mix powdered sugar, vanilla wafers, pecans, and orange juice. Form into balls and roll in coconut. They are ready to eat. Do not bake. Yield: 3 dozen.

ORANGE SLICE COOKIES

Flora Cox

My Borger friends request these cookies every time they visit.

2 cups margarine, softened
1 cup sugar
2 cups brown sugar
3 eggs
3 cups flour
1¹/₂ teaspoons baking
   powder

1¹/₂ teaspoons soda dis-
   solved in 4 tablespoons water
3 cups oatmeal
1¹/₂ cups coconut
1¹/₂ cups pecans, chopped
20 orange slice candy, cut (I
   use more)

Mix and blend all ingredients by hand in order listed. Divide into 3 to 4 parts and roll each in waxed paper. Chill. Slice and bake on greased cookie sheets at 325 degrees for 6–13 minutes. Yield: 8–10 dozen.

PECAN FROSTIES

Ray Sultemeier and Annie Lee West

2 cups flour
¹/₂ teaspoon soda
¹/₄ teaspoon salt
1 cup brown sugar

Filling:
1 cup pecans, chopped
¹/₂ cup brown sugar

1 egg
1 teaspoon vanilla
¹/₂ cup butter or shortening

¹/₄ cup sour cream

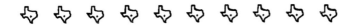

Sift flour, soda and salt and set aside. Mix sugar, egg, vanilla and butter together; stir in flour mixture. Roll into 1-inch balls; place 2-inches apart on ungreased sheets. Take finger and make print on round ball and put 1 teaspoon of the filling in the middle. Bake at 350 degrees for 12 to 14 minutes. Yield: 4 dozen.

PEPPERNUTS

Mary Pat Carter

2 cups sugar
1 cup butter or margarine
1 cup milk
1 tablespoon vanilla
Flour to make stiff dough,
    about 4 cups

3 teaspoons baking powder
1 teaspoon black pepper
1 teaspoon nutmeg
1/2 teaspoon cloves

Cream butter and sugar. Mix vanilla with milk. Sift flour, baking powder, pepper, nutmeg and cloves; add flour mixture slowly into butter mixture adding milk. Refrigerate for easier handling. Roll out dough into 1/2 to 3/4-inch ropes. Place ropes in refrigerator to stiffen dough. Cut in 1/4-inch slices and bake on an ungreased cookie sheet at 350 degrees for 10 to 12 minutes or until brown. Yield: about 200 little cookies.

PLAIN COOKIES

Pat Rumpf

This is my mother, Bernice Claxon's recipe for good plain cookies.

1 cup sugar
1/2 cup brown sugar
1/2 cup margarine
1/2 cup Crisco
1 egg
1 teaspoon vanilla

2 cups flour, sifted
Pinch of salt
2 teaspoons soda
2 teaspoons cream of tartar
Cinnamon (optional)

Cream sugars, margarine and Crisco; add egg and vanilla. Sift flour, salt, soda and cream of tartar and add to creamed mixture. Roll into balls and place on greased cookie sheets. Gently flatten balls with a fork. Bake at 350 degrees for 7 to 8 minutes. You can sprinkle cinnamon on top if desired. Yield: 6–8 dozen.

SANTA'S WHISKERS
Joycelyn Carter

1 cup margarine
1 cup sugar
2 tablespoons milk
1 teaspoon vanilla or rum
   extract

2½ cups flour
¾ cup red and green candied cherries, chopped fine
½ cup pecans, chopped fine
¾ cup flaked coconut

In a mixer bowl, cream margarine and sugar; blend in milk and vanilla. Stir in flour, candied cherries and nuts. Form into 2 rolls, each 2-inches in diameter and 8-inches long. Roll in coconut. Wrap and chill several hours or overnight. Slice 1/4-inch thick; place on ungreased cookie sheet. Bake at 375 degrees for 12 minutes or until golden. Makes about 5 dozen.

WHEATIE COOKIES
Ima Hobbs

This is Minnie Cox's recipe. She received a Merit Award and blue ribbon at the Blanco County Fair for her cookies.

1 cup sugar
1 cup brown sugar
1 cup Crisco
2 eggs, well beaten
2 cups flour

¼ teaspoon salt
½ teaspoon baking powder
1 teaspoon soda
2 cups coconut
2 cups Wheaties cereal

Cream sugars and Crisco; add beaten eggs. Sift together flour, salt, baking powder and soda and add to creamed mixture. Stir in coconut and Wheaties. Roll into small balls and place on ungreased cookie sheets about two inches apart. Bake at 350 degrees until light brown. Yield: 6 dozen.

HINT:
When rolling cookie dough, sprinkle board with powdered sugar instead of flour. Too much flour makes dough heavy.

Rolled Cookies

BUTTER COOKIES   *Stella Smith*

This is my very favorite cookie. It has been handed down from my Grandma Greenhaw.

2 cups sugar	Flour, enough to make a stiff
1 cup butter	dough, about 3¹/₂ cups
2 eggs	1 teaspoon soda
1¹/₂ teaspoons vanilla	

Cream butter and sugar; add eggs and vanilla. Sift flour and soda and add to creamed mixture. Roll out to 1/2-inch thickness on a floured board. Cut with biscuit cutter and place on lightly greased cookie sheets. Bake at 375 degrees for 10 minutes. Yield: 7 dozen 2-inch cookies.

NOTE: Chill dough for easier rolling.

JESSIE ELLIOTT'S COOKIES   *Betty Wood*

These cookies are not very sweet and need the frosting. They are excellent to decorate for the holidays with food coloring added to the frosting.

6 cups flour	2 cups shortening
2 scant teaspoons soda	4 eggs
4 teaspoons baking powder	2 cups sugar
¹/₂ teaspoon nutmeg	¹/₃ cup milk

Frosting:

¹/₂ cup butter	6 tablespoons milk
4 cups powdered sugar	1 teaspoon vanilla

Sift flour, soda, baking powder and nutmeg: cut in shortening like you would for pie crust. Add eggs, sugar and milk to flour mixture. It makes a stiff dough. Chill dough about one hour. Roll out dough and cut with cookie cutter. Place on greased cookie sheets. Bake at 400 degrees for 8 to

10 minutes until brown around the edges. Yield: 8–10 dozen.

Frosting: Cream the butter; add powdered sugar, milk and vanilla and beat until smooth and creamy. Frost cooled cookies.

TEA COOKIES
Shirley Lawson

These cookies taste like my Grandma Deison's tea cakes.

1 egg	¹/₄ teaspoon salt
1¹/₂ cups sugar	¹/₂ cup shortening
¹/₂ teaspoon soda	¹/₂ cup milk
1¹/₂ teaspoons baking	1 teaspoon vanilla
powder	3¹/₂ to 4 cups flour

Beat egg; add sugar, soda, baking powder, salt, shortening, milk and vanilla. Mix well. Add flour to make a stiff dough. Roll out on floured surface, approximately 1/4-inch thick. Cut out with cookie cutters in any design you wish. Place on lightly greased cookie sheets. Bake at 350 degrees for 10 to 13 minutes. When cool decorate as you desire. Yield: 6 dozen.

Candy

ALMOND BARK
Syd Burnett

³/₄ **pound white or dark chocolate, or candy making chocolate or 12-ounce package semi-sweet chocolate morsels**
²/₃ **cup roasted almonds or pecans**

Place chocolate in 2-cup glass measure or microwave-safe bowl. Heat in microwave at 60% power for 3 to 3¹/₂ minutes or until melted. Stir in almonds. Pour immediately onto waxed paper or aluminum foil. Spread thinly. Cool for approximately one hour and then break into pieces for serving. Yield: 1 pound.

Variation: Omit nuts and dip small pretzels or Ritz peanut butter crackers in melted chocolate.

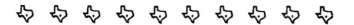

"SISTER ALICE'S BUTTERMILK CANDY" *Liz Carpenter*

2 cups sugar
1 cup buttermilk
1 teaspoon soda
1 tablespoon white corn
   syrup

¹/₄ cup butter
1 teaspoon vanilla
2 cups pecans, chopped

Mix sugar, buttermilk, soda, syrup and butter in a three-quart or larger saucepan. Cook to soft ball stage (240 degrees). Add vanilla and pecans; beat until mixture becomes opaque and starts thickening. Rapidly drop spoonsful on wax paper. Yield: about 3 dozen.

CHINESE CLUSTERS *Leslie Matus*

1 6-ounce package chocolate
   morsels, semi-sweet or
   sweet
1 6-ounce package
   butterscotch morsels

1 3-ounce can chow mein
   noodles
1 6¹/₂-ounce can cocktail
   peanuts

Place chocolate and butterscotch morsels in 1¹/₂ to 2 quart casserole. Microwave on medium, 50%, for 3 to 3¹/₂ minutes, or until melted. Stir until smooth. Stir in noodles and peanuts. Drop by teaspoons onto waxed paper. Let set until firm. Yield: 24 clusters.

DATE LOAF CANDY *Addie Paul*

This recipe has never failed, but like divinity it makes easier in brisk, cool weather.

3 cups sugar
1 cup milk
1 8-ounce box pitted dates

1 teaspoon vanilla
2 tablespoons butter
1 cup pecans

Put sugar and milk in saucepan and boil until it forms a soft ball in a bowl of cold water. Remove from heat and add dates. Place back on heat and boil until it forms a hard ball in cold water. Remove from heat, add vanilla and butter and beat until cool. Add nuts; pour onto waxed paper or wet cloth (I prefer the wet cloth). Roll and place in refrigerator until cold. Slice to desired thickness. Makes 2, 10 x 2-inch logs.

DINOSAUR FOOD

Joycelyn Carter

1/4 cup dirt (cocoa)
1/2 cup swamp water (milk)
2 cups crushed bones (sugar)
1/2 cup fat (butter)

3 cups grass (uncooked oatmeal)
1/2 cup squashed bugs (peanut butter)

Mix dirt and swamp water; add crushed bones and fat. Heat to a boil for 1 minute. Add grass and squashed bugs. Cool and place on waxed paper. Yield: 24 squares.

DIVINITY

Syd Burnett

4 cups sugar
1 cup light corn syrup
3/4 cup water
1/4 teaspoon salt

3 egg whites, beaten
1 teaspoon vanilla
1/2 cup nuts, chopped (optional)

Mix together sugar, corn syrup, water and salt in 1 1/2-quart microwave safe bowl. Cook in microwave on HIGH for 20 to 22 minutes, or until hard ball stage is reached. Stir once or twice during cooking. While syrup cooks, beat egg whites until stiff peaks form in large mixing bowl. Gradually pour hot syrup over egg whites while beating at high speed until mixture is thickened and candy starts to lose its gloss, about 12 minutes. Add vanilla and nuts to beaten mixture. Drop by teaspoons onto waxed paper. Candy may be tinted with food coloring for special occasions. Yield: 2 pounds.

EASY CHOCOLATE FUDGE CANDY

Joy Watson

This is real old-fashioned fudge.

4 cups sugar
4 tablespoons cocoa
Pinch of salt
1 cup evaporated milk (Pet)

4 tablespoons white Karo syrup
2 tablespoons margarine
2 teaspoons vanilla
2 cups pecans, chopped

Sift sugar, cocoa and salt together; stir in milk and syrup until well blended. Cook on medium heat stirring constantly. After mixture has reached rolling boil, test frequently in small bowl of cold water. Will cook quickly. When a small amount dropped in cold water forms a ball and does not separate when touched with the finger, remove from heat. Add butter and vanilla; whip until candy begins to get stiff. Add pecans and pour into buttered platter and cut into squares. Yield: 3 dozen squares.

ROCKY ROAD FUDGE   *Ola Matus*

My sister, Maxine Parrott, makes this every Christmas and all my family enjoy it.

2 6-ounce packages semi-sweet chocolate chips
1 14-ounce can sweetened condensed milk
2 tablespoons margarine
2 cups pecans, chopped
1 10½-ounce package miniature marshmallows

In heavy saucepan over low heat melt chips with Eagle Brand and margarine. In a large bowl combine pecans and marshmallows. Pour chocolate mixture into the nut mixture. Mix well. Spread into waxed paper-lined 13 x 9-inch pan. Chill 2 hours. Makes about 40 squares. Store loosely covered at room temperature.

HEAVENLY HASH   *Patsy Holloway*

½ bag Lite Wilton Chocolate Chips
½ cup pecans, roasted
½ cup small marshmallows

Melt chocolate chips in bowl in microwave for 2 minutes on HIGH. When melted, stir in pecans and marshmallows. Mix well. Drop by teaspoonfuls on waxed paper or foil. Let harden, then repeat with another half bag of chips. Yield: about 20.

CREAM CHEESE MINTS   *Dena K. Heider*

1 3-ounce package cream cheese, softened
2½ cups powdered sugar
Flavoring to taste, about ¼ teaspoon (vanilla, peppermint)
Food coloring, your choice

237

Mash cheese; mix in sugar. (If using more than one color and flavoring, separate into different bowls now). Add flavoring and color. Mix until like pie dough. Roll in small balls, then in granulated sugar. Press into mold; unmold at once. Shake sugar in mold if necessary to prevent sticking. Yield: 5 dozen.

MOCHA CLUSTERS

Lacey Lawson

1 cup semi-sweet chocolate pieces
1/3 cup butter or margarine
18 large marshmallows

1 tablespoon instant coffee granules
2 cups salted peanuts

Place chocolate pieces in 2-quart glass casserole. Microwave on MEDIUM (50%) for 1 1/2 minutes or until melted. Add butter and marshmallows. Microwave on HIGH (100%) for 1 1/2 minutes longer. Stir until smooth. Add coffee granules. Stir in peanuts. Drop by teaspoonfuls onto waxed paper. Chill until firm. Yield: 24 clusters.

PEANUT BRITTLE

Mary Dyer

I always make this at Christmas time and give to friends. It is so easy and almost always turns out well.

1 1/2 cups sugar
3/4 cup white Karo syrup
1 1/4 cups raw peanuts

3 tablespoons margarine or butter
1 teaspoon soda

Cook sugar and Karo syrup in skillet until soft ball stage. (When a ball forms when dropped in water). Add peanuts and continue cooking until color begins to change to amber. Turn off heat and stir in margarine. Stir well. Add soda and stir well until smooth. Pour on buttered cookie sheet. When cool, turn out on wax paper and break into small pieces. Yield: 1 pound.

MICRO PEANUT BRITTLE

Daisy Cox

1 cup sugar
1/2 cup white corn syrup
1 cup raw peanuts
1/8 teaspoon salt

1 tablespoon margarine
1 teaspoon vanilla
1 teaspoon baking soda

In a 1¹/₂-quart casserole, stir together the sugar, syrup, peanuts and salt, mixing well. Microwave on high for 7–9 minutes until light brown. Add margarine and vanilla and stir well. Microwave on HIGH 2 minutes more. Peanuts will be light brown and syrup will be very hot. Add baking soda and gently stir until light and foamy. Pour onto lightly-buttered cookie sheet. Let cool for an hour. When cool, break into small pieces. Yield: 3/4 pound.

PEANUT-BUTTERSCOTCH MASH   *Thelma Elm*

2 cups sugar
1¹/₂ cups miniature
  marshmallows
1 5-ounce can evaporated
  milk
1 12-ounce package butterscotch morsels
1 teaspoon vanilla

1 12-ounce package
  chocolate morsels
²/₃ cup chunky-style peanut
  butter
1 cup dry roasted peanuts,
  chopped

Combine sugar, marshmallows and milk in 1¹/₂-quart casserole. Cook on HIGH (100%) in microwave for 3 to 4 minutes, or until marshmallows are melted. Stir once or twice during cooking time. Stir in butterscotch morsels and vanilla. Stir until melted and well-blended. Spread in greased 2-quart utility dish. Cool slightly. Combine chocolate morsels and peanut butter in 1-quart glass measure or casserole. Heat on HIGH (100%) 1¹/₂ to 2¹/₂ minutes, or until melted. Stir halfway through cooking time. Blend in nuts. Spread over butterscotch layer. Cut before too hard. Yield: 20–24 candies.

Hint: For Cherry Chip Mash, use 10 to 12 ounces of cherry morsels instead of butterscotch morsels.

PEANUT PATTIE CANDY   *Cathy Woods*

3 cups sugar
1 cup white Karo syrup
1 cup water
4 cups raw peanuts

5 drops red food coloring
¹/₂ cup butter
1 teaspoon vanilla

Bring to boil sugar, syrup and water; add peanuts and food coloring. Cook

to half way between soft and hard ball stage (more toward the hard ball stage). Remove from heat and add butter and vanilla. Hand beat until thick. If too soft, put it back on the heat and bring to boil again. If too hard, add 1 teaspoon of hot water. Drop on waxed paper to form patties. Work fast, as it sets up fast. It really works best with two people making the patties, get a child to help out. Yield: 24–30 patties.

OLD FASHION WESTERN PRALINES   *Shirley Lawson*

The original recipe is torn, stained and yellow. I have made these pralines for many Christmases. All my children love these and I also send them to friends and relatives.

2 cups sugar	$^1/_8$ teaspoon salt
1 teaspoon soda	2 tablespoons butter
1 cup buttermilk, Bordens or Superiors	$2^1/_2$ cups pecan halves

Mix together sugar, soda, buttermilk and salt; cook until candy thermometer reaches 210 degrees and add butter and pecans stirring constantly. Cook until thermometer reaches 234 degrees (soft ball stage). Continue to stir. Remove from heat and let stand about 2 minutes. Beat with spoon until thick and creamy. Drop by tablespoonsful onto waxed paper. Let cool. Makes about 20 pralines.

MICROWAVE SOUTHERN PRALINES   *Cynthia Smith*

$1^1/_2$ cups light brown sugar, firmly packed	2 tablespoons butter or margarine
$^2/_3$ cup half and half	$1^1/_2$ cups pecan halves
$^1/_8$ teaspoon salt	

Combine sugar, half and half and salt in a deep 3-quart casserole; mix well. Stir in butter; microwave on HIGH (100%) for 7 to 9$^1/_2$ minutes or until mixture reaches soft ball stage, 235 degrees, stirring once. Stir in pecans. Cool 1 minute. Beat by hand until mixture is thick, about 3 minutes. Drop by teaspoonsful onto foil or waxed paper. Let harden. Store in air tight container. Yield: 16 pralines.

HILL COUNTRY TOFFEE

Ola Matus

¹/₂ pound pecans, chopped fine	¹/₄ teaspoon salt
1 cup margarine	¹/₂ teaspoon vanilla
1 cup sugar	1 6-ounce package semi-sweet chocolate chips

Place greased aluminum foil on a cookie sheet and spread with pecans, reserving 1/2 cup pecans. Combine margarine, sugar, salt and vanilla and bring to a boil. Cook over medium heat and stir frequently until mixture is brown in color and registers 290 degrees on a candy thermometer. Quickly pour over pecans and spread with spoon. Immediately sprinkle with chocolate chips and let stand 1 minute. Smooth chocolate with a spoon and then sprinkle with reserved pecans. When mixture has cooled, break into serving pieces. Yield: 1 pound.

MICROWAVE TURTLES

Mary Pat Carter

18 caramels, individually-wrapped	30 candy kisses (a 9-ounce bag contains 54)
18 pecan halves	1 tablespoon paraffin shavings
¹/₂ cup pecan pieces	

Unwrap 6 caramels and place in a circle on a buttered glass pie plate. Microwave on HIGH (100%) 30 to 40 seconds or until soft. Remove to foil-covered cookie sheet. Use 1 pecan half for turtle's head and four pieces for feet. Press into each caramel. Repeat for two other batches. Unwrap kisses and place in a 4-cup glass measure. Microwave on MEDIUM (50%) 5 minutes. Stir in paraffin shavings until they melt. Spoon chocolate over turtles. Makes 18.

Ice Cream

AMARETTO FREEZE

Agnes Stevenson

Vanilla ice cream
1¹/₂ ounces Amaretto liqueur
1¹/₂ ounces creme de cacao

Fill blender 3/4 full with ice cream and add Amaretto and creme de cacao. Blend until smooth. Serve in brandy snifters. Easy and very rich as a dessert. Serves 4.

SINFUL AND STOLEN DESSERT

Cynthia Smith

This is so good. I once saw a very refined lady turn up the bowl and lick the last drop!

1 quart Homemade Vanilla (Blue Bell) ice cream, softened
$^1/_3$ cup Amaretto

$^1/_8$ cup Triple Sec
$^1/_4$ cup creme de cacao
8 Oreo cookies, crushed

Combine ice cream, Amaretto, Triple Sec, and creme de cacao in mixer or blender. Pour into pie pan. Freeze. Serve frozen with Oreo crumbs sprinkled on top. Serves 8.

CARAMEL ICE CREAM

Leonard B. Talburt

To a rural Missouri lad, the Fourth of July was well worth the two or three weeks of impatient anticipations. Firecrackers, watermelon, ice cream and a crowded picnic ground mainly occupied the boy's mind. Caramel Ice Cream was the "Coup de Grace" that topped off the day that was nothing but sublime.

1 quart cream
1 cup milk
$^1/_2$ cup sugar

1 cup sugar (caramelized)
1 tablespoon flour
1 teaspoon vanilla

Cook all ingredients, except flavoring ten minutes. Cool, flavor and freeze. Serves: 8.

To caramelized the sugar, put it in a smooth saucepan and cook without water until a golden brown syrup is formed. Stir constantly to prevent burning.

EASY ICE CREAM

Mary Dyer

2 eggs
1/2 cup sugar
2 14-ounce cans sweetened
   condensed milk

1 teaspoon vanilla
Whole milk

Beat eggs and sugar together until fluffy; add vanilla. Add sweetened condensed milk; mix well. Add enough whole milk to fill one gallon freezer. If desired, sliced strawberries, peaches or bananas may be added when partially frozen. Makes 1 gallon.

Variation: For super rich ice cream, use 5 eggs, 2 cups sugar, 2 cans sweetened condensed milk and half and half to fill container.

DR. BILL CASTLE'S SUPER RICH HOMEMADE ICE CREAM is the same as the above super rich ice cream. Cynthia Smith writes:
   The first time I made homemade ice cream I thought, "What a nice fun family thing to do." Wrong! It was a terrible fight about when to stop the machine and when the ice cream is done. Then I poured the rock salt on the grass and killed it. But the ice cream is wonderful. Don't ask your husband to help.

TUTTI FRUITI ICE CREAM

Juanita "Teet" Hobbs

5 eggs
1 1/2 cups Imperial sugar
1 14-ounce can sweetened
   condensed milk
1 12-ounce can evaporated
   milk (Pet)
4 bananas, mashed

1 10-ounce bottle maraschino cherries, cut in fourths
1 cup pecans, chopped
1 envelope gelatin,
   dissolved in milk
Whole milk

Beat eggs until frothy; add sugar and beat very well. Add sweetened condensed milk, Pet milk and fruit and mix. Add gelatin. Pour into container and add whole milk to fill container. This is for old fashioned hand or electric freezer. Makes 1 gallon.

Sauces for Ice Cream

CHOCOLATE RUM SAUCE

Cynthia Smith

This keeps several weeks in the refrigerator and is best reheated to serve warm over ice cream.

1 6-ounce package semi-
 sweet chocolate morsels
1 tablespoon butter or
 margarine

1/2 cup light Karo syrup
1/4 cup half and half
1/4 teaspoon rum extract

Stir chocolate morsels, butter and Karo together. Microwave on HIGH for 2 1/2 minutes. Remove and stir until smooth. Blend in half and half and extract. Makes about 2 cups.

PRALINE SUNDAE SAUCE

Betty Wood

1 1/2 cups light brown sugar
2/3 cup white Karo syrup
4 tablespoons butter
1 16-ounce can Hershey's
 chocolate syrup

1 5-ounce can evaporated
 milk
1 cup pecans, chopped
Pinch of salt

Mix sugar, Karo syrup, butter and chocolate syrup in a saucepan and heat to boiling point, stirring constantly. Remove from heat and cool. When lukewarm, add milk, pecans and salt. Blend well. Store in jars in the refrigerator. Keeps a long time. Delicious over vanilla ice cream. Yield: 4 cups.

★ ★ ★ ★ ★

HINT:

Use leftover pieces of candy such as plain chocolate, mints or cream candies, to serve over ice cream or cake by melting in double boiler or microwave with a little milk. Heat until blended.

244

Nuts

MIMI'S KITCHEN'S CANDIED PEANUTS   *Wince Fincher*

1 cup sugar
¹/₂ cup water

3 cups raw peanuts

Combine sugar and water in a heavy saucepan. Cook over medium heat until sugar dissolves. Add peanuts. Cook, stirring continuously until liquid evaporates, about 15 minutes. Spread nuts on a greased baking sheet. Bake at 300 degrees for 30 minutes stirring every 10 minutes. Yields: 2 cups.

BAKED CARAMEL POPCORN   *Gwen Pickett*

1 cup butter or margarine
2 cups firmly packed brown
   sugar
¹/₂ cup white Karo syrup
1 teaspoon salt

¹/₂ teaspoon baking soda
1 teaspoon vanilla
Enough popped corn to fill
   9 x 12 pan

In a saucepan melt butter. Stir in sugar, syrup and salt and bring to a boil stirring constantly; boil without stirring for 5 minutes. Remove from heat; stir in soda and vanilla. Gradually pour over popped corn; mix well. Bake at 225 degrees for 1 hour, stirring every 15 minutes. Remove from oven. Cool. Yield: 3 quarts.

SPICED NUTS   *Joyce Ellis*

3 cups pecans
1 cup sugar
¹/₃ cup water
1 tablespoon cinnamon

¹/₂ teaspoon cloves
¹/₂ teaspoon salt
1¹/₂ teaspoons vanilla

Heat oven to 275 degrees. Grease cookie sheet. Spread nuts on prepared cookie sheet; bake 10 minutes. In medium saucepan, combine sugar, water, cinnamon, cloves and salt. Bring to boil; continue cooking for 2 minutes, stirring occasionally. Remove from heat; stir in vanilla and nuts. Using slotted spoon, remove nuts to foil or waxed paper. Separate with fork; let dry. Store in airtight container in cool dry place. Makes 4¹/₂ cups. 40 calories per tablespoon.

Heart Happy

LBJ BOYHOOD HOME

The family of Lyndon B. Johnson moved to Johnson City in 1913 and purchased the white frame "Gingerbread" house which is now known as the "Boyhood Home." It was here that Lyndon Johnson was exposed to politics at an early age through the influence of his father, Sam Ealy Johnson, Jr., who was a member of the Texas Legislature.

HELPFUL HINTS AND RECIPES
FOR "HEART HAPPY" FOODS
Heart Happy
(A happy heart is a healthy heart)

In this chapter are recipes for a variety of foods that have been tested for their nutritional values and fall within the guidelines set out by the American Heart Association and nutritionist alike.

SOUPS: Choose clear consommés and stock from vegetables and meat bones. Thoroughly chill and remove all fat before using.

Cream soups may be made with non-fat milk with the addition of flour, (2 teaspoons to 1 cup) thoroughly cooked until thick, then blended with various vegetables or vegetable purées.

MEATS: Meats should be served with all fat removed. Some methods of preparation for meat with a low fat content are roasting, pan broiling, braising, and cooking with liquids.

VEGETABLES: Wash, dry, chill until ready to cook. Cook in smallest amount of water and cook in the shortest possible time to preserve vitamins and color.

DESSERTS: All fruit desserts may be used; gelatin dishes, without any added cream, angel food cakes, sherbets and ices are okay.

Limiting the fat in your diet can start just this easily:

Choose fish, poultry without skin, lean meats, and low fat or better yet, non-fat dairy products instead of fatty meats and whole milk products as often as possible.

Try to drink and use 1/2% or even better skim milk and use in recipes whenever possible.

Reduce all kinds of fat in the diet, particularly saturated fats, such as butter, lard, bacon grease, cream shortening, and tropical oils.

Bake, broil, boil, grill, poach, or steam foods instead of frying.

Keep fat and oil to a minimum in cooking by using nonstick pans and vegetable cooking spray.

Limit cholesterol rich foods such as egg yolks and organ meats.

Increase vegetables, fruits, beans and whole grains in the diet.

The American Heart Association recommends that 30% of total calories in the diet come from fat with only 10% from saturated fat. The remaining 20% should come from monounsaturated fat and polyunsaturated fat.

HERB FILLED MUSHROOMS   *Committee*

24 large fresh mushrooms
1/2 cup white wine
2 beef flavor bouillon cubes
1/4 cup onion, finely
  chopped

2 packets Butter Buds, made
  into liquid
1/2 package herb-seasoned
  stuffing mix

Wash mushrooms, remove stems and reserve. In medium saucepan, combine wine and bouillon; heat till bouillon dissolves. Add mushroom caps, tops down; cover and simmer 2 to 3 minutes. Remove mushrooms and set aside; reserve wine mixture. Chop stems in separate pan; combine chopped mushrooms, onion, 1/2 cup of Butter Buds and 1/4 cup wine mixture. Cook over medium heat until vegetables are tender, 2 to 3 minutes. Stir in stuffing. Place 1 tablespoon stuffing on half of mushroom caps; top with remaining caps. Broil in oven 2–3 minutes, brushing occasionally with remaining 1/2 cup of liquid Butter Buds. Serves 6.

By using Butter Buds instead of butter you save 250 calories and 93 mg. of cholesterol per serving.

Nutritional Analysis: For 2 caps: 52 calories, 2 g. protein, 6 g. carbohydrates, trace fat, 515 mg. sodium.

HEART HAPPY DIP   *Committee*

1 8-ounce container plain
  yogurt
1 tablespoon dried onion
  flakes

1 tablespoon dried bell
  pepper
1 tablespoon dried parsley
1 tablespoon celery seed
1 tablespoon onion powder

Mix all ingredients and allow to stand and blend for at least 30 minutes. Serve with crispy cold vegetables. Makes 12 servings.

Nutritional Analysis per serving: 16.5 calories, 1.2 g. protein, 2.53 g. carbohydrates, 1.16 mg. cholesterol, 0.16 g. fat-unsat., .384 g. fat-total, 13.9 mg. sodium.

TANGY COTTAGE CHEESE DIP *Committee*

1 cup low-fat cottage cheese
1 packet Butter Buds
1 tablespoon Worcestershire sauce
4 teaspoons onion, minced

1 teaspoon horseradish
1 teaspoon caraway seeds
Freshly ground pepper, to taste
Dash paprika

Place cheese in blender. Cover and process at medium speed 30 seconds until smooth. Add Butter Buds, Worcestershire, onion, and horseradish; process 10 seconds until well mixed. Scrape into bowl and stir in caraway seeds and pepper. Garnish with paprika. Serve with vegetables as dippers. Yield: 1 cup. Serving: 2 tablespoons.

Nutritional Analysis: 25 calories per serving, 4 g. protein, 2 g. carbohydrates, 1.25 mg. cholesterol, trace fat, 185 mg. sodium. By not using butter you have saved 180 calories and 70 mg. cholesterol and no fat.

PARTY L0-CAL SPINACH DIP *Committee*

1 12-ounce carton 1% low-fat cottage cheese
1 10-ounce package frozen chopped spinach, thawed and drained
1/2 cup low-fat sour cream
1/4 cup dry vegetable soup mix

2 teaspoons grated fresh onion
1 teaspoon lemon juice
1 8-ounce can water chestnuts, drained and chopped

Position knife blade in food processor bowl; add cottage cheese. Process until smooth, scraping sides of processor bowl once. Place in a medium bowl, and set aside. Press spinach between paper towels until barely moist. Add spinach and remaining ingredients to cheese mixture; stir well. Cover and refrigerate 3 hours. Serve with unsalted crackers, breadsticks or raw vegetables. Yield: 3 cups.

Nutritional Analysis: Per tablespoon, 14 calories, 1.2 g. protein, 1.4 g. carbohydrates, 1.0 mg. cholesterol, 65 mg. sodium.

CHRISTMAS EGGNOG

Committee

1¹/₂ cup low fat milk
¹/₂ cup evaporated skim
   milk, undiluted
¹/₂ cup light rum or rum
   extract

4 ounces egg liquid
   substitute or amount equal
   2 eggs
2 packets Sweet'n Low
¹/₂ teaspoon vanilla
4 dashes nutmeg

Combine all ingredients except nutmeg in blender. Cover and process on low, 30 seconds, until frothy. Pour into cups and sprinkle nutmeg on top. Yield: 4 cups.

Nutritional Analysis: 158 calories per serving using extract and 187 calories using rum, 8.8 g. protein, 8.36 g. carbohydrates, 5.33 mg. cholesterol, 1.05 g. fat-unsat., 2.06 g. fat-total, 134 mg. sodium.

FRUIT SHAKE

Committee

²/₃ cup orange juice or
   pineapple juice
²/₃ cup non-fat plain yogurt
²/₃ cup strawberries

¹/₂ banana
6 ice cubes
2 packets Sweet'n Low or
   Equal

Combine all the ingredients in blender and pureé for 30 seconds until creamy and smooth. Yield: 4 servings of 3/4 cup.

Nutritional Analysis per serving: 59 calories, 2.4 g. protein, 12.5 g. carbohydrates, 0.7 mg. cholesterol, 0.1 g. fat-unsat., 0.3 g. fat-total, 27 mg. sodium.

PEACHY MILK SHAKE

Committee

¹/₂ cup vanilla ice milk
1 8-ounce can sugar-free
   peach halves

¹/₂ cup skim milk
¹/₄ cup crushed ice or 4 ice
   cubes

Combine all ingredients in blender and pureé for 30 seconds until smooth. Yield: 3 servings of 3/4 cup each.

Nutritional Analysis per serving: 78 calories, 3 g. protein, 15.6 g. carbohydrates, 4 mg. cholesterol, 0.3 g. fat-unsat., 1 g. fat-total, 41 mg. sodium.

PIÑA COLADA
Committee

³/₄ cup unsweetened
   crushed pineapple
³/₄ cup plain non-fat yogurt
¹/₂ cup crushed ice or ³/₄
   cup ice cubes

¹/₂ teaspoon coconut extract
1 packet Sweet'n Low
2 sprigs fresh mint

Combine ingredients in blender and pureé until smooth. Chill and garnish with mint. Yield: 2 servings of 1 cup.

Nutritional Analysis per serving: 93 calories, 4.5 g. protein, 19 g. carbohydrate, 2 mg. cholesterol, 0.1 g. fat-unsat., 0.2 g. total-fat, 61 mg. sodium.

COLD AVOCADO SOUP
Committee

2 10¹/₂-ounce cans chicken
   broth, chilled
2 ripe avocados, chilled

Dash lemon juice
1 ounce sherry, or to taste
Dill weed

Put chilled broth in blender. Dice avocados and add to broth with lemon juice and sherry. Blend well. Pour into cups and sprinkle with dill weed. Serve cold. Yield: 3 cups or 6 servings.

Nutritional Analysis per serving: 129 calories, 3.35 g. protein, 5.45 g. carbohydrates, .40 mg cholesterol, 8.12 g. fat-unsat., 10.8 g. fat-total, 323 mg. sodium.

CORN TOMATO SOUP
Committee

2 tablespoon oil (Canola)
¹/₄ cup onion, chopped
2 tablespoons flour
1 16-ounce can cream style
   corn

2 cups tomato juice
2 cups skim milk
Salt and pepper to taste
Parsley for garnish

In a 2 quart saucepan, heat oil over low heat and cook chopped onion until transparent. Stir in flour and cook stirring until thickened slightly. Pour mixture into blender with tomato juice and corn. Blend until smooth. Pour into 2 quart saucepan with the milk. Place over moderately low heat and cook stirring constantly. Do not allow to boil. Yield: 1¹/₂ quarts or 6 servings.

Nutritional Analysis per serving: 157 calories, 5.24 g. protein, 25.3 g. carbohydrates, 1.33 mg cholesterol, 4.03 g. fat-unsat., 5.14 g. fat-total, 757 mg. sodium.

CABBAGE SOUP

Committee

1 medium head cabbage, shredded
1 large onion, thinly sliced
1 large potato, pared and thinly sliced

3 cups skim milk
2 tablespoons margarine
Salt and pepper to taste

Place the vegetables in a heavy saucepan with a small amount of water. Cover and cook slowly until tender. Mash to a pulp; cabbage should retain some texture. Add milk, margarine, salt and pepper. Simmer 10 to 15 minutes. Serve hot. Yield: 1¹/₂ quarts or 6 servings.

Nutritional Analysis per serving: 140 calories, 6.36 g. protein, 20.6 g. carbohydrates, 2 mg. cholesterol, 3.11 g. fat-unsat., 4.28 g. fat-total, 218 mg. sodium.

MUSHROOM SOUP

Committee

1 pound fresh mushrooms, sliced
2 tablespoons oil
2 cups water
2 cups non-fat dry milk

1 tablespoon parsley flakes
1 teaspoon onion flakes
1 tablespoon flour
1 tablespoon sherry
Salt and pepper to taste

Slice caps and stems of mushrooms in thick pieces. Heat oil in heavy saucepan and sauté the mushrooms quickly until tender. Combine all other ingredients in blender and mix until thick and foamy. Add mushrooms and blend at lowest speed for 4 to 5 seconds or until mushrooms are chopped into fine pieces but not pulverized. Pour the mixture back into the saucepan and heat slowly, stirring with a wire whisk to keep from burning. Yield: 1¹/₄ quart or 5, 1 cup servings.

Nutritional Analysis per serving: 180 calories 11.6 g. protein, 20.1 g. carbohydrate, 4.8 mg. cholesterol, 4.76 g. fat-unsat., 6.06 g. fat-total, 264 mg. sodium.

SPINACH SOUP: Substitute one 10-ounce package of frozen chopped spinach for the mushrooms. Cook the spinach until it is broken up and follow recipe for Mushroom Soup.

Nutritional Analysis per serving: 172 calories, 11.5 g. protein, 18.9 g. carbohydrates, 4.8 mg. cholesterol, 4.65 fat-unsat., 5.79 g. fat-total, 310 mg. sodium.

CABBAGE APPLE SLAW   *Committee*

1 **packet Butter Buds mixed with 1/4 cup water**
¹/₂ **cup plain low-fat yogurt**
1 **tablespoon distilled white vinegar**
1 **tablespoon sugar or 1 packet Sweet'n Low**
3 **cups red cabbage, finely shredded**

1 **cup green apple, unpeeled and chopped**
1 **medium orange, peeled and chopped**
¹/₄ **cup celery, thinly chopped**
¹/₄ **cup walnuts, chopped**

In large bowl combine Butter Buds, yogurt, vinegar and sugar. Add remaining ingredients and toss to mix well. Chill. Yield: 6, 2/3 cup servings. By using butter substitute there is a savings of 125 calories and an additional 10 calories by using Sweet'n Low and 47 mg. of cholesterol saved.

Nutritional Analysis per serving: 95 calories, 3 g. protein, 14 g. carbohydrates, 3 g. fat, 150 mg. sodium.

DIJON DILL POTATO SALAD   *Committee*

¹/₂ **cup cholesterol-free reduced-calorie mayonnaise**
2 **tablespoons Dijon mustard**
2 **tablespoons fresh dill, chopped or 1¹/₂ teaspoon dried dill weed**

¹/₂ **teaspoon Tony Chachere's Creole seasoning**
1¹/₂ **pounds small new potatoes, cooked and cut-up**
¹/₂ **cup chopped red or purple onion**

253

Combine first five ingredients. Stir in onions. Cover and chill. Yield: 9, 1/2 cup servings.

Nutritional Analysis per serving: 151 calories, 2.82 g. protein, 29.5 g. carbohydrates, 3.22 mg. cholesterol, 2.20 g. fat-unsat., 2.89 g. fat-total, 117 mg. sodium.

LOW-CALORIE, NO FAT DRESSING *Committee*

1 tablespoon mixed
seasoning (Mrs. Dash)
1 cup buttermilk
1/4 cup tomato pureé
2 tablespoons ketchup

Garlic, to taste
1/4 cup wine vinegar
1/4 cup lemon juice
Fresh ground pepper to taste

Thoroughly blend all ingredients. Chill. Shake before serving. Yield: 2 cups. Use 1 tablespoon as needed.

Nutritional Analysis: 5.74 calories, .313 g. proteins, 1.11 g. carbohydrates, .281 mg. cholesterol, .025 g. fat-unsat., .074 g. fat-total, 86.1 mg. sodium.

SPANISH DRESSING *Committee*

1 teaspoon dry salad
dressing, French
1/2 teaspoon dry salad
dressing, Blue Cheese
1/4 cup fresh lemon juice

1/4 cup vinegar or wine
Few drops Tabasco sauce
Few drops Worcestershire
sauce
1 teaspoon sugar

Place all ingredients in covered bottle and shake. Minced onion and 2 tablespoons skim milk may be added for variation. Yield: 16 tablespoons. Use 1 tablespoon.

Nutritional Analysis: 7.71 calories, .067 g. protein, 1.78 g. carbohydrates, .085 mg. cholesterol, .181 g. fat-unsat., .232 g. fat-total, 27.1 mg. sodium.

ZERO DRESSING *Committee*

1/2 cup tomato juice
2 tablespoon lemon juice or
vinegar

1 tablespoon onion, finely
chopped
Salt, pepper, horseradish,
mustard may be added.

Mix all ingredients in covered bottle and shake well. Yield: 1/2 cup. Use 1 tablespoon.

Nutritional Analysis: 4.06 calories, .148 g. proteins, 1.08 g. carbohydrates, 0 mg. cholesterol, .008 g. fat-unsat., .014 g. fat-total, 71.6 mg. sodium (salt was added to recipe).

EASY HOLLANDAISE   *Cynthia Smith*

Low cholesterol — no eggs.

¹/₄ cup margarine	**2 tablespoons lemon juice**
¹/₈ teaspoon salt	**Dash cayenne pepper**
2 cartons (1 cup) Egg Scramblers	

Melt margarine in double boiler over hot but not boiling water. Add salt and Egg Scramblers stirring constantly until thickened. Gradually stir in lemon juice and continue to cook until thick. Add cayenne pepper. Serve hot. Yield: 8 servings or 1 cup.

Nutritional Analysis per serving: 151 calories, 3.53 g. protein, 1.43 g. carbohydrates, 0.5 mg. cholesterol, 11.2 g. fat-unsat., 14.7 g. fat-total, 228 mg. sodium.

MOCK SOUR CREAM   *Committee*

Use this sauce as a substitute for sour cream and it may be added to hot dishes at the last minute or serve it cold with the addition of flavorings or herbs, or as a salad dressing.

2 tablespoons skim milk	**1 tablespoon lemon juice**
1 cup low-fat cottage cheese	**¹/₄ teaspoon salt**

Place all ingredients in a blender and mix on medium high speed until smooth and creamy. Yield: 1¹/₄ cup or 5 servings.

Nutritional Analysis per serving: 36.5 calories, 5.36 g. protein, 1.83 g. carbohydrates, 3.25 mg. cholesterol, .231 g. fat-unsat., .735 g. fat-total, 244 mg. sodium.

SUPER TOMATO SAUCE

Janey Wiemers

1 12-ounce can tomato juice
1 garlic bud, crushed
$^1/_4$ cup Dry Vermouth, optional
1 teaspoon Worcestershire
   sauce

$^1/_2$ teaspoon parsley flakes
$^1/_2$ teaspoon dill weed
$^1/_2$ teaspoon marjoram
$^1/_2$ teaspoon dry mustard
$^1/_4$ teaspoon pepper

Combine ingredients in a saucepan and bring to a boil. Turn down heat and simmer 10 to 15 minutes. May be used as a spaghetti sauce, barbecue sauce, pizza base, over chicken or as a salad dressing. If used as a salad dressing add vinegar and oil. I usually double or triple the recipe. 6 servings.

Nutritional Analysis: For entire recipe. 68 calories, 16.5 g. carbohydrates, 0 mg. cholesterol, .75 g. fat-unsat., .299 g. fat-total., 1403 mg. sodium.

CASSEROLE Á LÁ TURKEY AND CABBAGE

Committee

1 pound ground turkey
1 medium onion, chopped
3 cups cabbage, finely
   shredded

$^1/_2$ cup long grain rice,
   uncooked
1 8-ounce can tomato sauce
2 packets Sweet'n Low
$1^1/_4$ cups water

Preheat oven to 350 degrees. In medium size non-stick skillet, brown turkey and onion. Drain if any fat. Transfer turkey and onion to $2^1/_2$-quart casserole and combine with remaining ingredients. Bake covered about 45 minutes. Yield: 4, $1^1/_4$ cup servings.

Nutritional Analysis per serving: 378 calories, 32.7 g. protein, 27.8 g. carbohydrates, 95.2 mg. cholesterol, 9.95 g. fat-unsat., 15.0 g. fat-total, 511 mg. sodium.

CRISPY BAKED CHICKEN

Committee

Cornflake crumbs give this skinless chicken a crisp coating. This is a great finger food; kids love it and it is great for picnics.

1 2–3 pound frying
   chicken, cut into serving
   pieces

1 cup Corn Flakes,
   crumbled
1 cup skim milk
Seasonings if desired

Preheat oven to 400 degrees. Remove all skin from chicken; rinse and dry pieces well. Season. Coat each piece with oil or in milk; shake to remove excess and roll in crumbs. Let stand briefly so coating will stick. Place chicken in an oiled baking pan. Line pan with foil for easy clean up. Do not crowd; pieces should not touch. Bake 45 minutes or more. Crumbs will form a crisp "skin." Yield: 8 servings.

Nutritional Analysis per serving: 291 calories, 42.2 g. protein, 3.92 g. carbohydrates, 127 mg. cholesterol, 6.18 g. fat-unsat., 10.5 g. fat-total, 172 mg. sodium.

HERBED TURKEY BURGERS

Committee

1 pound ground turkey
1/4 cup liquid Butter Buds
2 tablespoons chopped fresh parsley
2 tablespoons fine bread crumbs
2 teaspoons onion, finely chopped
2 teaspoons pimiento, chopped
1/4 teaspoon oregano
1/4 teaspoon garlic powder
1/4 teaspoon salt

Mix all ingredients together. Hand mold into 4 patties. Broil until done, 7–10 minutes turning once. Do not over cook. Yield: 4 servings.

Nutritional Analysis per serving: 270 calories, 30 g. protein, 2.78 g. carbohydrates, 95.4 mg. cholesterol, 9.84 g. fat-unsat., 14.9 g. fat-total, 288 mg. sodium.

TURKEY CHILI

Thelma Elm

1 pound ground turkey
1 medium onion, chopped
1/2 medium green pepper, chopped
1/4 cup celery, sliced
1 16-ounce can kidney beans, with liquid
1 15-ounce can stewed tomatoes
1 12-ounce can tomato juice
1 6-ounce can tomato paste
1 tablespoon Worcestershire sauce
1 teaspoon ground cumin or chili powder
1/2 teaspoon salt
1/4 teaspoon garlic powder

Place turkey and fresh vegetables in large skillet. Cook on medium 10 minutes, stirring and separating turkey as it cooks. Add remaining ingredients. Bring to a boil; turn down heat. Simmer 15 minutes, stirring occasionally. Yield: 6 servings.

Nutritional Analysis per serving: 310 calories, 27.4 g. protein, 27.8 g. carbohydrates, 63.5 mg. cholesterol, 7.10 g. fat-unsat., 10.7 g. fat-total, 1123 mg. sodium.

MACARONI AND CHEESE BAKE   *Committee*

1¹/₂ tablespoons margarine
¹/₄ cup flour
³/₄ teaspoon dry mustard
¹/₈ teaspoon ground red pepper
3 cups skim milk
1¹/₄ cups (5-ounces) sharp Cheddar cheese, shredded, divided

¹/₄ cup (1-ounce) Swiss cheese, shredded
¹/₂ teaspoon salt
¹/₈ teaspoon black pepper
5 cups large elbow macaroni (cooked without salt or fat)

Melt margarine in a large, heavy saucepan over low heat; add flour, mustard, and red pepper. Cook 1 minute, stirring constantly with a wire whisk. Gradually add milk; stir well. Cook over medium heat 10 minutes or until thickened and bubbly, stirring constantly; remove from heat. Add 3/4 cup Cheddar cheese and next 3 ingredients, stirring until cheese melts. Stir in macaroni; spoon into a 2-quart casserole. Sprinkle with remaining Cheddar cheese. Cover and bake at 350 degrees for 30 minutes. Let stand, covered, 10 minutes before serving. Yield: 12 servings of 1/2 cup.

Nutritional Analysis per serving: 166 calories, 8 g. protein, 18.8 g. carbohydrates, 16 mg. cholesterol, 6.4 g. fat, 226 mg. sodium.

TURKEY MEATLOAF   *Cynthia Smith*

1 pound ground turkey
¹/₄ to ¹/₂ cup skim milk
¹/₄ cup Egg Scramblers
¹/₂ cup onion, chopped
¹/₄ cup green pepper, chopped

¹/₄ cup bread crumbs
³/₄ teaspoon salt
¹/₂ teaspoon black pepper
¹/₂ teaspoon garlic powder
1 8-ounce can tomato sauce
1 slice bacon (optional)

Combine all ingredients except tomato sauce and bacon. Mold into a loaf. Place in a loaf pan that has been sprayed with non-stick vegetable spray. Pour tomato sauce over loaf and place the slice of bacon on top. Bake in a 350 degree oven for 45 minutes or until done. Yield: 4 servings.

Nutritional Analysis per serving: 440 calories, 36.4 g. protein, 27.7 g. carbohydrates, 97.7 mg. cholesterol, 13.5 g. fat-unsat., 20.2 g. fat-total, 1278 mg. sodium.

TURKEY SPAGHETTI PIZZA   *Cynthia Smith*

1 7-ounce package
   spaghetti, uncooked
1/2 cup skim milk
2 ounces egg substitute
Vegetable cooking spray
1/2 pound ground turkey
1 medium onion, chopped
1 medium green pepper,
   chopped
2 cloves garlic, minced

1 15-ounce can tomato sauce
   or no-salt-added tomato
   sauce
1 teaspoon Italian seasoning
1 teaspoon any salt-free
   herb seasoning
1/4 teaspoon pepper
2 cups fresh mushrooms,
   sliced
2 cups shredded part-skim
   mozzarella cheese

Prepare spaghetti as package directs; drain. In medium bowl, blend milk and egg substitute; add spaghetti and toss to coat. Spray 15 x 10-inch jelly roll pan with vegetable cooking spray. Spread spaghetti mixture evenly in prepared pan. In large skillet, cook turkey, onion, green pepper and garlic until turkey is no longer pink; drain. Add tomato sauce and seasonings; simmer 5 minutes. Spoon meat mixture evenly over spaghetti. Top with mushrooms and cheese. Bake in 350 degree oven for 20 minutes. Let stand 5 minutes before cutting. Refrigerate leftovers. Yield: 8 servings.

Nutritional Analysis per serving: 267 calories, 20 g. protein, 25.3 g. carbohydrates, 76.4 mg. cholesterol, 9.2 g. fat, 499 mg. sodium.

SKILLET SUPPER   *Committee*

1 cup elbow macaroni
1 pound lean beef or ground
   turkey
1 cup onions, diced
1 clove garlic, crushed
2 tablespoons oil
1 8-ounce can tomato sauce
1 teaspoon salt

1/4 teaspoon black pepper
1 cup ketchup
1 8-ounce can pieces and
   stems mushrooms, drained
2 tablespoons Worcestershire
   sauce
1/2 teaspoon Italian seasonings

Cook macaroni in boiling water according to package directions. Drain

259

and set aside. Sauté the meat, onion, and garlic in the oil until the meat loses its pink color and the onions are tender. Add salt, pepper, tomato sauce, ketchup, mushrooms, Worcestershire sauce and Italian seasoning. Bring mixture to a gentle boil, and then simmer for 5 minutes. Mix in the cooked macaroni and simmer for 5 more minutes. Yield: 8 servings.

Nutritional Analysis per serving: Beef: 265 calories, 16.8 g. protein, 18.1 g. carbohydrates, 49.3 mg. cholesterol, 7.96 g. fat-unsat., 14.4 g. fat-total, 1215 mg. sodium. Turkey: 240 calories, 17.5 g. protein, 18.1 g. carbohydrates, 47.6 mg. cholesterol, 7.83 g. fat-unsat., 11.1 g. fat-total, 1237 mg. sodium.

TURKEY STUFFED PEPPERS   *Committee*

2 medium-size green
  peppers
$1/2$ pound freshly ground
  raw turkey
$3/4$ cup onion, chopped
1 clove garlic, minced
Vegetable cooking spray
2 teaspoons reduced calorie
  margarine

1 tablespoon flour
$1/2$ cup skim milk
$1/2$ cup unpeeled tomato,
  chopped
$1/8$ teaspoon salt
$1/8$ teaspoon pepper
1 cup hot cooked long-grain
  rice

Cut tops off peppers. Discard seeds and membranes. Cook peppers in boiling water to cover 4 minutes; drain and set aside. Combine turkey, onion, and garlic in a large skillet coated with vegetable cooking spray; cook mixture over medium heat until browned, stirring to crumble. Drain and pat dry with paper towels; set aside. Melt margarine in a small, heavy saucepan over medium heat; add flour. Cook 1 minute, stirring constantly with wire whisk. Gradually add skim milk, stirring constantly. Cook mixture an additional $2^1/2$ minutes or until thickened and bubbly, stirring constantly. Combine turkey mixture, white sauce, tomato, salt, and pepper in a bowl; stir well. Spoon mixture into peppers. Place peppers in an $8^1/2$ x $4^1/2$ x 3-inch loaf dish, and bake at 350 degrees for 15 minutes. Serve over rice. Yield: 2 servings.

Nutritional Analysis per serving: 471 calories, 35.8 g. protein, 38 g. carbohydrates, 96.2 mg. cholesterol, 13.0 g. fat-unsat., 19.3 g. fat-total, 359 mg. sodium.

MARINATED GREEN BEANS

Genevia Bushnell

1 16-ounce can whole green
  beans, drained
1/2 cup liquid from beans
1/4 cup onions, chopped
1/2 teaspoon salt

1/2 cup wine vinegar
1/4 cup brown sugar
2 tablespoons Lo-Cal Italian
  dressing

Drain green beans, reserving 1/2 cup liquid. Combine bean liquid with remaining ingredients and bring to boil. Pour over beans and marinate in refrigerator overnight. Serve cold. Serves 4. Serve on a tray with assorted pickles, olives, cheeses and cold meats. Substitute cooked tender crisp carrot sticks for beans. This salad will keep for several days.

Nutritional Analysis per serving: 87.8 calories, 1.42 g. protein, 21.2 g. carbohydrates, .437 mg. cholesterol, .317 g. fat-unsat., .455 fat-total, 616 mg. sodium.

BAKED CARROT SQUARES

Committee

Vegetable cooking spray
1 cup sifted flour
1 teaspoon baking powder
1/4 teaspoon cinnamon
1/8 teaspoon nutmeg
1/8 teaspoon salt
6 packets Sweet'n Low

1/2 teaspoon soda
1 packet Butter Buds made
  into liquid
2 ounces egg substitute
1 cup carrots, grated
1 cup raisins

Preheat oven to 350 degrees. Spray 8-inch square pan with vegetable cooking spray. In medium bowl combine flour, baking powder, cinnamon, nutmeg, salt and Sweet'n Low. In separate bowl dissolve soda in Butter Buds; add to dry ingredients. Stir in egg substitute. Add carrots and raisins and mix well. Pour into prepared pan. Bake 30 minutes or until toothpick inserted in center comes out clean. Cool and cut into 2-inch squares. Yield: 16 servings.

Nutritional Analysis per serving: 60 calories, 1 g. protein, 14 g. carbohydrates, trace fat, 80 mg. sodium.

TWICE BAKED POTATOES Á LÁ COTTAGE CHEESE   *Committee*

4 medium potatoes, baked
1 cup low-fat cottage cheese
½ cup low fat milk
1 tablespoon onion, minced

Pepper, freshly ground
Dried parsley flakes
Paprika

Cut hot potatoes in half lengthwise; scoop out leaving skins intact for re-stuffing. Beat potatoes with cottage cheese, milk and onion. Spoon mixture into shells. Sprinkle with pepper, paprika and parsley flakes. Bake at 375 degrees for 10 minutes or until golden. Yield: 8 servings.

Nutritional Analysis per serving: 105 calories, 5.94 g. protein, 18.6 g. carbohydrates, 3 mg. cholesterol, .267 g. fat-unsat., .793 g. fat-total, 126 mg. sodium.

SCALLOPED POTATOES

Committee

4 cups raw potatoes, peeled
   and sliced thinly
1 onion, peeled and sliced
   thinly
1 tablespoon chopped parsley

3 tablespoons flour
1 tablespoon curry powder
Black pepper, freshly ground
3 tablespoons margarine
1½ cups skim milk

In a lightly oiled casserole, place a layer of potatoes. Sprinkle with flour and curry powder, then place a layer of onions. Sprinkling each layer with flour and curry powder, alternate potatoes and onions until all are used. Season with pepper. Heat milk and margarine together and pour over potatoes. Cover casserole and bake at 350 degrees for 1 hour, then remove cover and bake another half hour to brown. Yield: 6 servings.

Nutritional Analysis per serving: 180 calories, 4.5 g. protein, 1 mg. cholesterol, 6 g. fat-total, 103 mg. sodium.

SPINACH LASAGNA

Genevia Bushnell

One of my sons called the tofu in the recipe "fake food" but after eating this lasagna, he stopped by the next day to see if he could have another serving.

1 medium onion, chopped
2 garlic cloves, minced
1 tablespoon of olive oil
2 to 3 tablespoons of water
1 pound part-skim Ricotta cheese
1 pound tofu, drained and crumbled, (optional)
1/4 cup Parmesan cheese, grated
1 1/2 pounds fresh spinach, chopped and packed OR
   1 package frozen chopped, thawed and drained
2 egg whites, beaten
1/4 teaspoon black pepper, freshly ground
2 to 3 tablespoons fresh parsley, chopped
1/2 pound lasagna noodles, preferably whole wheat
Non stick vegetable cooking spray
6-ounces of Mozzarella part-skim cheese, grated
6 cups tomato sauce

Sauté the onion and garlic in the olive oil, adding water as needed to keep from sticking. Combine the Ricotta, tofu (if used), Parmesan, spinach, egg whites, pepper, parsley, onions and garlic, mixing well. Cook the lasagna noodles according to package directions. Spray a 13 x 9 x 2-inch casserole with cooking spray. Arrange a layer of cooked noodles on the bottom; top with 1/3 of the Ricotta mixture; sprinkle with Mozzarella, and spread with tomato sauce. Repeat layers twice more, ending with sauce. Cover pan with aluminum foil, crimping edges tightly. Bake at 350 degrees for 40 minutes; remove foil and bake 10–15 minutes more. Yield: 12 servings.

Nutritional Analysis per serving: 215 calories, 21 mg. cholesterol, 8 g. fat, 918 mg. sodium.

ZUCCHINI CASSEROLE WITH CHEESE *Committee*

2 pounds medium zucchini
   squash, sliced
1/2 cup onion, chopped
2 fresh tomatoes, sliced
2 tablespoons oil

1 16-ounce carton low-fat
   cottage cheese
1 teaspoon basil
1/2 teaspoon oregano
1/3 cup Parmesan cheese

Sauté zucchini and onion in oil. Whip cottage cheese with basil and oregano in blender. Place alternating layers of zucchini, cottage cheese and to-

mato in 1¹/₂ quart casserole dish. Top with Parmesan cheese. Bake at 350 degrees uncovered for 25 to 30 minutes. Yield: 6 servings.

Nutritional Analysis per serving: 173 calories, 14.6 g. protein, 12.4 g. carbohydrates, 4.89 g. fat-unsat., 7.80 fat-total, 397 mg. sodium.

GARLIC BAGEL THINS   *Committee*

2 (3¹/₂-ounce) plain bagels
2 tablespoons reduced-calorie margarine, melted
¹/₂ teaspoon garlic powder

Cut each bagel in half vertically using an electric knife, if possible. Place 1 bagel half, cut side down on flat surface; cut vertically into 8 slices. Repeat procedure with remaining bagel halves. Place slices on baking sheet. Combine margarine and garlic powder; brush over bagels. Bake at 325 degrees for 20 minutes until crisp and golden. Remove from pan; cool completely on wire rack. Yield: 32 crackers.

Nutritional Analysis per serving: 22 calories, 0.7 g. protein, 3.5 g. carbohydrates, 0.6 g. fat, 0 mg. cholesterol, 29 mg. sodium.

CARROT ORANGE BRAN BREAD   *Thelma Elm*

1 cup skim milk
2 cups Post Raisin Bran
1³/₄ cups all-purpose flour
¹/₂ cup sugar
1 tablespoon baking powder
¹/₂ teaspoon salt
1 tablespoon orange rind, grated
2 egg whites, slightly beaten
¹/₄ cup vegetable oil
1 cup carrots, coarsely grated

Pour milk over cereal in a large bowl; set aside. Mix flour with sugar, baking powder and salt; add orange rind. Mix in egg whites and oil to softened cereal. Add to flour mixture and mix just enough to moisten flour. Fold in carrots. Pour into greased 9 x 5-inch loaf pan. Bake at 350 degrees for 65 minutes. Cool in pan 10 minutes. Remove from pan and cool on rack. For easier slicing, wrap bread and store overnight before slicing. Yield: 12 portions or 12 slices.

Nutritional Analysis per serving: 180 calories, 4 g. protein, 32 g. carbohydrate, 0 mg. cholesterol, 5 g. fat, 210 mg. sodium, 2 g. dietary fiber.

JALAPEÑO CORN BISCUITS   *Cynthia Smith*

Non-stick cooking spray
$1/2$ cup plus 2 tablespoons unbleached flour
$1/2$ cup plus 2 tablespoons cornmeal
2 teaspoons baking powder
$1/4$ teaspoon salt
$1^1/2$ tablespoons chilled margarine, cut into
   10 small pieces
$1/4$ cup skim milk
$1/4$ cup plain, low-fat yogurt
$1/2$ teaspoon chopped jalapeño or fresh cayenne pepper
$1/4$ cup grated part-skim Mozzarella cheese

Preheat oven to 425 degrees. Lightly coat a baking sheet with non-stick cooking spray. In a food processor combine the flour, cornmeal, baking powder and salt, then add the chunks of margarine, and pulse the machine 5 to 6 times until the mixture is coarse and crumbly. Or combine these dry ingredients in a bowl, and cut in the margarine with a pastry cutter or two forks. Add the skim milk, yogurt, pepper and cheese, and stir until the batter is moistened and pulls away from the sides of the bowl. Transfer the batter to a lightly floured board, and knead the dough 5 to 6 times. Roll the dough out $1/4$-inch thick. Using a $1^1/2$-inch diameter cookie cutter, cut the dough into 12 biscuits. You will have to reshape and reroll the scraps of dough a few times to utilize all the dough. Place the biscuits on the prepared pan, and bake for 10 to 12 minutes, or until the biscuits are lightly browned. Yield: 12 biscuits or 12 servings.

Nutritional Analysis per serving: 71 calories, 2.3 g. protein, 10.5 g. carbohydrates, 1.4 mg. cholesterol, 1.4 g. fat-unsat., 2.5 g. fat-total, 90 mg. sodium.

RAISIN CINNAMON BISCUITS   *Committee*

1 cup flour, sifted
1 cup whole wheat flour
1 tablespoon baking powder
1 teaspoon cinnamon
3 packets Sweet'n Low

$1/4$ teaspoon salt
$1/4$ cup margarine
$1/2$ cup raisins
$3/4$ cup low fat milk

Preheat oven to 425 degrees. In medium bowl, sift together dry ingredi-

ents. With pastry blender, cut in margarine until mixture looks like oatmeal. Add raisins and stir to mix. Make a hole or well in center of the
flour mixture. Pour in milk. Stir quickly with spatula until dough is just
moist enough to leave sides of bowl and form a ball. Knead dough lightly
10 to 15 times; then roll or pat out on floured surface to $1/2$-inch thickness.
Cut into circles with biscuit cutter. Fit close together on non-stick baking
sheet. Bake 10–15 minutes or until golden. Cool on racks. Makes 12 biscuits.

Nutritional Analysis per serving: 106 calories, 3 g. protein, 18 g. carbohydrates, 3 g. fat, 152 mg. sodium.

BASIC MUFFINS   *Rita Reiner*

$2^1/4$ cups oat bran cereal
$1/4$ cup nuts, chopped
$1/4$ cup raisins or dates
1 tablespoon baking powder
$1/4$ cup brown sugar or
    honey

$1^1/4$ cups skim milk
2 egg whites or egg
    substitute
2 tablespoons vegetable oil

Preheat oven to 375 degrees. In a large bowl, combine the cereal, nuts,
raisins, and baking powder. Stir in brown sugar or honey. Mix the milk,
egg whites and oil together and blend in with the cereal mixture. Line
muffin pans with paper baking cups and fill with batter. Bake 15 to 20
minutes. Test with toothpick. It should come out moist but not wet.
Makes 12 muffins. Store in a plastic bag to retain moisture. Keep the muffins in the refrigerator if they will not be consumed within 3 days.

Nutritional Analysis: 117 calories, 4.11 g. protein, 15.7 g. carbohydrates,
.541 mg. cholesterol, 3.69 g. fat-unsat., 4.48 g. fat-total, 206 mg. sodium.

EGGLESS CORNBREAD MUFFINS   *Committee*

1 cup flour, sifted
$3/4$ cup yellow cornmeal
$1/2$ teaspoon salt
$2^1/2$ teaspoons baking
    powder

2 tablespoons sugar
Egg beater to equal 1 egg
1 cup skim milk
$1/4$ cup oil

Preheat oven to 425 degrees. Sift together the flour, cornmeal salt, baking powder and sugar. Add the Egg Beater, milk and oil stirring quickly and lightly until mixed. Do not beat. From the bowl, dip the batter into oiled $2^1/_4$-inch muffin tins or 8 x 8-inch pan or corn-stick pans. Fill each cup 2/3 full. Bake 20–30 minutes until golden brown. Makes 12 muffins.

Nutritional Analysis: 131 calories, 2.94 g. protein, 17.5 g. carbohydrates, .416 mg. cholesterol, 4.24 g fat-unsat., 5.33 fat-total, 186 mg. sodium.

BUTTERMILK PANCAKES   *Rita Reiner*
(Low cholesterol — not low fat)

6 egg whites or egg
   substitute to equal 3 eggs
3 cups 1% buttermilk or
   nonfat milk mixed with
   Saco buttermilk mix
6 tablespoons vegetable oil

1 cup self-rising flour
2 cups oat-bran cereal
1 tablespoon baking powder
3 tablespoons sugar
Pam

Mix all ingredients together. Bake on griddle sprayed with Pam. Serve with fresh fruit that has been put through the blender. This recipe will make a lot of pancakes. Makes 20–24. May be stored in freezer then just put in microwave.

Nutritional Analysis: For 2, $3^1/_2''$ pancakes, 207 calories, 7.44 g. protein, 24.1 g. carbohydrates, 2.7 mg. cholesterol, 6.94 g. fat-unsat., 9.08 g. fat-total, 438 mg. sodium.

HOMEMADE ANGEL FOOD CAKE   *Joycelyn Carter*

Low in calories and fat free!

$1^1/_2$ cups egg whites (10 to
   12 large eggs)
$1^1/_2$ cups sifted powdered
   sugar
1 cup sifted cake flour or
   sifted all-purpose flour

$1^1/_2$ teaspoons cream of
   tartar
1 teaspoon vanilla
1 cup sugar

Bring the egg whites to room temperature. Preheat the oven to 350 degrees. Sift powdered sugar and flour together 3 times. In a 3-quart mixer bowl beat egg whites, cream of tartar and vanilla with an electric mixer on medium speed until soft peaks form (tips curl). Gradually add sugar, about 2 tablespoons at a time, beating on high speed until stiff peaks form (tips stand straight). Sift about one-fourth of the flour mixture over the beaten egg whites. Lightly and gently fold the flour mixture into the beaten egg whites. Repeat the sifting over and folding in of the remaining flour mixture by fourths. Pour the batter into an ungreased 10-inch tube pan. Use a metal spatula or knife to cut through the batter and release any large air pockets. Place cake on the lowest rack of the preheated oven. Bake for 40 to 45 minutes or until the top springs back when lightly touched. The crust of the cake will be golden and slightly cracked. Immediately invert cake in the pan, standing the tube pan on its legs or resting the center tube over a tall-necked bottle. Cool the cake thoroughly. Loosen the sides of the cake from the pan; remove the cake. To serve, use a serrated knife to slice the cake into wedges. Makes 12 servings.

Nutritional Analysis: Each wedge 159 calories, 3 g. protein, 37 g. carbohydrates, 0 g. fat, 0 mg. cholesterol, 42 mg. sodium.

APPLESAUCE CAKE
Committee

Non-stick vegetable spray
3 tablespoons margarine, softened
1/3 cup molasses
1/4 cup brown sugar
1 egg
1 cup sugar-free applesauce
1/2 cup low-fat or non-fat buttermilk
1 1/2 teaspoons cinnamon
1/4 teaspoon salt
1 teaspoon baking powder
1 teaspoon baking soda
1/3 cup raisins
1 3/4 cups unbleached flour, sifted
1/4 teaspoon nutmeg
1/4 teaspoon cloves

Preheat oven to 375 degrees. Coat an 8-inch square baking pan with non-stick vegetable spray. In a bowl, combine the margarine with the molasses, brown sugar and egg. Mix until smooth. Stir in the applesauce and buttermilk. In another bowl, combine the remaining ingredients. Add the wet ingredients to the dry ingredients, stirring until the dry ingredients are well moistened. Pour the batter in the prepared pan. Bake for 35 minutes, or until a toothpick comes out clean. Yield: 12 servings.

Nutritional Analysis per serving: 141 calories, 3 g. protein, 24.7 g. carbohydrates, 17.5 mg. cholesterol, 2.5 g. fat-unsat., 3.5 g. fat-total, 185 mg. sodium.

LIGHT CARROT CAKE

Committee

With cream cheese frosting . . .

1³/₄ cups flour	2 eggs
²/₃ cup whole wheat flour	3 cups carrot, coarsely
2 teaspoons baking soda	shredded
1 teaspoon ground	¹/₂ cup raisins
cinnamon	²/₃ cup nonfat buttermilk
³/₄ teaspoon ground allspice	1 8-ounce can crushed
¹/₄ teaspoon ground nutmeg	pineapple in juice,
¹/₈ teaspoon salt	drained
³/₄ cup brown sugar, firmly	2 teaspoons vanilla extract
packed	Vegetable cooking spray
3 tablespoons vegetable oil	

Frosting:

¹/₂ cup sugar	¹/₂ teaspoon grated orange
2 tablespoons water	rind
1 egg white	¹/₂ teaspoon vanilla extract
1 8-ounce package Neufchâ-	
tel cheese, softened	

Combine first 7 ingredients in a bowl; stir well and set aside. Combine sugar and oil; stir well. Add eggs, one at at time, beating well with a wire whisk after each addition. Stir in carrot and next 4 ingredients. Add flour mixture; stir well. Spoon batter into a 13 x 9 x 2-inch baking pan coated with cooking spray; bake at 350 degrees for 35 minutes or until a wooden pick inserted in center comes out clean. Cool completely in pan on a wire rack. Spread frosting over top of cake. Yield: 18 servings, 3 x 2-inch pieces.

Frosting: Combine sugar and water in a small saucepan; stir well. Bring to a boil; cover and cook over medium heat 3 minutes. Remove from heat and set aside. Beat egg white at high speed of an electric mixer until soft peaks form; continue to beat while slowly adding hot syrup mixture in a thin stream to egg white. Beat until mixture is thick and glossy (about 4 minutes). Combine cheese, orange rind and vanilla in a large bowl; beat at high speed until light and fluffy (about 5 minutes). Add one-third of egg white mixture; beat at low speed just until blended. Fold in remaining egg white mixture. Yield: 1³/₄ cups.

Nutritional Analysis: Each square 262 calories, 6.0 g. protein, 41.2 g. carbohydrates, 41 mg. cholesterol, 8.2 g. fat, 234 mg. sodium.

KEY LIME PIE

3/4 cup graham cracker
crumbs
2 to 3 tablespoons water
1 package sugar-free vanilla
pudding mix (not instant)
7 tablespoons lime or key
lime juice

1 1/2 teaspoons grated lime
peel
1 1/2 cups skim milk
3 egg whites
1/4 teaspoon cream of tartar
1 1/2 tablespoons sugar
Non-stick cooking spray

Combine graham cracker crumbs and water until crumbly. Press the crumbs against the bottom and sides of an 8-inch pie plate that has been sprayed with non-stick cooking spray. Bake for 10 minutes at 350 degrees. Remove from oven and cool. In a saucepan combine the pudding mix, lime juice, and lime peel; gradually whisk in the milk, and cook over medium heat, stirring, until the mixture comes to a boil and thickens. Pour the thickened pudding into the baked pie shell. Beat egg whites with an electric beater until soft peaks form, then add the cream of tartar and sugar, and continue beating until the whites are stiff. Carefully spread the whites over the pie, and bake for 10 minutes, until lightly browned. Cool, then refrigerate until served. Yield: 8 servings.

Nutritional Analysis per serving: 93 calories, 3.7 g. protein, 17 g. carbohydrates, 0.8 fat-unsat., 1.3 g. fat-total, 0.8 mg. cholesterol, 182 mg. sodium.

CHOCOLATE BROWNIES

2 1/2 tablespoons margarine,
softened
1/3 cup sugar
1/4 cup unsweetened cocoa
powder

1 egg
1/2 cup less 1 tablespoon
sifted, unbleached flour
1 1/2 tablespoons chopped
walnuts

Preheat oven to 350 degrees. Lightly coat a 3 1/2 x 7 1/2 loaf pan with non-stick cooking spray. With an electric mixer, cream the margarine and sugar in a 1-quart bowl. Stir in the cocoa powder, then add the egg and blend on low for 30 seconds; scrape sides, and continue blending for 30 seconds more. Sift in the flour, and stir until well incorporated. Stir in nuts. Spread the batter evenly into the prepared pan. Bake for 18 minutes, or until a cake tester comes out slightly moist. Cool, then cut into 10 squares. Yield: 10 servings.

Nutritional Analysis: 91 calories, 1.9 g. protein, 12 g. carbohydrates, 3.2 g. fat-unsat., 4.5 g. fat-total, 20.8 mg. cholesterol, 40.8 mg. sodium.

BUTTERSCOTCH BROWNIES

Committee

3 tablespoons margarine, softened
1/4 cup brown sugar
1 egg
1 teaspoon vanilla
1/3 cup plus 2 tablespoons sifted, unbleached flour
Non-stick cooking spray

Cream margarine and brown sugar with an electric mixer. Mix in egg and vanilla. Stir in the flour until combined. Spread the batter in a 3½ x 7½-inch baking pan sprayed with non-stick cooking spray. Bake at 350 degrees for 15 minutes. Cool and cut into 10 squares. Yield: 10 servings.

Nutritional Analysis per serving: 78 calories, 1.3 g. protein, 9.6 g. carbohydrates, 21 mg. cholesterol, 2.9 g. fat-unsat., 3.8 g. fat-total, 49 mg. sodium.

APRICOT JAM

Committee

1 16-ounce can calorie reduced apricot halves
1 teaspoon unflavored gelatin
2 tablespoons sugar

Drain apricots, reserving juice. Measure fruit; add enough juice to make 1 cup. Pureé in blender. Measure 1 tablespoon of remaining juice into a saucepan; add gelatin. Let stand 5 minutes. Add pureéd apricots and sugar to gelatin. Heat to boiling over medium heat, stirring constantly. Pour into jar; cover. Store in refrigerator. 21 calories per tablespoon. Makes about 2 cups.

Sugar-free Apricot Jam: Omit sugar. After heating, stir in sugar substitute to equal 1/4 cup sugar. 16 calories per tablespoon.

FRESH BLUEBERRY JAM

Committee

2 tablespoons lemon juice
2 tablespoons water
1 envelope unflavored gelatin
1½ teaspoons arrowroot
2 cups blueberries, washed
9 tablespoons sugar

Combine lemon juice, water, gelatin and arrowroot in a sauce pan. Heat, stirring constantly, until gelatin and arrowroot dissolve. Add blueberries and sugar to gelatin mixture. Heat to boiling over medium heat stirring constantly. Boil 3 minutes. Pour into jars; cover. Store in refrigerator. Makes 1³/₄ cups at 18 calories per tablespoon. For frozen berries use 2¹/₂ cups.

Sugar-free Jam: Omit sugar. After heating, stir in sugar substitute to equal 1 cup sugar. 6 calories per tablespoon.

FRESH STRAWBERRY JAM   *Committee*

Use recipe above but substitute washed, hulled and sliced strawberries for blueberries.

* * * * *

HINT:
Chill soup and remove all fat before using.

* * * * *

HINT:
Cream soups may be made with non-fat milk; with the addition of flour (2 teaspoons to 1 cup) thoroughly cooked until thick, then blended with various vegetables or vegetable purees.

* * * * *

HINT:
Bake, broil, boil, grill, poach or steam foods instead of frying.

* * * * *

HINT:
Drink and use 1/2% milk or even better, skim milk in recipes whenever possible.

* * * * *

HINT:
Choose fish, poultry without skin, lean meats and non-fat dairy products instead of fatty meats and whole milk products.

Ranch Road 1

THE LBJ RANCH HOUSE

In 1951, then Senator Johnson bought this rambling white house and land, located along what was later known as "Ranch Road 1," from his Aunt Frank and Uncle Clarence Martin. Throughout the fifties and sixties, many improvements and additions were made. During the Presidential years, it became known as "The Texas White House." Many festive barbecues were hosted under the huge oaks along the Pedernales River.

One of my favorite times of the year in the Hill Country is Spring, slipping into early summer, while it's still pleasantly cool outside. Guests frequently arrive mid-afternoon and are greeted with tall glasses of iced spiced tea with sprigs of mint from our garden, and plates of sand tarts and lace cookies. The tea, served under the large live oak trees, is delicious (or equally good served hot in our best cups on a chilly winter afternoon in front of the fireplace).

Toward sunset we gather for a casual dinner in the front yard. The buffet tables are covered with patch-work quilts, topped by center-pieces of wildflowers gathered nearby. There may be bluebonnets, gaillardia, coreopsis — whatever the season provides — mixed with white daisies from the garden.

On the serving tables homemade jams, jellies and relishes surround a "country spread" of fried chicken, ham, black-eyed peas, pickled okra, garden vegetable salad, and scalloped potatoes. The vegetables vary according to what our garden produces; sometimes we serve stuffed squash, green beans or fried eggplant. I love to express the regional character, the flavor of this area whenever I can. We pass baskets of hot biscuits after guests are seated, and as is the custom, are invited to select for themselves.

Nowhere are the "fruits of the land" presented more vividly and deliciously than on the dessert table. The Pedernales valley is home to many pecan trees, as well as marvelous peach groves. So pecan pie and a piping hot peach cobbler, topped with a generous scoop of ice cream, are mainstays. Last, but not least, there is usually a good old-fashioned buttermilk pie — reflecting pioneer frugality and which is still a favorite down through these many years.

Lady Bird Johnson

"The Red Book" is the official cookbook at the LBJ Ranch.

GRANOLA   *"The Red Book"*

Luci really likes this snack.

¹/₂ cup vegetable oil
4 cups rolled oats
1 cup sliced almonds
2 cups whole wheat flakes

¹/₂ cup sesame seeds
³/₄ cup honey
1 teaspoon vanilla

Heat oil in a heavy skillet. Place oats and almonds in the skillet and stir constantly over medium heat for 5 minutes to roast a little. Add whole wheat flakes and sesame seeds. The sesame seeds are a must in this recipe. Keep stirring and heating for about 10 minutes or more. Add honey and vanilla and stir for 2 to 3 minutes or more. Store in air tight container. Do not make more than 3 or 4 days ahead as it does not keep well. Makes 8 cups. 230 calories per cup.

CURRY DIP   *"The Red Book"*

1 pint mayonnaise, not salad dressing
1 tablespoon Worcestershire sauce

3 tablespoons chili sauce, Heinz
2 teaspoons curry powder
¹/₂ teaspoon garlic salt
¹/₂ teaspoon pepper

Mix all ingredients. Serve with a raw vegetable platter of celery, carrots, cauliflower, yellow squash, turnips, mushrooms or tiny tomatoes. Lady Bird likes curry. Makes 2 cups.

PICADILLO MEAT DIP   *"The Red Book"*

1 pound ground meat, lean
1 whole onion, chopped
1 cup tomatoes fresh or canned, chopped
2 garlic cloves, pressed
1 tablespoon vinegar
¹/₄ teaspoon ground cumin
1 teaspoon salt

1 bay leaf
¹/₂ teaspoon oregano or 1 teaspoon cinnamon and a pinch of cloves
2 whole jalapeños, chopped
¹/₂ cup raisins
¹/₂ cup almonds, slivered

Place meat in frying pan and when it begins to release the fat, add both

275

the onion and garlic. When the meat has browned, add all but the raisins and almonds and simmer for 30 minutes. Next add raisins and almonds, simmer these for 5 to 10 minutes. This can be used as a taco filling or it is good as an accompaniment to scrambled eggs. If it is used as a dip you would thin it with tomato juice. This may be frozen. Serves 6–8.

CHEESE WAFERS
Lady Bird Johnson

1 cup margarine or butter	1 teaspoon cayenne pepper
2 cups flour	1/2 teaspoon salt
8-ounces sharp cheddar cheese, grated	2 cups Rice Krispies

Cut butter into flour; add cheese and seasonings; fold in cereal. Drop by small rounds on ungreased cookie sheet and flatten with spoon. Bake at 350 degrees for about 15 minutes; do not let them get too brown. Makes 6 dozen.

TEXAS TRASH
"The Red Book"

One of Lady Bird's favorites. Keeps it on hand all the time.

1/2 box Cheerios	1/2 cup bacon drippings
1 box Rice Chex or any Chex cereal	1 tablespoon garlic salt
	1 tablespoon Savory salt
1 box tiny pretzel stix	1 tablespoon Tabasco sauce
1 pound pecans, or mixed nuts	1 tablespoon Worcestershire sauce
1/2 cup margarine	

Mix Cheerios, Chex and pretzels together. Add nuts. Melt margarine and bacon drippings, then add seasonings. Put nut-cereal mixture in large pan. (I use a turkey roaster). Pour liquid mixture over the cereal mixture. Place in 350 degree oven for 20 to 25 minutes. Stir often. Makes 10 pints.

SPICED TEA
Lady Bird Johnson

I like to serve this to guests on a cold winter's day here at the Ranch — just as I did at the White House.

6 teaspoons tea or 8 tea bags   2 cups boiling water

Pour water over tea and let cool. Strain and add:

1 small can frozen lemon
  juice
1 small can frozen orange
  juice

1¹/₂ cups sugar
2 quarts water
1 stick of cinnamon

Simmer mixture for 20 minutes. If too strong, add water. Add extra sugar to taste. Makes 16 to 20 cups.

COLD SQUASH SOUP "The Red Book"

Lady Bird substitutes yogurt for whipping cream in this recipe.

¹/₄ cup butter
1¹/₂ cups onion, finely
  chopped
1 quart small summer
  squash, sliced
2 cups chicken broth

¹/₄ teaspoon sugar
2 cups whipping cream or
  yogurt
Salt and pepper
Pinch of nutmeg
Parsley or chives, chopped

Melt the butter; add the onion and cook on low heat until soft but not brown. Add the squash and chicken broth. Cook until squash is tender. Add sugar. Put mixture through a sieve or pureé in the blender. Cool. Add the cream and season with salt, pepper and nutmeg. Chill; serve very cold sprinkled with chopped parsley or chives . . . good. Double two times to serve twenty-three people. Serves 6–8, 1 cup servings.

COLD YOGURT SOUP "The Red Book"

3 cups yogurt
¹/₂ cup half and half
1 egg, hard cooked and
  finely chopped
6 ice cubes
¹/₂ cup cucumber, finely
  chopped
¹/₂ cup green onion, finely
  chopped

1 teaspoon salt
¹/₂ teaspoon pepper
¹/₂ cup raisins soaked in 1
  cup cold water
1 tablespoon parsley,
  chopped
1 tablespoon fresh dill,
  chopped or 1 teaspoon dry

Put yogurt in mixing bowl with the cream, egg, ice cubes, cucumber, onion, salt and pepper. Stir well. Add the drained raisins and cold water. Refrigerate for several hours. Serve with chopped parsley and dill. Serves 8, 1/2 cup servings.

CHICKEN SALAD
Lady Bird Johnson

Use only chicken breast. Mix the salad just before serving.

5 **cups of white meat of chicken, cut in medium size pieces with scissors. Add broth to keep moist.**
5 **hard boiled eggs, diced**
5–6 **stalks of celery, stripped and diced**
³/₄–1 **cup of toasted almond slivers (toast but do not butter or salt. Can be done ahead and stored in air tight jar.)**
5-ounce **can of water chestnuts cut in nice small pieces**

Mix all of the above ingredients in a large bowl — lightly — with a fork. Add . . .

2 **strong dashes cayenne pepper**
1 **teaspoon, or more, of curry powder**
1 **teaspoon of Grey Poupon mustard and enough mayonnaise to moisten salad mixture**

Serves 10–12.
Optional ingredients to be added last include:

1¹/₂ **cups of white seedless grapes**
1 **cup pineapple chunks, drained and cut in small pieces**
4 **tablespoons of chutney (mango) any good commercial brand will do**
5-ounce **can of pitted ripe olives**
2 or 3 **teaspoons of capers**

MOLDED CRANBERRY SALAD
Lady Bird Johnson

2 cups cranberries
1 cup cold water
1 cup sugar
1 envelope unflavored gelatin

¹/₄ cup cold water
¹/₂ cup celery, chopped
¹/₂ cup nuts, chopped
¹/₂ teaspoon salt

Cook cranberries in 1 cup of water for 20 minutes. Stir in sugar and cook

5 minutes longer. Soften gelatin in 1/4 cup cold water; add to hot cranberries and stir until dissolved. Set aside to cool. When mixture begins to thicken, add chopped celery, nuts and salt. Turn into mold that has been rinsed with cold water. Chill in refrigerator until firm. Unmold on serving plate. Garnish with salad greens if desired. Serves 6.

BARBECUE SAUCE   *Kermit and Tillie Hahne*

This sauce was developed by Kermit and Tillie Hahne at the LBJ Ranch at Stonewall where they prepare and cater the food on many occasions.

1 large onion chopped
2 cups of water
1 pound margarine
1 cup vinegar
1 tablespoon prepared
  mustard

1 tablespoon paprika
1 tablespoon chili powder
1 tablespoon Worcestershire
  sauce
1 46-ounce can tomato juice

Boil onion in water and then strain. Add all ingredients to onion and boil all this together and let it cook down and thicken some. Makes 8–10 cups.

JAMES DAVIS' SEASONING FOR MEATS   *"The Red Book"*

This is especially good on Prime Rib and is used often at the Texas White House. James Davis was a long-time employee of the Johnson family, serving in many capacities.

1 cup salt
1 cup black pepper
1/3 cup Accent

1/3 cup garlic powder
1/3 cup onion powder

Mix all ingredients and rub into meat before cooking. Makes about 3 cups.

SWEET-SOUR DRESSING   *"The Red Book"*

1/4 cup vegetable or olive oil
2 tablespoons sugar or 3
  packages of Equal
2 tablespoons vinegar or
  wine vinegar

1 tablespoon parsley,
  snipped
1/2 teaspoon salt
Dash of pepper
Dash of red pepper sauce

Shake all ingredients in tightly covered jar. Refrigerate. Makes 1/2 cup.

LBJ RANCH DEER MEAT SAUSAGE   *Lady Bird Johnson*

A favorite recipe at the LBJ Ranch is for deer meat sausage. The finished product is recommended for late Sunday morning breakfast with scrambled eggs, hominy grits, hot biscuits and boiling hot coffee. Or, it can be served for a late-afternoon snack in hot biscuits.

1/2 deer, ground (100 lbs.)	20 ounces black pepper
1/2 hog, ground (100 lbs.)	8 ounces red pepper
25 ounces salt	2 ounces sage

Mix together for 200 pounds of sausage.

SHRIMP SQUASH CASSEROLE   *Lady Bird Johnson*

1 1/2 pounds (3 cups) yellow squash	1/2 cup whipping cream or small can evaporated milk, chilled
3/4 cup raw shrimp, peeled and deveined	1 tablespoon instant minced onion
2 tablespoons butter	1/2 cup coarse bread crumbs
2 tablespoons flour	1/4 cup grated Parmesan cheese
1/2 teaspoon salt	1 tablespoon butter
1/8 teaspoon black pepper	
1 cup chicken broth or bouillon cube	

Wash and dry squash. Cut crosswise into 1/4-inch slices. Thoroughly rinse shrimp under cold water. Drain. Heat the 2 tablespoons butter in sauce pan. Blend in flour, salt and pepper. Cook until it bubbles. Remove from heat and add chicken broth gradually, stirring constantly. Bring to boil for 1 or 2 minutes. Blend in cream and onions. Mix in the raw shrimp. Put in layer of squash in bottom of a 1 1/2-quart casserole and spoon half of the shrimp sauce over squash. Repeat layer with remaining squash and shrimp sauce. Cover tightly and set in a 400 degree oven for 30 minutes. Meanwhile, toss crumbs and Parmesan cheese with melted butter. After 30 minutes, remove casserole from oven and reduce heat to 350 degrees. Remove cover and top with bread crumbs. Return to oven 15 minutes or until crumbs are golden brown. Serves 8.

LIMA BEANS   *"The Red Book"*

Fresh lima beans or canned	Flour
Butter	Milk
Mushrooms	Cheddar cheese, grated

Cook and drain lima beans. Put small amount of butter in sauce pan and melt. Add mushrooms and sear for 5 minutes. Add flour and milk to make thick sauce. Add grated cheese and let melt, then add lima beans. Serve hot. Serves 4.

CORN PUDDING   *"The Red Book"*

If this cooks too long it turns to water.

2 **cups milk or light cream**	3 **eggs, well beaten**
2 **cups canned corn, cream**	1 **tablespoon sugar**
or kernel	1 **teaspoon salt**
2 **tablespoons butter, melted**	1/4 **teaspoon pepper**

Add milk, corn, butter, sugar and seasonings to eggs that have been beaten. Turn mixture into greased casserole dish and bake in moderate oven, 350 degrees, 45 minutes or until set. Serves 6.

LBJ RANCH SCALLOPED POTATOES   *"The Red Book"*

3 **cups potatoes, pared**	1 1/4 **cups milk**
1 **teaspoon salt**	1 1/4 **teaspoons salt**
2 **tablespoons flour**	1/4 **teaspoon paprika**
3–6 **tablespoons butter**	1/4 **teaspoon dry mustard**

Preheat oven to 350 degrees. Drop potatoes in boiling water. Add salt and cook for 8 minutes. Drain well. Grease a 10-inch baking dish. Place 1/3 of potatoes in baking dish. Sprinkle with flour and dot with butter. Add second layer and repeat flour and butter, then final layer and repeat. Heat milk and add to it the seasonings. Pour milk mixture over potatoes. Bake about 35 minutes. Serves 6.

SPINACH GOURMET   *"The Red Book"*

This is a favorite of Lady Bird Johnson but Mrs. Johnson only uses fresh mushrooms, never canned.

1 **pound fresh spinach or Swiss chard or 1, 10-ounce package, cooked and drained**	1 **small clove garlic, crushed**
1 **4-ounce can button mushrooms or fresh**	1/2 **teaspoon salt** **Dash of pepper**
1 **teaspoon instant minced onion**	1/3 **cup dairy sour cream** 1 **tablespoon half and half; or milk**

Prepare and cook spinach as directed above; chop and drain completely. Mix spinach, mushrooms, onions, garlic, salt and pepper in saucepan. Blend sour cream and half and half and then pour over spinach mixture. Heat just to boiling. Serves 4–6.

SPINACH SOUFFLÉ

Lady Bird Johnson

¹/₄ cup onions, chopped
1 cup spinach, cooked and
   chopped
¹/₂ cup of thick white sauce

3 eggs separated
¹/₂ cup cheddar cheese,
   grated

White sauce:
2 tablespoons butter
2 tablespoons flour
1 cup milk or cream

¹/₂ teaspoon salt
¹/₈ teaspoon pepper

Sauté onions in small amount of butter. In medium sauce pan on low heat melt butter for white sauce and add flour stirring until well blended. Remove from heat. Gradually stir in milk. Return to heat. Cook, stirring constantly, until thick and smooth. Blend in salt and pepper. Beat egg yolks until thick and lemon colored. Stir into white sauce and add spinach and cheese. Fold in stiffly beaten egg whites and turn into greased casserole. Set in pan of hot water and bake in moderate oven, 350 degrees, about 50 minutes. Serve at once. Serves 4–6.

HOT SPINACH CASSEROLE

Lynda J. Robb

One of the first dishes Lynda learned to cook, and how hilarious it was recalling all the times the recipe "flopped," as she was "apprenticing" in earning her "degree" in cooking. Many times Lynda utilized this good way of getting the children to eat spinach, which they didn't really like, but which was good for them. Even Chuck's father who hates spinach would eat it this way.

2 packages frozen, chopped
   spinach
4 tablespoons butter
2 to 3 tablespoons onion,
   chopped
2 tablespoons flour
¹/₂ cup evaporated milk
³/₄ teaspoon celery salt
³/₄ teaspoon garlic

1 teaspoon Worcestershire
   sauce
Dash cayenne pepper
Black pepper
1 6-ounce roll jalapeño
   cheese
Bite-size bread crumbs,
   sautéed in butter

Cook 2 packages spinach; drain well; save 1/2 cup cooking liquid. Melt butter and sauté onions; add flour and mix well. Gradually add milk and spinach liquid stirring continuously. Blend in seasonings; add jalapeño cheese and stir until melted. Add spinach; mix well and place into a casserole dish. Top with bread crumbs. Cook at 350 degrees for about 30 minutes or until bubbly. Serves 6–8.

STUFFED SQUASH   *"The Red Book"*

2 pounds yellow squash
2 onions, chopped
1 clove garlic, minced
³/₄ cup toasted bread
  crumbs, rolled finely
6 slices bacon, fried and
  crumbled

1 teaspoon sugar
Salt and pepper
Dash cayenne pepper
1 teaspoon Worcestershire
  sauce

Cook whole squash with onion and garlic until tender. Drain well. Half squash and scoop out pulp. Arrange halves in baking dish. Mash pulp and mix with bread crumbs, bacon and seasonings. Fill squash halves. Top each with a dot of butter and bake at 350 degrees for 15 minutes. Serves 6–8.

BISCUITS   *"The Red Book"*

1 cup flour
¹/₄ cup milk
1 tablespoon Crisco

2 teaspoons baking powder
2 teaspoons sugar
1 teaspoon salt

Mix and sift dry ingredients. Add half of Crisco and milk and beat. Add enough flour to knead well. Roll out on floured board; fold over and roll again. Melt remainder of Crisco in baking pan; place cut biscuits in pan and brush with melted Crisco. Makes 6 large or 12 small biscuits.

FLUFFY SPOON BREAD   *"The Red Book"*

2 cups milk
¹/₂ cup cornmeal
2 tablespoons butter

¹/₄ teaspoon salt
3 eggs, separated

Place well greased deep baking dish in 350 degree oven to heat. Bring milk to a boil. Slowly stir in cornmeal. Simmer gently for 5 minutes. (Make certain there are no lumps). Add butter and salt. Remove from heat and let stand 5 minutes. Stir in well beaten egg yolks. Fold in stiffly beaten egg whites. Turn into heated baking dish. Bake at 350 degrees for 25 minutes or until set and golden brown. Serves 4–6.

DINNER ROLLS
"The Red Book"

2 packages dry yeast	**²/₃ cup shortening**
2 cups lukewarm water	**1 teaspoon salt**
2 eggs	**7 cups flour**
¹/₂ cup sugar	

Dissolve yeast in 1/2 cup warm water. Melt shortening. Beat eggs, sugar, 1¹/₂ cup water and shortening together. Sift flour and salt and add to egg mixture with yeast mixture. Batter will be stiff. Knead a few times and put dough into large bowl which has been buttered with melted butter; cover and put into the refrigerator overnight or leave out to rise. After the dough has doubled in size punch down and make out into rolls the size of ping pong balls. Put these on a greased baking pan and when the rolls have doubled in size, bake them in a 375 to 400 degree oven until brown. This will make several dozen rolls. If you make them larger, as they do at "The Ranch" you will have 20 to 30 large rolls.

TINY QUICHES
"The Red Book"

This is fixed when the girls are at the ranch.

Filling:

¹/₂ cup bacon bits, home made	**¹/₂ cup half and half**
¹/₂ cup Swiss or Monterey Jack cheese, grated	**¹/₂ teaspoon salt**
	Dash Tabasco
	Dash nutmeg
1 tablespoon dried parsley	**1 tablespoon Parmesan cheese**
2 eggs, well beaten	**Paprika**

Crusts:

1 3-ounce package cream cheese	**¹/₂ cup margarine**
	1 cup flour, sifted

Soften margarine and cream cheese to room temperature and blend together. Stir in flour. Chill 1 hour. Shape into 2 dozen one-inch balls. Place in tiny muffin tins, greased lightly with salad oil. Press dough on bottom and sides. Layer bacon, cheese and parsley in unbaked crust. Beat together the next five ingredients and pour over bacon, cheese and parsley mix. Sprinkle Parmesan cheese and paprika on top. Bake at 325 degrees for 25 to 35 minutes. Quiches baked in regular size muffin tins take 10–15 minutes longer. Makes 12 regular size or 24 small.

FLOATING ISLAND   *"The Red Book"*

Lady Bird and Lynda's favorite. Always Christmas dinner dessert.

4 egg whites	**¹/₂ cup sugar**
4 ounces sugar (¹/₂ cup)	**6 egg yolks**
¹/₄ teaspoon maple extract	**3 ounces sugar (¹/₃ cup)**
2 cups milk	

Make a meringue with egg whites and 4 ounces of sugar. Add maple extract. Spoon 6–8 ice cream scoop sizes of meringue into simmering milk. Cook a minute on each side. Drain on paper towels. Make a caramel with 1/2 cup sugar and a tablespoon of water. Pour over meringues. To prepare custard: mix egg yolks and 3 ounces sugar. Over this pour the hot milk. (Strain any remaining pieces of egg whites). Stir over low heat to thicken custard. Do not boil. Pour custard into shallow serving dish. Arrange meringues over the top. Refrigerate one hour before serving. Serves 6.

GRAPENUT PUDDING   *"The Red Book"*

3 cups milk, scalded	**1 teaspoon vanilla**
³/₄ cup sugar	**¹/₂ cup Grapenuts**
2 eggs, beaten	**¹/₂ cup raisins, use more**
¹/₈ teaspoon nutmeg	**Grapenuts if not used**
1 pinch salt	**¹/₈ teaspoon nutmeg on top**

Mix all ingredients except the last nutmeg; sprinkle the nutmeg on top. Bake at 350 degrees in a Pyrex bowl sitting in water for approximately 1 hour. Serves 8.

SOUFFLÉ GRAND MARNIER   *"The Red Book"*

8 egg yolks, lightly beaten	**10 egg whites, beaten**
²/₃ cup sugar	**¹/₄ teaspoon cream of tartar**
¹/₂ cup Grand Marnier liqueur	

Preheat oven to 400 degrees. Beat in a double boiler over boiling water the egg yolks and sugar. Continue to beat until the mixture forms a broad ribbon as it runs from a lifted spoon. Add the liqueur. To arrest the cooking, transfer the mixture to a bowl and beat it over ice until cooled. Beat the egg whites until foamy. Add cream of tartar and continue to beat until stiff, but not dry. Fold the egg yolk mixture into the whites. Mound the mixture in a soufflé dish. Bake 12 to 15 minutes, until firm, and serve at once. Serves 8–10.

PRUNE CAKE
Lady Bird Johnson

¹/₂ cup Crisco
1 cup sugar
2 eggs
1¹/₃ cups flour
¹/₂ teaspoon soda
¹/₂ teaspoon salt

¹/₂ teaspoon nutmeg
¹/₂ teaspoon allspice
¹/₂ teaspoon cinnamon
¹/₂ teaspoon baking powder
²/₃ cup sour milk or buttermilk
²/₃ cup prunes, chopped

Cream shortening; add sugar and eggs; beat well. Mix dry ingredients and add alternately with sour milk to creamed mixture. Add chopped prunes. Bake in 2 waxed paper lined cake pans for 25 minutes at 350 degrees. Serves 12.

Frosting:
2 tablespoons butter
2 tablespoons prune juice
1 tablespoon lemon juice

¹/₂ teaspoon salt
¹/₂ teaspoon cinnamon
1¹/₂ cups powdered sugar

Cream butter, add prune and lemon juice, salt, and cinnamon. Beat in powdered sugar gradually.

BUTTERMILK PIE
"The Red Book"

6 eggs, separated
3 cups sugar
³/₄ teaspoon salt

1 cup flour
6 cups buttermilk
Cinnamon

Prepare three pie shells. Beat egg yolks; add sugar and salt. Stir flour into part of buttermilk; stir until smooth. Add to egg mixture. Add remaining buttermilk. Fold in very stiffly beaten egg whites. Pour into unbaked pie shells; sprinkle with cinnamon. Bake at 350 degrees for 35 minutes. Yield: 3 pies.

LBJ RANCH PEACH COBBLER
"The Red Book"

4 cups peaches, peeled and
   sliced
³/₄ cup sugar
1 tablespoon butter

1 teaspoon cinnamon
Extra butter, sugar and
   cinnamon

Stir first four ingredients together and heat. Do not boil. Pour into 8 x 8-inch pan. Dot with more butter. Cover with top crust. Sprinkle cinnamon and sugar on top and bake for 30 minutes at 400 degrees. Serves 6.

Top Crust:

3 cups flour
$^1/_4$ cup sugar
1 teaspoon salt

1 cup Crisco
1 egg, plus enough water to
   total $^1/_2$ cup

Mix flour, sugar and salt together. Add Crisco and blend until in crumbs. Add egg and water mixture and gather into a ball. Roll out for top crust. Remainder of dough will keep well in refrigerator.

PECAN PIE   *Lady Bird Johnson*

$^1/_3$ cup butter
$^3/_4$ cup brown sugar, firmly
   packed
1 cup light corn syrup

3 eggs, slightly beaten
1 teaspoon vanilla
$^1/_4$ teaspoon salt
1 cup broken pecans

Prepare one pie shell. Cream butter and brown sugar. Beat in the rest of the ingredients. Pour into an unbaked pie shell. Bake in a moderate oven, 375 degrees, for 30 to 45 minutes. Makes 1, 9-inch pie.

MRS. JOHNSON'S LACE COOKIES   *Lady Bird Johnson*

Just perfect for that special tea or brunch.

$^1/_2$ cup flour
$^1/_2$ cup coconut
$^1/_4$ cup Karo syrup (red or
   blue label)

$^1/_4$ cup brown sugar, firmly
   packed
$^1/_4$ cup Mazola margarine
$^1/_2$ teaspoon vanilla

Mix flour with coconut. Cook over medium heat, stirring constantly, Karo syrup, sugar and margarine until well blended. Remove from heat and stir in vanilla. Gradually blend in flour mixture. Drop by teaspoonfuls three to four inches apart on ungreased cookie sheet. Bake at 325 degrees for 8 to 10 minutes until lightly browned. Cool 1 minute and remove. Cool on racks. Makes 4–5 dozen, 2″ cookies.

LEMON SQUARES   *"The Red Book"*

These are another favorite of Lady Bird Johnson's and she serves them often and sends them out when she provides refreshments for some occasion away from home. They are rich and delicious.

Crust:

2 cups flour

1/2 cup sugar

1 cup butter

Custard:

2 cups sugar

1 teaspoon baking powder

4 tablespoons flour

3 eggs, beaten

Juice and rind of 2 lemons

Mix the three crust ingredients as for pie crust, and pat into a 9 x 18-inch jelly roll pan. Bake at 350 degrees until very light brown, about 15 minutes. Mix custard ingredients in order given; pour over baked crust. Bake for 15 to 20 minutes or until set. Sprinkle with powdered sugar. Makes 5 to 6 dozen.

SAND TARTS

"The Red Book"

1/2 pound butter

4 tablespoons powdered sugar

2 tablespoons water

3 cups flour

1 cup pecans, chopped

2 teaspoons vanilla

Blend butter and sugar; add other ingredients. Roll with the hand to finger size and turn into half moons. Bake on ungreased cookie sheet about 15 minutes in 350 degree oven. Roll in powdered sugar. Makes 5–6 dozen.

SUGAR COOKIES

Lynda J. Robb

These cookies Lynda makes every Christmas for the family and friends who come to visit. A Robb Christmas tradition — and the decorating of the cookies is a fun family project.

2¼ cups flour, sifted

1/2 teaspoon salt

3/4 cup butter or margarine

1¼ cups sugar

1 egg

2 teaspoons vanilla

Sift flour and salt onto wax paper. Beat butter, sugar and egg until fluffy; then add vanilla. Stir in flour mixture to make stiff dough and wrap in wax paper. Chill at least 3 hours or until firm enough to roll. Roll out dough on lightly floured pastry board and cut out with floured cookie cutters. Place 1-inch apart on greased cookie sheet and decorate with colored sugars. Bake at 350 degrees for 8 minutes or until brown on the edges. Cool on wire rack. Makes 3 dozen cookies. May decorate with icing after baking.

PEACH ICE CREAM

Lady Bird Johnson

With our Stonewall peaches this makes our very favorite "company dessert" — a summer treat without equal.

1 quart cream
1 pint milk
3 eggs
1 cup sugar

¹/₂ gallon soft peaches, peeled, mashed, and well sweetened

Make a boiled custard with cream, milk, eggs and sugar. When cool add the peaches. This makes one-gallon of ice cream which is most delicious.

BUTTERMILK SHERBET

"The Red Book"

This recipe takes a little extra time for the best results, but it is worth it and is an excellent finale' to a Mexican dinner.

1 quart buttermilk
2 tablespoons grated lemon rind
¹/₄ cup lemon juice

¹/₂ cup sugar
1¹/₂ cups white Karo syrup
¹/₂ teaspoon salt

Combine in large bowl the above ingredients and beat well. Place ingredients in 2 refrigerator ice cube trays until partly frozen; then pour into a cold bowl and beat with a wire whisk until smooth. For best results freeze and beat the sherbet three times in all. Makes 1–1¹/₂ quarts.

LBJ RANCH PICKLED OKRA

"The Red Book"

3 pounds okra, whole
6 hot peppers
6 cloves garlic
1 quart vinegar

1¹/₃ cups water
¹/₂ cup salt
1 tablespoon mustard seed

Wash okra and pack in clean jars. Add hot peppers and garlic to each jar. Bring remaining ingredients to a boil. Cover okra with hot liquid, filling to 1/2-inch of top of jar. Adjust lids. Process in boiling water for 10 minutes. Makes 3 pints.

★ ★ ★ ★ ★

HINT:
For just a squirt of lemon juice, poke a hole in one end and squeeze.

Stocking Up,
Preserving, Canning

PERRY MUSEUM

The log cabin which houses Perry Museum was constructed on a land grant received by Cicero Rufus Perry as a veteran of the Texas Revolution. It was moved into Johnson City in 1972, having been located one and a half miles west.

Both Perry and his father served under Sam Houston. Perry was only thirteen and a half years of age. Later, he became a captain in the Texas Rangers, very knowledgeable in the ways of the Comanche Indians.

The Perrys raised eight children in the cabin and occupied it from 1860 to 1898, the year of his death.

MASTER BISQUICK MIX   *Neatta Cade*

9 cups flour
1/3 cup baking powder
1 tablespoon salt
2 teaspoons cream of tartar

4 tablespoons sugar
1 cup dry milk
2 cups shortening

Put all dry ingredients in large plastic container with lid. Shake hard several minutes to blend. Add shortening in chunks. Close container and shake hard until mixture is crumbly. Use in recipes just as you would Bisquick. Makes 10 cups.

EAST TEXAS MAYHAW JELLY   *Cynthia Smith*

Prize Winning . . . This is an East Texas "must" for breakfast. Mayhaw is tricky to harvest and it grows on bushes in the swampy areas of East Texas. Just as it is well known that under every Agarita bush in the Hill Country there hides a rattlesnake, likewise under many Mayhaw bushes you might encounter a water moccasin! Mayhaws are harvested by placing a sheet on the ground under the bush and beating the bush with a stick to make the berries fall. In some really swampy areas the berries will be floating on the water and they can be scooped up.

3 pounds mayhaws or 4 cups prepared juice
5 1/2 cups sugar or 2 pounds and 6 ounces sugar
1 box Sure-Jel fruit pectin

To prepare fruit: Crush berries one layer at a time. Add 4 cups water, cover and simmer 10 minutes, stirring occasionally.

Jelly: Measure sugar and set aside. Stir fruit pectin Sure-Jel into fruit juice and let it come to a boil. Make sure pot is very large as the fruit will boil over. Immediately stir in all the sugar and let it come to a full rolling boil, one that cannot be stirred down. Boil for one minute at a hard rolling boil, stirring constantly. Remove from heat; skim off foam with metal spoon and then ladle into glass jars. Let jelly stand to cool. This jelly can be frozen. Yields: 6 cups.

OLD FASHIONED PEACH PRESERVES   *Joy Watson*

2 quarts hard ripe peaches,
   peeled and sliced
6 cups sugar

4 teaspoons Fruit Fresh
6 teaspoons Sure-Jel

Combine fruit, sugar, Fruit Fresh and Sure-Jel; bring slowly to a boil, stir-

ring frequently. Boil gently until fruit becomes clear and syrup thickens, approximately 40 minutes. As mixture thickens, stir frequently to prevent sticking. Pour boiling hot into sterilized jars; adjust caps. Yields: Seven, 1/2 pints.

PRICKLY PEAR JELLY
Mavis Lemons

Pick cactus pears (red bulbs of cactus) in late summer or early fall when they are red and ripe. Be sure to take a good pair of tongs, some leather gloves and a bucket or dishpan. Place fruit in a clean sink and spray with clear water until well washed. With a sharp knife and fork cut each pear in half. Place washed fruit in cooking pot and cover with water. Bring to boil over high heat then simmer about 25 minutes or until fruit looks slightly shrivelled and juice is good red color. Strain juice through colander lined with cheese cloth.

3 cups juice	**Juice of one lemon**
1 box Sure-Jel	**$3^1/_2$ cups sugar**

Add Sure-Jel to the juice and bring to a hard boil over high heat; add lemon juice and sugar. Bring to full boil and boil 3 to 5 minutes. Skim off foam. Pour into jelly glasses and cover immediately with 1/8 inch melted paraffin. Cool and cover with lids. Yield: 3 pints.

Variation: Cynthia Smith calls her jelly, Cactus Pear Jelly. Burn off stickers and peel fruit, using rubber gloves. Cut fruit in fourths and simmer for one hour. Uses $3^3/_4$ cups juice, $^1/_2$ cup lemon juice, $1^1/_2$ boxes Sure-Jel and 6 cups sugar. Caution: Watch for rattlesnakes when in areas where there are rocks and cactus.

PICKLED CACTUS
Ava Johnson Cox

This was used at the White House. It is very good over scrambled eggs and cheese as a relish. It is so good it will make you go slap Pappy.

Cactus, young	**$^1/_2$ vinegar, equal amount as**
Garlic	**water**
Onion, sliced	**$^1/_2$ water, equal amount as**
Jalapeño, as much as desired	**vinegar**
Leaf river fern or parsley	

Burn off the thorns of the cactus and slice into julienne strips. Soak in salt water overnight. Drain off salt water. Pack cactus, garlic, onion, jalapeño, and leaf river fern. Bring vinegar and water to boil; pour over vegetable mixture. It can be eaten while hot or packed in canning jars and sealed.

292

PICKLED CABBAGE   *Holly Lawson*

1 head cabbage, cut in   1 to 2 cloves garlic
  wedges   1 cup white vinegar
2 jalapeño peppers   2 cups water
1 small onion, cut in wedges 3 tablespoons pickling salt
Fresh dill

Wash cabbage; drain and pack in wide mouth jars with other vegetables.
Boil vinegar, water and pickling spices for 5 minutes. Pour over vegetables
in jars and seal. Process for 5 minutes in boiling water bath. Let season for
several weeks. Yield: 3 pints.

JALAPEÑO CARROTS   *Cynthia Smith*

1¹/₂ pounds carrots   1 jalapeño, diced, half to
2 teaspoons dill seed   each jar
1 teaspoon celery seed   1 garlic pod, half to each jar
2 teaspoons mustard seed   2 cups water
                              1 cup white vinegar

Prepare two pint jars. Put 1 teaspoon of dill seed, 1 teaspoon mustard
seed, 1/2 teaspoon celery seed, half the jalapeño and half the garlic pod in
each jar. Peel carrots; slice in circles or strips or leave whole and pack into
jars. Bring water and vinegar to a boil. Pour over carrots. Seal. These can
be processed for 5 minutes in boiling water bath. Yield: 2 pints.

VEGETABLE TRASH   *Ava Johnson Cox*

*The committee visited with Mrs. Cox a couple of hours one morning to get
some of her recipes. She gave us samples to taste as we wrote down each recipe.
This is a sweet relish and goes good with brown beans. Mrs. Cox is a cousin
to Lyndon B. Johnson our 36th president.*

4 large cucumbers, cleaned   Green and red peppers,
4 large squash, cleaned   cleaned, to taste
4 large onions, peeled   ¹/₄ cup salt
4 large carrots, peeled   2 cups Imperial sugar
4 ribs celery, cleaned   1 cup white vinegar, 80%
4 medium green tomatoes,   2 tablespoons pickling
  cleaned   spices

The vegetables can be sliced, chopped or ground, whatever you prefer.
Place vegetables in large container and sprinkle salt over them. (If vegetables are a few days old may use a little more salt). Let soak at least 1

hour and drain. Bring sugar, vinegar and pickling spices to boil until sugar dissolves. If not sweet enough for you add more sugar. Add vegetables to sugar-vinegar mixture and bring to a boil; simmer until vegetables lose their color and pack in jars and seal. If you pick your vegetables when the moon is on the increase they will keep their color. Yield: 3–4 quarts.

PEGGY'S EASY PICKLES
Cynthia Smith

1 gallon jar hamburger
   sliced dill pickles
5 pounds sugar

1 2-ounce jar Tabasco sauce
4 garlic sections, sliced

Drain pickles; save about half the juice. Start adding sugar, jugglin' it in until you have added almost 5 pounds of sugar. (I usually leave out 2 or 3 cups). Add a small jar Tabasco (again I do not add the full jar because it makes them too hot). Add garlic. You need to add some juice back to help dissolve the sugar as added but don't add much until all sugar is in, then, fill jar with the juice. Turn jar up and down daily; leave on bottom one day and top the next day for about 4 days or until pickle slices are clear and crisp. Refrigerate. Yield: 1 gallon.

CRISP SWEET PICKLES
Joycelyn Carter

1 gallon sour pickles, sliced
   thin
5 pounds sugar

1 box mixed pickling
   spices, tied in small bags
3 cloves garlic, peeled

Pour off juice on pickles but do not drain in colander or anything that drastic. Slice pickles and put back in jar or in a clean (maybe new would be a better word) plastic dish pan, if you have room in refrigerator for it. Add other ingredients and with wooden spoon or your hand (never use metal for any of this), stir every day for eight days. Then put in convenient size containers (if there is any left) to keep refrigerated. Cannot be heated to seal containers hence the refrigeration. After 3 to 4 days they taste pretty good but are not crisp. The added time in the syrup makes them crisp. Yield: 1 gallon.

ZUCCHINI PICKLES
Mavis Lemons

Serve as a relish with meats, sandwiches, in salads or as an appetizer on fresh, crisp lettuce leaves.

1 quart white vinegar
2 cups sugar
1/4 cup salt
2 teaspoons celery seed
2 teaspoons tumeric

1 teaspoon dry mustard
4 quarts zucchini, sliced,
   and unpeeled
1 quart onions, sliced

Bring vinegar, salt, sugar and spices to a boil. Pour over zucchini and onion slices and let stand one hour. Put on heat and bring to a boil. Cook gently for 3 minutes. Pack in hot, sterilized jars, seal at once. Makes 6–7 pints.

Variation: (1) To make dilled zucchini pickles, substitute 2 teaspoons dill seed for tumeric.

(2) Omit tumeric and add 2 teaspoons mustard seed and 2 teaspoons dill seed and increase salt to 1/2 cup coarse salt. Mix salt with water and soak vegetables one hour; drain. Follow above directions except process in boiling water, enough to cover the jars, for 10 to 15 minutes. Cool.

GREEN TOMATO SAUCE
Joy Anderson

This recipe was sent to my mother, Mamie Garner (who is ninety years old this year) soon after she and Daddy married. You know how young brides always ask their mothers for family tried-and-true recipes. I have this in "Mama Pogue's" own handwriting. The recipe is copied as it is written.

1 galon of green tomatos	1 half teaspoon all spice,
1 quart of onions	sinamon, clovs, black
1 and half cups vinegar	pepper
1 and half cups suggar	2 green peppers
1 cup water	

Chop tomatos, onions, pepper up fine and mix all and cook til juice is thick put more vinegar suggar if you like. Yield: 6–8 pints.

GREEN TOMATO RELISH
Mavis Lemons

1 peck green tomatoes, ground	2 quarts vinegar
1 cup salt	7¹/₂ cups sugar
1 medium head cabbage	2 tablespoons celery seed
6 green peppers	2 tablespoons mustard seed
6 medium onions	1 tablespoon whole cloves

Mix 1 peck of ground green tomatoes with salt; let drain in cloth bag overnight. In the morning, grind vegetables. Mix tomatoes and vegetables in large kettle and add vinegar, sugar and spices. Cook until onions are tender, about 20 minutes; seal in hot, sterilized jars. Makes 10–12 pints.

This 'n That

JOHNSON CITY LIBRARY

The Johnson City Library was organized in the early 1940s and moved to its present location in 1971. At one time it was two separate buildings, one being a law office and the other a cafe. The Library is supported by the people of Johnson City and surrounding area and has always been a major project of the Johnson City Women's Civic Club. It also receives funding from the city and county.

PLAY DOUGH OR MUDDING DOUGH   *Sallye Baker*

This will entertain small children.

3 cups flour
1 cup salt
2 tablespoons oil

1 cup water (add more if
   needed)

Use your hands to mix all the ingredients; work dough until it is smooth
and holds together. Store in a plastic bag or in a large covered jar. Cut it;
roll it; shape it; build with it; stick toothpicks in it; use cookie cutters in it.

EDIBLE PLAYDOUGH   *Betty Wood*

1 cup water
2 tablespoons oil
1 cup flour

1/2 cup sugar
1 package Kool-Aid, any
   flavor

Mix together water and oil. Microwave on HIGH for about 2 minutes.
Remove and add flour, sugar and Kool-Aid. Mix ingredients together
with a spoon. Use to make whatever you want. When it comes time to
clean up — EAT IT!

FLUBBER   *Vanessa Luce*

A fun treat for family, friends and little people.

4 envelopes of gelatin
3 small packages of Jello, any flavor
3 cups of boiling water

Mix gelatin and Jello in boiling water. Pour into a jelly roll pan or cookie
sheet with sides. Refrigerate until hardened. Cut with your favorite cookie
cutters. Will not melt at room temperature. A fun treat and also nutri-
tious.

DOUGH ART RECIPE   *Joycelyn Carter*

*This is the recipe we used to make the Christmas ornaments at the LBJ Med-
ical Center for "Lights Spectacular, Hill County Style."*

1¹/₂ cups hot water (as it
   comes from the tap)

1 cup salt
4 cups flour

Put the hot water and salt into a bowl and stir for 1 minute. The salt does
not dissolve completely. Add the flour and stir until the water is absorbed.
Turn the dough onto a pastry board or table and knead a few minutes.

The dough is ready when it is smooth and pliable. Keep the dough in a sealed plastic bag so it will not dry out as you use it. Refrigerate if not using right away. Roll out like pie dough and cut into shapes with cookie cutters. The dough can also be made into shapes by rolling and putting together. Where dough joins add water. Bake the thin dough at 300 degrees for about one hour. The formed dough may take one to four hours. They can be painted, glazed and glued. To make hanging ornaments make a hole in the dough with a toothpick or insert half of a paper clip.

SPICED CUTOUT ORNAMENTS

Sallye Baker

These add a spicy fragrance to any room. They can be hung on kitchen window or on cabinet pulls. At Thanksgiving I use a turkey or pumpkin cookie cutter. At Christmas I use assorted cutters. Ornaments may be used on gifts or tree.

$3/4$ cup cinnamon	1 tablespoon nutmeg
1 tablespoon allspice	1 cup applesauce
2 tablespoons ground cloves	

Mix all ingredients in a bowl and stir. The dough will be stiff. Roll out on waxed paper like pie dough. Cut out shapes with cookie cutters. Place on ungreased cookie sheet. Dry 5 days uncoverd. Turn over everyday to let underside dry. Make holes in cutouts with straw or toothpick to run ribbon through for hanging. Contains no flour.

BAKING POWDER

Committee

2 tablespoons cream of tartar	1 tablespoon baking soda
	1 tablespoon cornstarch

Mix together. Measure it the same as baking powder.

MIRACLE MEAL FOR BIRDS

Vanessa Luce

This gives bug eating birds their protein in the winter.

1 part flour (1 cup)	1 part peanut butter (1 cup)
3 parts yellow corn meal (3 cups)	Lard (about 1 cup)

Mix flour, corn meal, and peanut butter together. Add lard (has to be old fashion lard) and combine until the mixture will make firm balls. Make into 1-inch balls. Place in a section of tree limb that has had several large holes drilled in it, horizontal or vertical. Hang the feeder from a tree limb.

CHEMICAL GARDEN
Thelma Elm

6 tablespoons liquid bluing
6 tablespoons water
6 tablespoons salt
1 tablespoon ammonia

3 or 4 rocks, clinkers or
  pieces of coal
Cake coloring (optional)

Combine bluing, water, salt and ammonia. Place rocks in an old pie pan and slowly pour the mixture over the rocks. Crystals start to grow very soon and will continue as long as the liquid stays. If you want a little color, add a few drops of cake coloring to the rocks. Set the pan where you can watch it daily.

PLANT FOOD
Dena Heider

1 teaspoon baking powder
1 teaspoon Epsom salt
1 teaspoon salt peter

$1/2$ teaspoon household
  ammonia
1 gallon tepid water

Use only every 6 weeks for watering plants or the leafy ones will crowd you out and the flowering ones will bloom themselves to death.

Another mixture that will promote growth and flowering is put cow patties (chips) in 5 gallons of water for a day or two then water your household plants once a week with the solution. Sadie Sharp

Cut flowers will last longer if you snip the stems at an angle or add an aspirin to the water. If flowers start to wilt, put in very hot water to revive.

DEER REPELLENT
Paula Housman

2 eggs
1 or 2 green onion tops
2 cloves garlic
1 tablespoon chili powder

2 cups water
1 gallon warm water
Yellow soap

Blend eggs, onion tops, garlic, chili powder in two cups water. Add mixture to one gallon of warm water that has been mixed with yellow soap. Splash on plants to prevent deer from eating them. Repeat after a rain.

PAINT REMOVER
Holly Lawson

My brother, Robbie Penick, gave me this recipe. It really works! It leaves the wood smooth and rich compared to sanding. After using apply Briwax in the shade you want; repaint or varnish.

4 cups water, divided
2 cups cornstarch

5 tablespoons lye (read all instructions on can)

Boil 2 cups water and take off heat. Add cornstarch, stirring until dissolved. Heat second 2 cups of water and take off heat; add lye, stirring until dissolved. Let cool then mix the two mixtures together. Use rubber gloves (mixture will burn or irritate hands). Paint a small section at a time. Let the mixture remain on the wood awhile but do not let it dry. Wipe off with paper towel. If it does dry, it has to be taken off with extra water and elbow grease. When working with lye be very careful and follow all instructions on the label.

HAND LOTION
Pearl Preston by Jane Mills

My mother had what she called "tatters" on the back of her hands in the winter. This helped her a lot to keep the tatters under control.

1½ pints soft water
1 ounce gum tragacanth
1 ounce rose water

1 ounce glycerine
1 ounce bayrum

Heat water to boiling; pour over the gum tragacanth. Allow to stand twenty-four hours. Beat well with an egg beater and add remaining ingredients. Beat thoroughly. Place in air tight container. Store in cool place.

NOTE: gum tragacanth is a white or reddish, tasteless, odorless gum used in pharmacy.

LILY WHITE HAND LOTION
Committee

¾ cup rosewater
¼ cup glycerine

¼ teaspoon cider vinegar
½ teaspoon honey

Pour all ingredients into a bottle and shake. Keep bottle handy and rub a few drops into hands after washing. Glycerine and honey are the oldest moisturizers known.

HOMEMADE WALLPAPER CLEANER
Pearl Preston by Jane Mills

This came from my mother's files. She used to hang wallpaper for people. I can remember every spring we had to clean our wallpaper to get rid of the coal film.

1 cup flour
½ cup water
2 tablespoons salt

2 tablespoons vinegar
1 tablespoon kerosene

Mix flour and water into a smooth paste. Add salt, vinegar and kerosene to paste. Cook until thick enough to knead. Let set until cool enough to handle. This makes a dough like substance. Start at ceiling and wipe down. Knead dough after each swipe.

FIRE ANTS: Grind up grapefruit peel and mix with water. Stir up fire ant mound and dig it out and pour grapefruit mixture into mound.

CLEAN SINK DRAINS: First clean coffee maker with vinegar. Sprinkle 1/2 cup baking soda into drain. Follow with hot vinegar from cleaning coffee maker. The "fizz" does the cleaning. Let set about 30 minutes before running water through the drain. Jane Mills.

CLEAN HANDS: Wash hands with a paste of soda and water to remove fish or onion scent from them. Can also be used to scour pots and pans. Sadie Sharp.

To rid hands of onion odor, rub with salt or vinegar then rinse with cold water and wash in hot water.

When hands are stained from the gardening, add a teaspoon of sugar to the soapy lather you wash them with.

Old Home Remedies

LINIMENT   *Pearl Preston by Jane Mills*

1 pint turpentine	The whites of three eggs
1 pint of apple vinegar	¹/₂ tablespoon salt
1 cake of camphor gum	3 tablespoons mineral salts

Mix all together and shake thoroughly.

ARTHRITIS: Gather mud from stream that runs through a mountain. Make a mud pack out of it and put it on the sore place. This is supposed to take the soreness out.

SPRAINED ANKLE, FOOT OR ARM: Make a mud pack out of red clay (soil) mixed with vinegar. Next place the pack on the sprain. Put a paper grocery bag (brown) over it and tie a bow made from butchers twine. This takes the swelling out. (Cynthia Smith — "I wore this!")

CHICKEN POX: Undress the child and roll him under the chicken roost: This is supposed to stop the itching. Never tell the child what your intentions are, or you will never catch the child!

CUTS: Let your best dog lick any cut you may have. This is a sure and quick cure for the cut.

EAR ACHES: Boil a cockroach in oil and then use the oil the roach was boiled in for drops or on a piece of cotton to stop the pain of earache.

COLD: Starve a cold and stuff a fever. Cross a creek backwards.

HEADACHES: 10 sniffs from a pair of dirty socks should do it.

LOCK JAW: In horses only: Take the horse and hit him in the head with the flat end of an ax. This should un-lock the jaw.

NOSE BLEED: A nickel placed under your tongue is supposed to stop nose bleed. Sadie Sharp.

STINGS: For relief from stings wash immediately with Clorox.

FOR SLEEP: 1 teaspoon powdered milk
                 1 teaspoon brewer's yeast
                 2 teaspoons molasses or honey
                 Stir into a cup of warm milk
Another: 3 teaspoons apple cider vinegar
                 1 cup honey
                 Take 2 teaspoons at bed time.

LAXATIVE HOME BREW: Boil cup of water and add level teaspoon of Swiss Kress Herbs. Let stand 3 minutes and strain. Add a teaspoon of honey and a few drops of lemon.

COUGH: Boil lemon for 10 minutes. Add 2 tablespoons glycerine to juice and fill the rest of the glass with honey. You can also use lemon juice, sugar and small amount of liquor.

TIRED EYES: Soak cotton pads in warm milk and place on eyes for 10 minutes.

Hint by Dena Heider: If your eyes feel tired or sore, lay down and close your eyes and rub Vicks on the eye lids. Keep them closed until the burning ends.

Household Hints

Stains or discolorations on aluminum utensils can be removed by boiling a solution of 2 to 3 tablespoons cream of tartar and either lemon juice or vinegar to each quart of water in the utensil for 5 to 10 minutes.

Burned food can be removed from an enamel pot by filling the pot with cold water and adding 2 to 3 tablespoons salt, stirring until dissolved. Let set overnight. The next day cover and bring water to a boil.

When food boils over in the oven, sprinkle salt on the burned surface. This will stop smoke and odor from forming and make the spot easier to clean.

New cast-iron cookware should always be seasoned before using. Rub the interior and exterior with oil or shortening and place in a 250 to 300 degree oven for several hours. Wipe off oily film and store. If scouring is necessary after using the utensil, re-season the surface immediately to prevent rusting. If utensil has rusted, wash in hot soapy water, then treat as new cookware.

Always turn saucepan and skillet handles toward the back of the range to prevent accidents.

Lower oven temperature 25 degrees when using heat-proof glass dishes to ensure even baking.

For a quick and easy clean up for a gas grill after use, turn the burner to high for about 10 minutes. This will burn off residue.

To remove smoke stains from brick, make a paste of cornstarch and Clorox. Brush on, let dry, then brush off.

There is no need to scrub the fireplace so often if you throw salt on the logs occasionally. This will reduce the soot by two-thirds.

Old nylon stockings make great dust cloths, so do old T-shirts.

Tie cloves in a cheese cloth and hang in closet. They work as well as moth balls and smell better.

Boil 1 tablespoon of whole cloves in a pan of water for a few minutes to freshen the air in the house. Try adding a little orange or lemon peel.

Refrigerated candles will not drip and cause clean up headaches after your next candlelight dinner.

Your new white tennis shoes will last longer if sprayed heavily with starch when you first get them.

Next time you go on a picnic take a vinyl tablecloth instead of a blanket to spread on the ground vinyl side down. It will keep out any ground moisture.

Wet newspaper can be dried in the microwave — one section at a time is better.

Pour the saltwater from making ice cream on weeds on gravel side walk.

Add 1 teaspoon of vanilla to a gallon of paint to cut down the odor of the paint.

If you get gum on clothes or carpet, take an ice cube and rub it on the gum. It will harden the gum for easy removal.

When the bathroom mirror steams, cut an onion and take the sliced side and rub it on the mirror. The mirror will no longer steam over.

Salt water used in washing wicker furniture keeps it from turning yellow and it is also good for cleaning straw mats.

Use baking soda on a damp cloth to make kitchen appliances shine.

Old Hints

GARDEN: A garden planted on Good Friday will be productive.

HAIR: Hair cut when the moon is coming big will grow faster and when the moon is waning will grow slower.
To make hair lighter in color rinse the hair in lemon juice.
To make hair darker use a vinegar rinse.

RAIN COMING: When you see more scorpions around.
When the cows are lying down.
When you see box turtles cross the road.
When the Purple Sage blooms.

COLD WEATHER: Thick bark on a tree.

GOOD LUCK: When you see a Roadrunner running from right to left.
From left to right is BAD LUCK.

Index

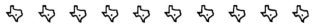

Index

Index